Reflections on Surah
AL-BAQARAH
A Thematic Understanding

ANIS AHMAD

THE ISLAMIC FOUNDATION

Reflections on Surah al-Baqarah: A Thematic Understanding

First published in England by
The Islamic Foundation
Markfield Conference Centre
Ratby Lane, Markfield
Leicestershire, LE67 9SY United Kingdom

Tel: +44 (0) 1530 249230

Quran House, PO Box 30611, Kenya

P.M.B 3193 Kano, Nigeria

Website: www.kubepublishing.com
Email: info@kubepublishing.com

© Anis Ahmad 2024 All rights Reserved
   2nd impression, 2025

The right of Anis Ahmad to be identified as the author of this work has been asserted by him in accordance with the Copyright, Design and Patent Act 1988.

Cataloguing in-Publication Data is available from the British Library

ISBN Paperback 978-0-86037-983-6
ISBN Ebook 978-0-86037-988-1

Cover Design and Typesetting: Nasir Cadir
Stock Image: Istock

Printed by: Elma Basim, Turkey

Contents

- Preface — 1
- Introduction to *al-Baqarah* — 7
- An Overview: Five Thematic Groups of Verses — 12
- The Change of Leadership — 15
- Guidance on Social Ethics — 17
- The Uniqueness of Qur'anic Guidance — 17
- Preservation of the Qur'an — 20
- The Earlier Scriptures — 21
- The Most Appropriate Universal Guidance (*Hidayah*) — 24
- The Universality of the Qur'an — 27
- *Taqwa* is a Prerequisite of *Hidayah* — 29
- The Ethical Empowerment of Human Beings — 32
- The Role of Guidance (*Hidayah*) in Achieving *Taqwa*, Virtue, Piety and Servitude — 34
- *Taqwa* as a Behavioural Practice, Objective of all Acts of Devotion and a Key Theme in the Qur'an — 40
- The Real Success (*Falah*) — 44
- The Culture of *Infaq* — 45
- Two Types of Human Conduct and Behaviour: Disbelief (*Kufr*) and Hypocrisy (*Nifaq*) — 47
- The Meaning of Hypocrisy (*Nifaq*) — 49
- The Inimitability of the Qur'an — 53
- The Wisdom (*Hikmah*) in the Challenge to Produce Something Like the Qur'an — 54
- Comprehensiveness of the *Din* — 56

» Lessons from the Story of Prophet Adam ﷺ	61
» Iblis's Modern Forms of Temptations: Cultural Colonialism and Entrepreneurial Capitalism	63
» The Fourfold Implication of *Khilafah*: What *Khilafah* is and is not	65
» The Leadership Role of Earlier Peoples: The Case of Bani Isra'il	67
» In the Wilderness of Sinai	69
» *Shirk* (Associating with Allah) and *Nifaq* (Hypocracy), The Two Major Transgressions that Lead to Helfire	73
» Realizing *Tawhid* in the Social Sphere	74
» The Transgressions of the Israelites	76
» Allah's Mercy and the Israelites' Response	77
» A Universal Message: *Tawhid* as the Common Ground	79
» The Israelites' Practice of Double Standards	82
» The Negative Effects of the Israelites' Cultural Assimilation in Egypt	83
» The Response of the Jewish Community in Madinah	84
» Immediacy Instead of Ultimacy	86
» The Dialogical Approach	90
» Implications of the Covenant: Serving Allah Through *Salah* and *Zakah*	94
» Serving Parents as a Demand of *Tawhid*	96
» The Qur'anic Model of Extended Family	98
» The Rights of the Marginalized: The Culture of *Ihsan*	100
» The Ethics of Communication	101
» The Culture of Using Communication in a Dignified Way	104
» The Status of Earlier Sacred Laws	105
» Religious Pluralism and the Right to Worship in an Islamic Polity	111
» Similarity of and Constancy in the Message (*Da'wah*) of all the Prophets	113
» The Conferment of Leadership on Prophet Ibrahim ﷺ	115
» A Dialogue Based on the Abrahamic Faith	116
» *Sibghat* Allah: From Physical Identity to Ideological Identity and from Symbolic Colours and Signs of Devotion to Substantial Transformation and Exemplary Conduct	117
» Allah's Colour	118
» The Leadership Role of the Muslim *Ummah*	119
» Conferment of the Leadership Role of the Muslim *Ummah*	121
» The *Ummah* as a Model of Justice (*'Adl*) and Moderation (*Wasatiyyah*)	123
» The Obligations of the Leadership of Mankind	127
» The Culture of Gratitude, Perseverance and Remembrance	128
» The Culture of Ethical Intelligence and Striving (*Jihad*)	131

- » Continuity and Change in the *Shari'ah* — 133
- » The Unreasonableness of the People of the Book — 136
- » The Culture of Research, Reason, and Introspection — 136
- » Qur'anic Pointers — 138
- » Is Religion a Personal Matter? — 140
- » The Culture of Righteousness, Piety, and Allah-consciousness: The *ayat al-Birr* — 141
- » The Sanctity of Life and Legal Equality: The Principle of Justice (*'Adl*) and Excellence (*Ihsan*) — 145
- » Implications of the Qur'anic Ordinance: The Principle of Legal Equality — 148
- » Social Justice — 148
- » The Supremacy of Law and the State — 149
- » Social and Legal Fairness — 151
- » The Dimensions of Piety — 153
- » Fasting and the Inculcation of Allah-Consciousness — 154
- » The Culture of *Tazkiyah* in Financial, Trade and Economic Transactions — 159
- » Liberation from Superstitions — 160
- » War Ethics — 161
- » The Prohibition of Self-infliction of Harm — 163
- » The Globalisation of *Da'wah* and Islamic Brotherhood — 164
- » Two Types of Personality — 170
- » The Holistic Personality — 174
- » The Unity of Humankind — 176
- » The Culture of Benevolence (*Infaq*) and Social Engagement — 179
- » The Culture of Benevolence — 182
- » War Ethics — 184
- » The Dynamics of Faith and Migration (*Hijrah*) — 186
- » The Gradual Removal of Social Evils through *Ma'ruf* — 190
- » The Institutionalization of Social Engagement — 192
- » The Building of a Compassionate Family — 197
- » Family Ethics — 199
- » A Graceful Family Life — 201
- » Striving to Achieve Justice and Peace — 204
- » The Leadership of Mankind — 206
- » The Role of Reason, Revelation and Miracles — 210
- » Encouragement of Social Engagement and the Culture of Spending on Others (*Infaq*) — 212

- » The Beauty of the Verse of the Throne (*Ayat al-Kursi*) — 213
- » Religious Freedom — 215
- » *Rushd* and *Taghut* — 216
- » Experiential Truth — 219
- » Manifestation of Faith in *Infaq* (Spending on Others for Allah's Sake) — 223
- » The Gift of Wisdom — 225
- » The Culture of Almsgiving (*Sadaqah*) — 230
- » The Secular Concept of Corporate Social Responsibility vs. The Culture of *Infaq* and *Sadaqah* — 233
- » Establishing an Interest-free Society — 233
- » No Gender Disparity in Legal Matters — 236

Preface

Al-Baqarah the first *surah* revealed in al-Madinah, and the longest *surah* in the Qur'an, in a comprehensive way touches on several major themes of the Qur'an. *Tawhid* remains the key theme throughout the *surah* and at other place in the Qur'an. *Tawhid* provides the foundation of faith, society, economic and political order as well as the basis of culture and civilization Islam wants to realize. In Makkah the Islamic *da'wah* (message) addressed the centuries old traditions of polytheism, tribalism, superstitions, and materialism. And this happened in a land which was originally the center of the pristine Unity and transcendence of Allah (*tawhid*). It was here that Ibrahim and Isma'il ﷺ erected the foundations of the House of Allah around eight hundred years before Dawood and Sulayman ﷺ built the Temple at al-Quds. The Kaaba as the House of Allah was a reminder (*ayah*) of *tawhid*. But *tawhid* the original faith of mankind got diluted and polluted when Bani Isma'il and Bani Isra'il (the children of Israel) and the followers of Isa ﷺ [Jesus] deviated from the original teachings and indulged in attributing divine character to not only their Prophets but even considered their religious leaders as immune (*ma'sum*) and as intermediary between them and their Lord. Makkans took pride in their being descendants of Ibrahim and Isma'il ﷺ but unfortunately they too adopted polytheistic practices.

The environment in Madinah was no different. The native tribes of the Aws and Khazraj practiced polytheism but the Jewish settlements around al-Madinah with their pride as people of the Book, in the final analysis, were equally involved in superstitions and polytheistic practices.

Al-Baqarah revives the original teachings of Ibrahim and Isma'il ﷺ and invites both the polytheists and the children of Israel to the original and True Path to Success. It addresses socio-economic, political, legal, and spiritual issues in a multi-cultural and pluralistic Madinah society. The *surah* also contains the *ayah* **"And have fear of the day when you shall return to Allah, and every human being shall be fully prepared for whatever (good or evil) he has done and none shall be wronged"** *al-Baqarah* 2: 281, reported to be the last revelation received by the Prophet ﷺ.

Ahadith of the Prophet ﷺ assign great significance to this *surah*. It is said that if it is recited in a home, it protects its inhabitants from misguidance and evil coming from satan. Due to its importance and comprehensiveness some *sahabah* (companions) took several years to study *al-Baqarah* in order to grasp fully its meaning.

The *surah* instructs on matter of faith (*iman*) and devotion (*'ibadah*), its major focus is on ethical leadership of mankind. Earlier this leadership role was given to the children of Israel, the *surah* declares transfer of leadership role to the Muslim *ummah*. The new social order, it wants to erect is based on the centrality of family. Matters related with family, marriage, mediation, divorce, and inheritance and rights of wife and husband are enumerated. Additionally, the role of jihad in the context of an ethical order is elaborated upon.

It also refers to historic events, particularly the rise and fall of the children of Israel, but not as a historical narration. Its purpose being to encourage change, learning from history and the establishment of a peaceful, fair and ethically responsible order.

Humanity, at a global level, is faced today with numerous critical social, economic, political, and cultural issues. The gap between the haves and have nots is ever increasing. A very small number of people control 85% wealth of the world. Man-made health hazards have lead to the emergence of a variety of viruses that harm the quality of life. The ethical and moral decay in society is also reflected in the dilution of family values. This is further complicated by the insistence of the normalisation of same-sex relationships, on a global level, that does not give room for an alternative ideology to voice its right to exist or dissent.

Al-Baqarah provides direct guidance, clear injunctions and rational grounds for a gradual removal of social evils through the discernment of good (*ma'ruf*), virtue (*birr*), conscious realization of Allah's obedience (*taqwa*), comprehension of fairness, equity, and justice (*'adl*) in human conduct and social transactions. It also provides guidance in matters of international law. In brief *al-Baqarah* contains a treasure of universally applicable principles, specific legislations and general guidance on a large variety of socio-economic, political and cultural issues

These brief reflections on *Surah al-Baqarah* should not be considered as formal *tafsir* exegesis, but an effort to learn, as a student of the Qur'an, thematic relationships between issues and topics faced by humankind in the past as well as in the so-called modern age. The fact of the matter is the Qur'an was revealed in the daylight of history but due to its universality, it transcends the finitude of time. It is not sent to a specific group of people living in a given period and place. Its universal principles and legislations are addressed to the whole of humanity irrespective of time and space. This makes it a unique sacred text, not a creation of the human mind or scribes. Every single letter and word of it is fully preserved in written form, and protected by Allah, it is memorized and recited by its followers without any gap in time.

We believe no translation of the Qur'an in any human language can convey fully the total meaning of the Divine revelation for the simple reason all human languages are finite. These reflections are meant only to introduce the thematic unity of the Qur'an. The Arabic text must always be kept at hand when going through these preliminary reflections. For no other reason but continuity of thought the Arabic text is not included in this series of reflections. The fact of the matter is no translation in any language can holistically substitute the original text of the Qur'an. Translations can only help in understanding one or another dimensions of meaning of the text to a certain extent.

These reflections of a layman pave the way to a more systematic, in-depth study of the known exegeses of the Qur'an, available in most of the world languages. English rendering of the meaning of the Qur'an, used in this series of reflections is from Dr Zafar Ishaq Ansari's *Towards Understanding the Qur'an Abridged Version of Tafhim-al-Qur'an*, Islamic Foundation, Leicester, UK (2006).

I thank Allah for His special favor and blessings in allowing me to put down these reflections. I appreciate assistance provided to me in review of the manuscript by brother Muhammad Arshad Baig and Dr Sohaib Zafar Malik. I also appreciate sincere contribution of Mr. Huzaifa Khalid who typed the manuscript. I thank my family particularly my wife Anisa and my children for their understanding and patience to allow me to be away from them for long hours in my library to work on the manuscript. My niece Asma took time to read the manuscript and made valuable suggestions. May Allah reward all of them for their sincerity, patience, sacrifice, and assistance. Also, I thank Kube and Haris for their impressive production of this volume. I pray to Allah to accept this humble effort to share His *Hidayah* with my fellow human beings, particularly the youth. I will gratefully welcome any comments and suggestions from the readers of this volume. I dedicate these reflections to my mentors Maulana Sayed Abul A'la Mawdudi and Prof. Isma'il Raji al-Faruqi.

May Allah forgive me for any human omissions and allow me to complete this series of reflections on the rest of the Qur'anic *surahs*.

وما توفيقى الا با الله

Prof. Anis Ahmad Ph D
May 23, 2023

Reflections on *Surah al-Baqarah*

A THEMATIC UNDERSTANDING

Introduction to *al-Baqarah*

In just seven short verses (*ayat*), *Surah al-Fatihah* summarizes the core message of the Qur'an. It establishes Allah's Supremacy, Providence, Compassion and Care for His creation, particularly human beings who are gifted with the capacity to distinguish between right and wrong. Out of His compassion, Allah has not left human beings without guidance in all the phases of their existence. In *al-Fatihah*, the seeker of Truth supplicates the Lord of the worlds to guide them to the Straight Path (*al-sirat al-mustaqim*). The first two verses of *Surah al-Baqarah* apparently offer a response to this supplication: *"This is the Book there is no doubt in it, it is guidance for the Allah-conscious (muttaqin)"* (al-Baqarah, 2: 2).

Al-Baqarah is the longest *surah* of the Qur'an, and most of it was revealed in Madinah during the first two years after the emigration (*hijrah*). The last four verses of this *surah* were not revealed in Madinah but due to their thematic similarity, and following the instruction of the archangel Jibril, they were placed here by the Prophet ﷺ. The name of the *surah*, like the names of other *surahs*, is taken from a specific reference made to something in the *surah* itself and, in this case, reference is made to a cow. The word *al-Baqarah* appears in verse sixty-seven of this *surah*, after which it is named.

> ### The Focus of the Makkan *Surah*s
>
> The focus of the Makkan *surahs* is on a critical analysis of the belief system of the rejectors of Truth (*Kuffar*) and the polytheists (*mushrikun*). The Makkan *surahs* are short but extremely powerful; they have the impact of a forceful river in a rocky mountainous terrain. The Madinan *surahs* such as *al-Baqarah*, are also persuasive but are like the subtle power of water, which rubs on solid and impermeable rocks, and gradually reduces them to pebbles and sand.

In the Makkan *surahs,* the focus is on *da'wah* and a critical analysis of the belief system of the Makkans. Based on evidence from the history of the rise and fall of human civilizations, the invalidity of the belief system of the Makkans and the truthfulness of the Islamic, or the original Abrahamic faith (*tawhid*), is one of the major themes of this *surah*. The Makkan *surahs* are short but extremely powerful; they have the impact of a forceful river in a rocky mountainous terrain. The arrogant Makkans who were adamant about their disbelief and association of idols with Allah perhaps needed an intellectual jolt through an extra forceful and powerful speech. The disbelievers and idolaters are compared to rocks due to this obstinate and headstrong attitude. The Madinan *surahs* such as *al-Baqarah*, are equally persuasive but are like the subtle power of water, which rubs on solid and impermeable rocks, and gradually reduces them to pebbles and sand. This invisible power of Truth ultimately triumphs and overwhelms the evil powers.

Yathrib, later known as *Madinat al-Nabi*, or Madinah, not only had a different climate and landscape to Makkah but the composition of its population was also different. It had old settlements of migrants from Yemen, and Israelite tribes. The prolonged war of Bu'ath between the native tribes of Aws and Khazraj had worn them out and weakened them. Even though the Jews were internally divided, they cleverly exploited the differences between the Aws and Khazraj and became power brokers. In general, the people of Madinah shared the belief system of the Makkans. However, under the influence of the Jews, they shared with the latter their expectation of a Prophet ﷺ, mentioned in the Jewish Scripture. Against this backdrop, six people from Khazraj visited Makkah in the tenth year of Prophethood and were approached by the Prophet ﷺ who called them to accept Islam. They embraced Islam and the following year a larger group of people from both Aws and Khazraj came to Makkah not only to embrace Islam but also to invite the Prophet ﷺ to move to Yathrib and become their leader. This opened a new avenue for *da'wah* and, within the next two years, the ground was prepared for the Prophet's migration to Yathrib which became a stronghold of Islam.

Before the Prophet's migration, the Jews of Madinah were preparing to install 'Abdullah ibn Ubayy ibn Salul, from the tribe of Khazraj, as the ruler of Madinah. The Prophet's migration to this city greatly disturbed their plans. The covenant of Madinah signed with the Jewish tribes consolidated the Prophet's authority as head of the city-state of Madinah and ended any prospect of 'Abdullah bin

Ubayy becoming the king of the Aws and Khazraj tribes. This drove him to become a Muslim outwardly, but he remained a hidden enemy of Islam and the leader of the hypocrites in Madinah who always tried to harm the interests of the Muslims.

In order to appreciate the unique style of the Qur'an, one has to understand the purpose of the Divine revelation. Madinan revelations thus address a variety of emerging social, economic, security and governance issues faced by the newly founded polity. Quite often matters of faith are elaborated and then guidance is provided on some emergent social or economic issues, and further down a comment is added to the previous subject, while in the same continuation, reference is made to a security problem, and the following passage may refer to a legal issue. A person unaware of the total historical context may find it difficult to connect all these statements or to understand the logical link between such statements. But a careful study of these statements unveils an understandable thematic link.

> The main task of the Prophet ﷺ was to bring a substantial and sustainable qualitative behavioural change in people. It was not a matter of introducing some new ways of worship but rather a total transformation of society and the mindset of its people from disbelief to belief in Allah. This required simultaneous focus on a variety of social, economic, ethical, political, and legal issues. This is why quite often, in just one Qur'anic verse, several issues are addressed. However, the presence of more than one topic in a given narrative always calls for increased concentration and thinking. Unless one is aware of this unique style of the Qur'an, one cannot properly appreciate the flow of ideas and the internal thematic link running in the Book.

The purpose of Revelation (*wahy*), or the Qur'an, is to instruct and guide human beings to the path of success in this world and the Hereafter, through re-confirming the original teachings brought to mankind by the earlier Messengers of Allah which, due to various reasons, were either lost or distorted. At the same time, it provides comprehensive directives (*Shari'ah*) that are fully preserved in their original form and practically demonstrated by the final Messenger of Allah ﷺ in social, economic, political and legal matters.

It is also a unique feature of the Qur'an that it is recorded and preserved in its original form. It is not a book of history or biography of the Prophet ﷺ nor is it the result of the Prophet's personal contemplations. In order to understand it in depth, it is helpful to first consider the context of the revelation itself and then contemplate on the internal link between the Qur'anic verses. The Qur'an does refer to certain historical events but not in a chronological sequence for it is not a historical record of social development at any specific time and place. It only points to major ethical and moral factors that were responsible for those events as its historical evidence of the conflict between the forces of truth and evil, between *ma'ruf* (well-known good) and *munkar* (disagreeable), *haqq* (right, truth) and *batil* (wrong, untrue), *'adl* (fairness) and *zulm* (oppression, injustice). A comparison of these events provides flashes of guidance wherever similar situations arise.

Madinan society presented a pluralistic setting whereby the believers had their own spiritual, social, psychological, cultural, legal, and economic needs and concerns, while the hypocrites and the neighbouring Jewish communities also had their own historical, cultural, and legal issues and challenges. *Al-Baqarah* and other Madinan *surahs* address these complex existential issues and provide directives, on a variety of topics, that may be applied universally.

The whole *surah* was revealed during the first two years after the Prophet's *hijrah* (migration) to Madinah. Verse 281 is an exception; it was the last revelation to the Prophet ﷺ but it was not revealed in Madinah. It was placed in *al-Baqarah* following the instruction of the archangel Jibril. *Al-Baqarah* also happens to be the longest *surah* in the Qur'an.

An Overview:
Five Thematic Groups of Verses

Al-Baqarah elaborates on the basic tenets of faith (*aqidah*) which were already summarized in *Surah al-Fatihah*. It invites both the idolaters and the People of the Book, settled in and around Madinah, to reflect on the authentic faith of Prophet Ibrahim ﷺ i.e. the Oneness of Allah (*tawhid*) and belief in the Afterlife (*Akhirah*), and embrace it.

Thematically, the *surah* can be divided into five major groups of verses. The first group elaborates on faith (*iman*) and its manifestations in the conduct and behaviour of the believers (*mu'minun*). It also refers to the polytheists (*mushrikun*) and the People of the Book (the Jews and Christians) who vehemently resisted the Islamic message, due to their own biases, dislike of Islam, vested interests, historical baggage and the myth of their genetic superiority as the 'Chosen People'.

The first group of verses begin by introducing the Book as Divine Guidance (*hidayah*) from Allah, Who is the Lord (*Rabb*) and Owner (*Malik*) of the Universe to those who sincerely seek the Truth and path to success (*al-sirat al mustaqim*) in order to win Allah's favour in this world as well as in the Hereafter. This first group of verses

(1-39) informs us about three broad categories of people: (1) those who recognize the Truth, embrace it and value it, these are believers (*muʾminun*); (2) those who knowingly refuse the Truth and insist on retaining the way of their forefathers, their ancient traditions, and their tribal customs. They consciously reject the evident Truth and keep following multiple functional gods; these are idolaters or polytheists (*mushrikun*); (3) the People of the Book, i.e. the people of earlier revelations *ahl al-kitab*, namely the Torah (*Tawrat*) and the Gospel (*Injil*). These Scriptures had already predicted the coming of a final Prophet ﷺ, but the scholars of these Scriptures suppressed the truth and kept it hidden from their followers. Although some of them embraced Islam, their hearts remained loyal to the faith of their forefathers. Outwardly they showed their attachment to Islam and the Prophet ﷺ, but they were hardened disbelievers inwardly who always tried to harm the Muslim community from within; these are the hypocrites (*munafiqun*).

The second major theme included in this group of verses relates to the origins of humanity and the purpose of their creation as ethically responsible agents or vicegerents of Allah (*khalifah*). It also underscores the role of Satan (*Shaytan*) in distracting human beings from the straight path of Allah and the struggle between good (*maʿruf*) and evil (*munkar*). One is reminded, through the story of Adam or that of Abel (Habil) and Cain (Qabil), of the traps Satan uses to misguide human beings and that seeking Allah's protection and help (*istaghfar istiʿadha*) can always save believers from going astray.

The next group of verses (40-121) specifically invites the People of the Book (*ahl- al-kitab*) to ponder on the Qur'an which validates the original and uncorrupted teachings of their own Scripture and also corrects the additions and changes they introduced in their Sacred

Law. It also reminds them of the Prophesy in their Scriptures about the advent of the final Messenger.

The Israelites are also reminded of their continuous ungratefulness and their rebellious conduct and behaviour toward Allah's commands and their own Prophets, some of whom they even tortured or killed. These verses point out their cunning use of intellect to avoid following their own Scripture whenever it conflicted with their desires and vested interests.

Evidence is provided of how the Israelites violated their own Sacred Law which explains why they were removed from their role as leaders of the nations of the world. Consequently, leadership was entrusted to the best of nations, the middlemost nation of Islam, under the leadership of the final Messenger of Allah ﷺ.

Although the address is to the Israelites, it is also a warning to the Muslim *ummah* and an invitation to learn from what happened to the Israelites and not fall into the traps of the devil. The Prophet ﷺ also warns the believers to avoid following the way of the Israelites if they want to be successful in the Hereafter.

The Qur'anic warning to the Muslims not to follow the course of the Israelites is supported by concrete historical facts. For example, they worshipped an idol in the shape of a calf made of gold as instructed by al-Samiri, they were ungrateful to Allah's blessings when He provided *manna* and *salwah* during their long wandering in the desert and they also abandoned fighting for the sake of Allah. They even started reciting their Book in a way that served their purpose, *"Those who do not recite the Book as it ought to be recited, in fact they reject it, they are the losers"* (al-Ma'idah, 5: 121).

Since the Israelites were stripped of the role of leading other nations, the next group of verses (122-162) addresses the ethical and moral leadership role of the Muslim *ummah*.

The Change of Leadership

Before declaring the transfer of leadership from the Israelites to the Ishmaelites, the Qur'an elaborates on the principles upon which this change was made. It refers to the exemplary devotion, sacrifice, commitment to the cause, and struggle made by Prophet Ibrahim ﷺ in establishing the Oneness (*tawhid*) of Allah.

In this respect, the Qur'an recalls how the first centre of *tawhid* was established by Prophets Ibrahim and Isma'il in Makkah. They both built the Kaaba as a symbolic house of *tawhid* (*Bayt Allah*) which became the central sanctuary established by the forefathers of Prophets Musa, Dawood and Ya'qub. This remained the centre toward which the Israelites faced in their prayers until Prophets Sulayman and Dawood built a Temple in Jerusalem. The Qur'an also informs us that when Prophets Ibrahim and Isma'il were building the simplest possible structure as a centre of worship toward which the devotees may face, both made a supplication for a messenger to come from the progeny of Prophet Isma'il ﷺ. They also reconfirmed that they were both Allah's servants or Muslims. In other words, neither Prophet Ibrahim ﷺ nor Prophet Isma'il ﷺ had anything to do with Judaism or Christianity. Both of them declared themselves to be servants of Allah who submitted to Him as Muslims.

The change of the *qiblah* towards the Kaaba, therefore, was not a deviation but rather a revival of the genuine faith of Prophet Ibrahim ﷺ. It also indicates that leadership is not a matter of inheritance or succession. It is based on having excellence in service to Allah and acting with god-consciousness (*taqwa*), justice ('*adl*) and fearing accountability on the Day of Judgement. Hence, leadership is based on merit, not blood relation. Total surrender to Allah's good pleasure (*rida*) is the key. Through their conduct and behaviour, Prophet Ibrahim ﷺ, and

Prophet Isma'il ﷺ proved, their total acceptance of Allah's directives. They were given leadership (*imamah*) and viceregency (*khilafah*), and whoever after them acquires these qualities also qualifies for *imamah* or *khilafah*. It is not by genealogical succession.

The message conveyed is simple, the *qiblah* established by Prophet Ibrahim ﷺ and Prophet Isma'il ﷺ in Makkah, which became with the passage of time the house of hundreds of idols, was originally built on the foundations of an uncompromising *tawhid*, which meant that the believers had an obligation to liberate and cleanse it from the pollution of idolatry.

The following verses (163-246) provide guidance on social, legal, and devotional matters in order to establish justice, peace and Allah's authority (*hakimiyyah*) on His land in all walks of life. Here the Qur'an demolishes the pre-Islamic, dualistic worldview of dividing space and time into sacred and profane. Islam does not divide life in terms of worldly, secular materialistic activities and religious devotions. It wants unity in life: *"Enter in Islam in totality"* (al-Baqarah, 2: 208). The dualism of Jewish, Christian and Polytheistic people as well as the dualism of later philosophies in life, has been totally rejected by the Qur'an. This group of verses focuses on *tawhid* (163-176); social responsibility and the integration in one's life of worship (*'ibadah*), good works (*a'mal salihah*), the obligatory-due (*zakah*), spending on others (*infaq*), Allah-consciousness (*taqwa*) and righteousness (*birr*) (2: 177).

The *ayah al-birr* elaborates not only dimensions of virtue in terms of *ibadah* or worship and rituals but provides in terms of *'ubudiyah'* or servitude, a holistic and comprehensive meaning of *taqwa*, *'adl* and *ihsan*. It tells a believer to observe *huquq* of Allah as well as *huquq* of His creations.

Guidance on Social Ethics

Surah al-Baqarah is rich in its guidance on social ethics. It provides guidelines on human relations as well as how to resolve human conflicts and differences, which are also part of any civil order. The following verses provide directives regarding retaliation (*qisas*) and blood-money (*diyyah*) (178-179); they also touch upon the prohibition of bribery, provide instructions on pilgrimage (*hajj*) and *jihad*, the prohibition of games of chance and intoxicants, the rights of orphans, social obligations, marriage, divorce and what constitutes permissible family relations as well as the prohibition of marrying idolaters whether men or women. Then directives on the rights of a wife and children are provided (219-242) as well as the permission to strive for the liberation of the Kaaba from the idolaters who, by any definition, could not be the custodians of the centre of *tawhid* (243-283).

The last group of verses (284-286) recaptures the essence of *tawhid* and designates authority and sovereignty over the whole universe to its sole Creator and Owner, Allah. It further affirms that true faith consists of total obedience to Allah and imitation of His Messenger, and that one should always seek Allah's forgiveness and help in all one's efforts and endeavours as Allah alone is the One Who helps in all matters. The *surah* ends with a comprehensive supplication (*du'a*) for forgiveness, forbearance and success in this world and the Hereafter.

The Uniqueness of Qur'anic Guidance

Every single Qur'anic verse contains a treasure-trove of knowledge and wisdom. For the sake of convenience and to attain a thematic understanding of this *surah*, the present study of *al-Baqarah* will be done through focussing on its verses in small clusters. We shall start with some reflections on the first five verses.

"*Alif, Lam, Mim. This is the Book, there is no doubt in it; it is a Guidance for the pious (muttaqin). For those who believe in the existence of that which is beyond the reach of perception, who establish prayer and spend out of what We have provided them. Who believe in what is revealed to you and what was revealed before you, and have firm faith in the Hereafter. Such are on the true guidance from their Lord; such are the truly successful*" (al-Baqarah, 2: 1-5).

In these first five verses, the letters, *Alif, Lam, Mim* are known as the disjointed letters (*al-huruf al-muqata'ah*) and their real meaning is known only to Allah, though Qur'anic scholars have offered various interpretations for them. They are, therefore, left as they are, without any speculation about their real meaning.

The second verse touches on a major theme: the significance of Scripture in guiding human beings. The Qur'an refers to itself as the Book. It implies that, in order to achieve success, human beings need Divine guidance in the form of a recorded book. The human mind alone is not adequate to decide what is ethical and what is not. Human beings need an objective and universal understanding of what is ultimately good (*ma'ruf*) and what is evil or unacceptable (*munkar*).

It also raises another question: can speculation (*zann*), conjecture and philosophical thought lead to a universal consensus on truth? And is it fair to impose an individual and personal view regarding the truth, which is bound to be subjective, on all human beings? Are human reason and emotional intelligence alone capable of guiding human beings in their decisions regarding social, political, economic, legal, or other matters?

All these questions are answered by this Qur'anic verse, namely that neither individual nor collective reason–by nature limited and confined–can make an objective judgement on what is ultimately good or evil. Therefore, the objective criterion of Truth is the Book of Allah, who is the Almighty and the Ultimate Authority, who transcends all subjective considerations and He alone can define for human beings what is right and what is wrong.

The verse states that this is the book which alone can play this role and provide guidance to humankind in a totally objective yet fair manner. It also elaborates that without a doubt this Qur'an is the Book that contains nothing uncertain, unverified or conjectural; it contains only what is revealed by God and it is indeed all the Guidance that human beings need until the Day of Judgement.

It is further elaborated that those who follow it, achieve true *iman* and *taqwa*. This category of people is called the believers (*mu'minun*). However, to benefit from the Book, the believers should have conviction about five things: they must believe in matters that are beyond their sense experience but reported by the truthful and trustworthy (*sadiq* and *amin*) Messenger of Allah ﷺ. For example, Allah is seeing and His grip encompasses everything, but the reality of this grip and what is meant by His hand is a suprasensible matter that escapes human comprehension; that Paradise (*Jannah*) exists and that the Day of Judgement shall take place, are true but one cannot tangibly verify these truths.

The believers must confirm their faith by performing the five obligated daily prayers; spending their wealth in the way of Allah; holding on to the Qur'an as their guide in all matters and believing in the truthfulness of the original revealed Scriptures as being sent from Allah.

The second category of people includes those who are not

prepared to leave their old practices, customs and traditions, or their forefathers' ways. These people deliberately disregard the truth and Allah's guidance. These are the unbelievers (*kuffar*) who knowingly refuse to accept the truth and consciously embrace falsehood and Allah does not stop them from going astray. They have eyes but they cannot differentiate between light and darkness; they also have ears, but they block their ears from hearing the truth.

The third category of people includes the followers of Judaism and Christianity who recognise the Prophet ﷺ but refuse to believe in him out of arrogance. And the fourth category of people includes those who pretend to be Muslims and, hence, attend the communal prayers but, due to their enmity towards Islam, their real intention is to harm the Muslim community because hypocrisy (*nifaq*) lies deep in their hearts. The Qur'an mentions elsewhere that they shall be in the lowest level of *Jahannam*

Preservation of the Qur'an

The statement "*This is the Book, there is no doubt in it, it is a guidance for the pious*" (al-Baqarah 2: 2), though revealed orally to the Prophet ﷺ refers to the Qur'anic revelation as *al-Kitab*. The *surah* begins with a statement of fact: this Book of guidance contains only the truth and there is no doubtful material in it. It is a Book that contains no speculation, doubt or human imagination. Historically speaking, it is the only Book among the Divine Scriptures that assigns to itself a title, i.e. *al-Qur'an*, and is still in its original form. Each word of the Qur'an was received directly by the Prophet ﷺ through Allah's Messenger Gabriel (Jibril) and was immediately committed to memory by the Prophet ﷺ and, without any gap, conveyed by the Prophet ﷺ to the Companions, particularly to those who were designated as scribes (*kuttab al-wahy*) committed to preserving it in writing. The Qur'an, we are told, is also preserved in its original form, in Heaven: "*No, indeed this is a Reminder. So, whoso wills may give heed to it. It is contained in scrolls highly honoured, most exalted and purified, born by the hands of scribes, noble and purified.*" ('Abasa 80: 11-16). These three levels of its preservation (instant memorization, writing it down by the scribes, and its preservation in Heaven are further vouched by Allah Who says: "*Indeed, it is We Who have revealed it and it is indeed We Who are its guardian*" (al-Hijr 15: 9). Among the revealed Scriptures, the Qur'an is the only Book which is kept in the *lawh al-mahfuz* (the secure tablet) in heaven, in its complete form. *Al-Kitab* also indicates that the Book– with its comprehensiveness, relevance and applicability–is the final message; it is not a mere book but the Book or *al-Kitab*, the true Guidance for the whole of mankind (*hudan li'l-nas*). As the final, most comprehensive Guidance, it relieves mankind from all earlier sacred laws and guidelines sent from time to time which were not preserved in their original revealed form. Scriptures of all major world religions, according to their own scholars, do not exist today in their pristine original form.

The Earlier Scriptures

According to the editors of *The New English Bible with Apocrypha*, (1970), "the Old Testament consists of a body of literature spread over a period extending from the twelfth to the second century B.C. No manuscript of the Old Testament from the earlier part of this period have been preserved; Indeed, most of it must have been handed down by oral tradition from generation to generation." Similarly, the New Testament travelled a long journey until, in the year 1611 under the directions of King James, a group of fifty-four theologians after comparing Greek, Hebrew and Latin versions came up with the King James version which we have today. The Scriptures of the Buddhists, Hindus and Zoroastrians were also orally communicated from generation to generation for centuries before their written records were made. The only exception is the Qur'an, which was preserved from the beginning in two uninterrupted forms, i.e. its memorization and its transcription by the scribes appointed by the Prophet ﷺ himself, and in his presence.

While most of the Scriptures of the world religions went through a prolonged period of oral tradition and translations from one language to another, the Qur'an is the only Book that is preserved in its original language and recited partly in daily congregational or individual prayers, and in its entirety in the month of Ramadan.

The Scriptures of Jews and Christians, as they exist today, are essentially recollections compiled by scribes who were not the direct recipients of the Scripture from their own Prophets. The scribes of the New Testament never saw, met or directly heard from Prophet 'Isa ﷺ.

The Qur'an also bears witness that it is the speech of Allah and not a subjective "inspiration" of the Prophet ﷺ. This is evidenced by the following verses: *"This Book, beyond doubt was revealed by the Lord of the Universe"* (al-Sajdah, 32: 8); *"This is a revelation from the Most Merciful the Most Compassionate"* (Ha-Mim al-Sajdah, 41: 2); *"We have revealed this Book to you (Muhammad) with Truth, so serve Allah, offering Him sincere devotion"* (al-Zumar, 39: 2); *"Tell them: 'It is the spirit of holiness (Jibril) that has brought it down, by stages from your Lord, so that it might bring firmness to those who believe and guidance to the Right Way, and give glad tidings of felicity and success to those who submit to Allah"* (al-Nahl, 16: 102); *"We revealed it (on) a Blessed Night, for We were intent on warning"* (al-Dukhan, 44: 2) that affirm the Qur'an as revelation from Allah. Furthermore, the matter of preservation of the Last Revelation is guaranteed by the Sender Himself as shown by the following verse: *"Indeed it is We who have revealed it and it is indeed We who are its Guardian"* (al-Hijr, 15: 9).

It is important to understand the theme conveyed in these two verses: *"This is The Book. There is no doubt in it. It is a guidance for the God-fearing"* (al-Baqarah, 2: 2-3). First, by naming itself 'the Book' and not just a book, it overrules earlier Scriptures that came from the same source and simultaneously resolves several points of confusion regarding the nature of the Qur'anic revelation (*wahy*). It is a Revelation and not a subjective personal *inspiration* for Revelation is an objective experience, coming from beyond and not from within. The word *al-Kitab* simply means a written document. The word Qur'an, *qara'a yaqra'u,* means that which is recited or collected together which eliminates the possibility of it being an oral tradition for a prolonged period as was the case of practically all world Scriptures. It also stands for the recorded, recited, documented and verified text, containing the revelations sent down during twenty-three years, and directly recited by the Prophet ﷺ in congregation, without a single deviation, and heard by thousands of his followers, multitudes of whom memorized and recited it in exactly the same manner.

This is why from Morocco to Indonesia and across the globe, there are millions of handwritten, decorated manuscripts and beautifully printed copies of the Qur'an which contain no discrepancies whatsoever.

The Most Appropriate Universal Guidance (*Hidayah*)

The Book describes itself as *huda*, or guidance, which is another recurring theme in the Qur'an. It is addressed to those who strive to be Allah-conscious (*muttaqi*). Apart from its obvious meaning of guidance, the word *huda* also refers to insight, vision, proof, evidence, and a clear and straight way. Furthermore, *hidayah* means to guide someone with kindness, benevolence, and sincerity. The word *hidayah*, in its various forms, appears in around two-hundred and ninety places in the Qur'an. This clearly indicates Allah's love and kindness towards His servants by showing those who seek the truth True Guidance which guarantees success in this world and the Hereafter.

That the Qur'an is the Ultimate guidance from Allah for all seekers of Truth is elaborated in several other places in the Qur'an, for example, *"And it is a guidance (huda) and mercy (rahmah) for the believers"* (al-Naml, 27: 77); *"Ta-Sin. These are the verses of the Qur'an and a clear Book. A guidance (huda) and good tiding (bushra) for the believers"* (al-Naml, 27: 1-2) and *"Mankind! Now there has come to you an exhortation (maw'izah) from your Lord, a healing (shifa') for the ailments of the hearts, and a guidance (huda) and (rahmah) for those who believe"* (Yunus, 10: 57). In other words this *hidayah* is a comprehensive guidance which covers the principles of governance as well as directives on behavioural matters. It heals by removing enmity, hate, hypocrisy, jealousy, malice, rancor, and greed from the heart and provides consolation. Its discourse (*maw'izah*) excels in politeness, simplicity, and it penetrates the heart and soul effecting a measurable transformation.

The first recipients of Allah's *hidayah* are His Prophets themselves: *"And We bestowed upon Ibrahim (Abraham), Ishaq (Issac) and Ya'qub (Jacob), and each of them did We guide (hadayna) to the*

Right Way as We had earlier guided Nuh to the Right way and (of his descendants We guided), Dawood (David) and Sulayman (Solomon), Ayyub (Job), Yusuf (Joseph), Musa (Moses) and Harun (Aaron). Thus do We reward those who do good, and Zakariya (Zechariah), Yahya (John), 'Isa (Jesus) and Ilyas (Elias), each one of them was of the righteous, (and of his descendants We guided) Isma'il (Ishmael), al-Yasa' (Elesha), Yunus (Jonah) and Lut (Lot). And each one of them We favoured over all mankind," (al-An'am, 6: 84-86).

All the Prophets of Allah were deputed to guide their people to the Right Way (*al-din*) or the noble path of the *Shari'ah* in the most appropriate way. However, ultimately *hidayah* is acquired by people only when Allah so wills: *"(O Prophet ﷺ) you cannot grant guidance (la tahdi) to whom you please. It is Allah who guides (yahdi) those whom He wills. He knows best who are amenable to guidance,"* (al-Qasas, 28: 56).

This simply means Prophets of Allah and the believers have an obligation to introduce, inform and invite people to the Right Way with all possible and suitable means, but guidance or *hidayah* is subject to certain conditions. One important prerequisite is the desire or intention of a person or a people to seek guidance: *"Did We not show him the two highroads (good and evil)"* (al-Balad, 90: 8-10). The choice is left to human beings as is evidenced in the following verse: *"Verily We created men out of a drop of intermingled sperm, so that We might try him, and We therefore endowed him with hearing and sight. Surely, We showed him the Right Path regardless of whether he chooses to be thankful (shakiran) or unthankful (kafura)"* (al-Dahr/al-Insan, 76: 2-3).

As mentioned earlier, though human beings are gifted with the faculties of sense perception, reason, and the freedom of will, human reason falls short of providing ultimate guidance due to its own limitations and finitude. It is only Allah, the Creator and Lord of all animate and inanimate beings, Who can provide transcendent universal guidance, through His Prophets and Messengers: "*Even so We revealed to you, (O Prophet ﷺ) a spirit (wahy) by Our Command. You knew neither what the Book nor what the faith was. But We made that spirit a light whereby We guided those of Our servants whom We please to the Right Way. Surely, you are directing (la-tahdi) people to the Right Path. The way of Allah to Whom belongs the dominion of all that is in the heavens and the earth. Lo it is to Allah that all things ultimately revert*" (al-Shura, 42: 52).

The Prophets of Allah always pray to Him to keep them on the right path and help them in presenting His *hidayah* to people as it ought to be presented: "*Say as for me my Lord has guided me on to a Straight Way, the right din, the way of Ibrahim who adopted it in exclusive devotion to Allah and he was not of those who associate others with Allah*" (al-An'am, 6: 161). One attribute that every single believer should have is to pray continuously for steadfastness and *hidayah*: "*They pray to Allah: Our Lord! Do not let our hearts swerve towards crookedness after you have guided us to the right way and bestow upon us Your Mercy for You are the Munificent Giver*" (Al 'Imran, 3: 8).

All earlier Prophets received *hidayah* from Allah which they delivered, in the best possible way, to their peoples. Referring to Prophet Musa ﷺ the Qur'an states: "*Surely We revealed the Torah, where there is Guidance (huda) and Light (nur)*" (al-Ma'idah, 5: 44) and it further states: "*And we sent Jesus the son of Mary after those Prophets, confirming the Truth of whatever there still remained of the Torah. And we gave him the Gospel, wherein is Guidance and Light...*" (al-Ma'idah, 5: 46).

These explicit Qur'anic statements assert again and again that the Islamic or Qur'anic teachings are not derived from earlier Scriptures, rather the Qur'an as well as all the earlier Scriptures originate from one and the same source: Allah. Hence, the basic message of all the

Prophets of Allah is always one and the same: to obey the guidance and instructions of the Creator and not to follow in the footsteps of Satan, or one's own desires, whims and pleasures. In other words, *tawhid* must prevail over the entirety of human conduct and behaviour, as taught and commanded by all the Israelite Prophets and others who were sent to different nations of the world.

The apparent and obvious differences and discrepancies that exist in the earlier Scriptures are due to their lack of preservation by their followers. The scholars of these Scriptures added and altered many teachings within these Scriptures.

Since these earlier Scriptures were not preserved in their original form, it is natural that their teachings differ from some of the teachings of the Qur'an. The Jews and Christians believe in God the Creator and the Lord, yet a good number of them believe in the God Who manifested Himself in Ezra ('Uzayr) and Jesus, peace be upon them. The Abrahamic concept of God, though, insists that none is like Him nor can anyone share in His Person or Divinity. Aware of these claims by the Jews and Christians, the Qur'an invites them to use their cognitive and emotional intelligence to ponder on the life examples of Prophets Ibrahim, Yaq'ub, Musa and 'Isa and their firm belief in uncompromising *tawhid* which rejects the divinity of any created being.

The Universality of the Qur'an

Prophets were generally sent to specific people: *"We sent Noah to his people (and directed him) warn your people before a grievous chastisement comes upon them"* (Nuh, 71: 1); *"And call to mind when Jesus son of Mary said: O children of Israel, I am Allah's Messenger to you I verify the Torah which has come before me and I give you the glad tidings of a Messenger who shall come after me, his name being Ahmad"* (al-Saff, 61: 6). Before the advent of Jesus a large number of Messengers and Prophets were sent specifically to the Israelites to remind and warn them. The Jewish and Christian Scriptures, too, address the lost followers of Israel.

On the other hand, the Qur'an as Scripture and the Prophet ﷺ as Messenger are not just for the Quraysh of Makkah or the Ansar of Madinah but for the whole of humanity. The earlier Scriptures contain several universal teachings, but their context and addressees were primarily a specific people such as the Israelites. The Qur'anic *Shari'ah*, on the contrary, is universal. It is founded on universal principles which were applicable at the time of the Prophet ﷺ and his Rightly guided successors but equally relevant today and until the Day of Judgement.

The Difference between Islamizing and Arabizing

The Prophet ﷺ is not an Arabian Prophet ﷺ who, consequently, came to Arabize people. He is the Prophet ﷺ of Islam who came to Islamize the Arabs as well as mankind as a whole. The final Messenger ﷺ was not sent only to guide the people living in one country or one continent, but also to lead and guide the whole of humanity. *"(O Prophet ﷺ) We have not sent you forth but as a heralder of good news and a warner of all mankind (kafatan li'l-nas). But most people do not know"* (Saba', 34: 28). Similarly, the Prophet ﷺ was declared as the carrier of compassion, kindness and love for the whole world. *"We have sent you forth as none but mercy to people of the whole world"* (al-Anbiya', 21: 107).

While earlier books were addressed to specific people, the Qur'an as the final, comprehensive, and universal guidance is *hidayah* for the whole of mankind. *"This is a plain exposition (bayan) for mankind (li'l-nas) and guidance (huda) and admonition (maw'izah) for the Allah-fearing"* (Al 'Imran, 3: 138). That the Qur'an is not specific to a particular people or a place but a guidance for the whole of mankind is repeated again and again in the Qur'an. *"During the month of Ramadan, the Qur'an was sent down as a guidance (huda) to the people (of the world) with Clear Signs of true Guidance and as the Criterion (between right and wrong)"* (al-Baqarah, 2: 185). However, in order to benefit from *hidayah*, the seeker of Truth has to develop the quality of Allah-consciousness, an ever-present awareness of His presence and being watched by Him.

> Unlike other Scriptures which address a specific people, the Qur'an addresses the whole of mankind and not only their spiritual or ritualistic matters but also their social, economic, political as well as legal issues. The Qur'an talks about itself as *al-Hidāyah*, the Guidance, in more than two-hundred and eighty places.

Taqwa is a Prerequisite of *Hidayah*

Another major theme linked with *hidayah*, which is highlighted here, is *taqwa* or Allah-consciousness (doing one's best to please Him and to avoid His anger). *Taqwa* is mentioned by the Qur'an as a prerequisite for benefiting from this *hidayah*. This *taqwa*, or the desire to achieve it, facilitates the journey of the seeker of Truth (*haqq*). The word *taqwa* is often, literally translated as God-fearing while as a comprehensive Qur'anic terminology it also refers to a desired quality of Allah-consciousness.

The root word *waqa* means to protect, preserve, guard, shield and to keep one safe from detriment or loss. But its recurrent use and emphasis in the Qur'an compels one to regard it as one of the key concepts and a major theme with implications of visible behavioural change in a believer's conduct. Its role in making the act of worship (*'ibadah*) meaningful is clearly indicated by the Qur'an: "*Believers, fasting is enjoined upon you as it was prescribed upon those before you that you may become Allah-conscious (la'allakum tattaqun)*" (al-Baqarah, 2: 183). With reference to the sacrifice of animals after *hajj* Allah says, "*It is neither their meat nor their blood that reaches Allah; It is your taqwa that reaches Him*" (al-Hajj, 22: 37). The message or *da'wah* that the Prophet ﷺ conveyed to people focussed on *taqwa*: "*I am a trustworthy messenger to you. So have Allah's taqwa and obey me*" (al-Shu'ara', 26: 125-126). The same is reemphasized in the following verse, "*O you who believe, have taqwa of Allah as is His right to have taqwa*" (al-Imran, 3: 102) or "*Have taqwa of Allah as much as you can*" (al-Taghabun, 64: 16). These Qur'anic verses focus on *taqwa* in the sense of performing acts of worship and devotion *par excellence*, i.e. in their most perfect and beautiful way. This aspect is further reflected in the following verses: "*For sure Allah is with those who hold Him in taqwa and do good (muhsinun)*" (al-Nahl, 16: 128).

Those who choose *taqwa* and do good deeds win Allah's favour: "*There will be no blame on those who believe and do righteous deeds for whatever they might have partaken (in the past) as long as they refrain from the things prohibited and persist in the faith and do righteous deeds and continue to refrain from whatever is forbidden and submit to Divine Commandments and persevere in doing good fearing Allah. Allah loves those who do good (muhsinin)*" (al-Ma'idah, 5: 93).

Taqwa in the Qur'an is directly linked with the attitude and behaviour of the believers: "*Those who obey Allah and His Messenger and fear Him and avoid disobeying Him such indeed shall triumph*" (al-Nur, 24: 52).

Taqwa as a behavioural outward practice is expected to be equally reflected in the believer's acts of worship (*'ibadah*) and in their financial and personal matters: "*Believers! have fear of Allah (ittaqu Allah) and give up all outstanding interest if you do truly believe*" (al-Baqarah, 2: 278). That such obedience to Allah must be reflected in one's conduct and behaviour is a leitmotif in the Qur'an. All the Prophets of Allah demanded this one thing from their followers: "*Fear Allah (fatttaqu Allah) and obey me and do not follow the biddings of those who go to excesses*" (al-Shu'ara, 26: 150-151).

The impact of *taqwa* on the believer's behaviour is also reflected in their speech and loyalty to Allah as opposed to their loyalty to nationalism, regionalism, and communalism. Allah makes clear in the Quran: "*Believers avoid being excessively suspicious, for some suspicion is a sin. Do not spy nor backbite one another. Would any of you like to eat the flesh of his dead brother? You would surely detest it. Have fear of Allah (wa'ttaqu Allah). Surely Allah is much prone to accept repentance, is Most Compassionate. Human beings, We created you all from a male and a female, and made you into nations and tribes so that you may know one another. Verily the noblest of you in the sight of Allah is the most Allah-conscious (atqakum) of you. Surely Allah is All-Knowing, All-Aware*" (al-Hujurat, 49: 12-13).

Those who have *taqwa* are declared to be ultimately successful: "*Believers be steadfast, and live in steadfastness, stand firm in your faith, and hold Allah in fear (wa'ttaqu Allah), so that you may attain true success*" (Al 'Imran, 3: 200).

The Qur'an as guidance (*hidayah*) provides universal ethical solutions to the individual and collective needs of human societies, and the same is fully preserved in the practice of the Prophet ﷺ as a role model of *taqwa*. In other words, *taqwa* means following the Qur'an and Sunnah of the Prophet ﷺ.

The Essence of *Taqwa*

The kind of *taqwa* the Qur'an expects from the believer has nothing to do with abandoning the world and leaving their natural needs in favour of a world of so-called spirituality and piety. *Taqwa* means achieving the best ethical and moral conduct, practice, and behaviour in all human transactions while having the sense of Allah's constant presence.

The Ethical Empowerment of Human Beings

Since the purpose of the creation of human beings and jinn, as clearly stated in the Qur'an, is to wilfully serve and obey Allah, therefore the jinn and humans are gifted with free will. With reference to human beings, the Qur'an says: *"And we have shown him the two highways [i.e. the path of virtue and the path of vice]"* (al-Balad, 90: 10). Prophet Adam ﷺ was empowered with the knowledge of things as well as the freedom of will. By contrast, angels due to their constitution, are not given the choice to disobey. Human beings are empowered to excel in doing good but, at the same time, they are given the option to act otherwise. The story of Adam's creation–his empowerment through knowledge and the bowing down of the angels to him on Allah's command–shows the significance and power of knowledge. The Qur'an elsewhere mentions that those who are knowledgeable cannot be equal to those who are not: *"Are those who know equal to those who do not know?"* (al-Zumar, 39: 9). We are also told that it is the knowledgeable who have more fear of Allah (*khashyah*): *"From among His servants ('ibad), it is only those who know that fear Allah"* (Fatir, 35: 28). The first test related to exercising this freedom of will, as Muhammad Iqbal (1877-1938) calls it, was when Adam and Eve were asked to avoid going near a tree. Due to forgetfulness and the temptation of Satan, they failed to follow Allah's instructions. But as soon as they realized their mistake they returned to Allah, Who taught them how to repent and their repentance was accepted. They were then asked to follow the original plan of living on earth as the deputy (*Khalifah*) of Allah. They were asked to follow the guidance (*hidayah*) sent to them, from time to time, through Allah's angel: *"We said: Get you down from here, all of you and guidance shall come to you from Me; then, whoever will follow My guidance (huda) need have no fear nor shall they grieve"* (al-Baqarah, 2: 38). This ethical empowerment to act virtuously or wickedly is only given to human beings and the jinn.

It is due to the unceasing and boundless love and mercy of Allah towards His servants that He provides humankind with continuous guidance, in order for them to succeed in this world and Hereafter. Throughout the history of mankind, guidance was sent down to people through selected pious persons, the Messengers of Allah, as is mentioned in the Qur'an: *"Surely We revealed the Torah, wherein there is guidance (huda) and light (nur)…"* (al-Ma'idah, 5: 44); *"And We gave him Gospel (al-Injil) wherein is Guidance and Light and which confirms the truth of whatever there still remained of the Torah, and a guidance (huda) and admonition (maw'izah) for the Allah-fearing (muttaqin)"* (al-Ma'idah, 5: 46).

The Role of Guidance (*Hidayah*) in Achieving *Taqwa*, Virtue, Piety and Servitude

Guidance invariably focuses on the core message of observing loyalty to the Creator alone. The source of guidance, throughout the history of humankind, according to the Qur'an has been only one i.e. Allah the Owner of all Universes: *"We raised a Messenger in every community (to call them) serve Allah and shun the Evil one (al-taghut), thereafter* Allah *guided (hada) some of them while others were overtaken by error"* (al-Nahl, 16: 36).

Although human beings are gifted with intellect and the capacity to observe, collect information and classify it, human reason and experience alone fall short, due to their limitations and finitude, which prevent it from being authentic enough to provide comprehensive and universal guidance on how to live a meaningful life. Divine guidance, stemming from the All-Knowing alone, therefore, has the capacity to lead to the path of success, righteousness, piety and *taqwa*: *"As for those who were led to the guidance (ihtadu), Allah increases them in their guidance (huda) and causes them to grow in Allah-consciousness (taqwahum)"* (Muhammad, 47: 17). Having a sincere desire along with exercising the right effort, therefore, seem to be a pre-condition for benefitting from Allah's guidance. In *al-Fatihah*, this sincere desire is fully expressed and Allah did not leave such a supplication unheeded: *"And whosoever has faith in Allah, Allah directs his heart along the Right Path (yahdi). Allah has knowledge of everything"* (al-Taghabun, 64: 11).

Responding to human beings' basic need for guidance, two aspects are underscored right at the beginning of *Surah al-Baqarah*. First, here is the Guidance (the Book) and, second, this Book alone can lead to success in this life and in the Hereafter if the seekers of Truth, or the *muttaqin*, are sincere. A recognition of the kindness of Allah in providing guidance to the seekers of Truth demands humble behaviour and a grateful attitude from the believers; an attitude which makes them more and more observant of and committed to Allah's obedience: *"All praise be to Allah Who has guided us on to this. Had it not been for Allah, Who granted us right guidance, we would not be on the Right Path"* (al-A'raf, 7: 43) and similarly the following verse: *"... it is the guidance (huda) for the muttaqin"* (al-Baqarah, 2: 2).

An Illustration of *Taqwa*

The attitude and behaviour of *taqwa* are beautifully illustrated in a discussion between 'Umar, the second Rightly-guided caliph, and the well-known Companion Ubayy ibn Ka'b. 'Umar asked him what is *taqwa*? Instead of giving a direct answer, Ubayy said to 'Umar: "When you walk on a pathway full of shrubs and thorns what do you do?" 'Umar responded we protect our dress from being torn by the shrubs. Ubayy ibn Ka'b then said: "This is exactly the way of *taqwa*", i.e. that a person should be watchful in all his behaviour and allow no lapses in his ethical conduct.

"If you persist in misbehaving how will you guard yourself (fakayfa tattaqun) against the (woe of) the Day that will turn children

grey-haired" (al-Muzammil, 73: 17). In the verse above the Qur'an further refers to the meaning of *taqwa* in terms of acting ethically in this world in order to shield oneself from punishment on the Day of Judgement. And similarly, *"And those who feared (ittaqu) disobeying their Lord, shall be driven in companies to Paradise..."* (al-Zumar, 39: 73).

When we read this Qur'anic verse in conjunction with the next one it seems that *taqwa* is the main purpose of worship as well as of all forms of servitude (*'ubudiyyah*) to Allah, because a servant (*'abd*) cannot have more than one master at one and the same time. This further reinforces *tawhid* both in terms of the Existence and Attributes of Allah, and that the acts of worship increase *taqwa* in the believer: *"And whoso venerates the sanctity of all that has been ordained as signs of Allah surely does so because of the true piety of the hearts (taqwa al-qulub)"* (al-Hajj, 22: 32).

One of the most comprehensive elaborations of *taqwa* and truthfulness (*sidq*) can be seen in *Surah al-Baqarah*, in the famous *ayat al-birr*: *"Righteousness (birr) does not consist in turning your faces towards the East or towards the West, true righteousness consists in believing in Allah and the Last Day, the Angels, the Book, and the Prophets, and in giving away one's property in love of Him to one's kinsmen, the orphans, the poor and the wayfarers, and to those who ask for help, and in freeing the necks of slaves, and in establishing prayers and dispersing the zakah (true righteousness is attained by those) who are faithful to their promises once they have made it, and by those who remain steadfast in adversity and affliction at the time of battle (between Truth and falsehood). Such are the truthful (sadaqu) ones, such are the Allah-conscious (muttaqun)"* (al-Baqarah, 2: 177).

> ### The Scope of *Birr*
>
> According to *al-Baqarah* 2: 177, the scope of *birr* includes,
> 1. Belief in the articles of faith;
> 2. Observance of rights (*huquq*) of Allah through acts of worship (*'ibadah*);
> 3. Observing the rights of other people (*huquq al-'ibad*), social engagement, and responsibility towards the needy;
> 4. Constancy in one's ethical conduct and behaviour.

This rather long verse in *al-Baqarah* contains a treasure trove of wisdom and guidance relating to virtue and *taqwa*, matters of faith, worship, and social dealings. First, it refers to the scope of *birr* (virtue, piety, purity, and righteousness) and that it is not confined to strictly observing the prayer. In very simple words, it points out that virtue is not confined to turning one's face toward the East or West. Pre-empting that this statement may reduce the value and centrality of *salah*, later in the same sequence the establishment of prayer is underscored to ensure that the believer remains fully aware of its importance and should not think that mere fulfilment of social responsibilities can be a substitute for the prayer which is an obligatory act (*faridah*) of worship.

The *ayat al-birr* also highlights the significance of faith (*'aqidah*) as an integral part of *birr*, *taqwa* and *sidq*. It mentions that there can be no virtue, goodness, or piety if one does not affirm one's belief in *tawhid*, the Hereafter, prophethood, the existence of angels and the Revealed Book. Here the word Book is used not in plural but in singular thus referring to the Qur'an alone. After enumerating these articles of faith, the focus of *birr* and *taqwa* is shifted to the believer's social ethics and responsibility, not as a *charity* but, as an *obligation*.

The verse also prioritizes social and financial responsibility and obligations toward the next of kin (*aqriba'*), the extended family and near relatives, who are defined elsewhere in *Surah al-Nur* 24: 61 as one's parents, brothers and sisters, uncles and aunts, cousins, etc. The point that pertains to *taqwa* here is that what matters is not to spend from surplus wealth, which may carry less importance for a person, but rather to spend from that wealth which one loves and values. Here a revolutionary concept is introduced of sharing what one loves with relatives as an obligation. Usually, whatever is surplus and over and above one's need, at a given time, is given to others. Here, on the contrary, it is said that one should give what one values for himself, (*mimma tuhibun*) to the deserving.

Birr and *taqwa* also require that one spends on the orphans, a usually neglected segment of society. Again, it is not left to one's own personal judgement, but the verse carries the force of an obligation. Therefore virtue, piety and *taqwa* can be measured, for example, by the believer's attitude toward the orphans. Supporting and helping orphans is thus one key performance indicator (KPI) of *taqwa*.

Similarly, social obligations include helping those in need (*masakin*), especially those who do not stretch their hand for help out of self-esteem and embarrassment. The believers are asked to go looking for those in need to help them out, again not as an act of *charity* but as an *obligation*. The scope of social obligations is further extended to those who are compelled to ask for help, the wayfarers, and those who are deprived. Needless to say that Islam does not encourage mendicancy and it strives to alleviate poverty and reduce dependency by empowering people to be self-reliant and learning to manage their livelihoods. *Zakah* is a mandatory permanent institution created for this purpose. Sincere gift (*sadaqah*) and spending on others (*infaq*) are voluntary contributions in the way of Allah, and serve the same purpose. Both are an indicator of the level of a believer's *taqwa*.

In the same vein, another vital area is touched upon the social and collective obligation of the believers to eliminate slavery from society. So the verse makes a specific command which stipulates that *taqwa* requires not only performing acts of worship and taking care of the near ones, the orphans and the needy but it is also a matter of getting free those who are bonded, enslaved and deprived of their physical, religious, cultural and intellectual freedom, or their liberties and human rights. Here, virtue, righteousness and Allah-consciousness are directly linked to emancipating those who are deprived and oppressed. The emancipation which is meant here is not confined to physical slavery but also includes cultural, religious, intellectual and economic colonialism, the violation of human rights as well as covert cultural and intellectual colonialism, imperialism, eurocentrism, and the so-called new world order, which aim to subjugate the people of the world economically, politically, intellectually and culturally.

Having touched on these vital issues and establishing an internal link between Allah-consciousness (*taqwa*), righteousness (*birr*) and truthfulness (*sidq*), the verse then refers to constancy (*istiqamah*), steadfastness (*sabr*), and firm resolution (*'azm al-'umur*) of the believers in their social matters.

Let it be reiterated, *taqwa* in the Qur'an does not refer to any kind of asceticism or denial of the world. In most world religions, piety is considered a sign of spirituality which is reflected in one's withdrawal from society and material life. Spiritual elevation is linked to self-mortification and physical discomfort. Therefore, celibacy, continuous fasting, ongoing vigil, standing exposed to the heat of the sun, or knee-deep in freezing cold water, sleeping on a bed of iron nails, eating only one chickpea in a day, (as done by the Buddha) and such other practices are observed in order to achieve spirituality, piety and enlightenment. The above Qur'anic understanding of *taqwa* does not approve of any of these so-called ways of purification of the soul for achieving enlightenment. An outstanding statement on the meaning of *taqwa* is made right at the beginning of *Surah al-Nisa'* in the context of marital relations which are considered, in some religions, too worldly and carnal: "*O people, have God-fearingness (taqwa) of your Lord who created you from a single being and out of it created its mate and out of the two spread many men and women. Have Allah's taqwa in whose name you plead your rights and heed the ties of kinship. Surely, Allah is ever watchful over you*" (al-Nisa', 4: 1).

Taqwa as a Behavioural Practice, Objective of all Acts of Devotion and a Key Theme in the Qur'an

Taqwa, here, refers to living a normal family life and getting involved in procreation, not just as a biological activity but as an indication of *taqwa* to the extent that an authentic tradition of the

Prophet ﷺ referring to marriage states that: "Whoever shies away from my Sunnah, (i.e. married life and having a balanced lifestyle) is not of me." In other words, a person who consciously rejects getting married and prefers to live alone is regarded by the Prophet ﷺ as a person who does not belong to his *ummah*.

This is why, *taqwa* is mentioned right at the beginning along with the other important theme of guidance (*hidayah*). The Book offers guidance to all those who desire to be God-fearing (*muttaqi*) and act with full awareness of the presence of their Lord around them. They seek guidance and help from Him and He showers His blessings and guidance and help on them: *"Allah will find a way out for him who fears Allah (yattaqi Allah) and will provide him sustenance from where he never even imagined"* (al-Talaq, 65: 2-3).

It is due to the importance and centrality of *taqwa*, as a behavioural trait, that the Qur'an wants the believers to practise and observe it to live a meaningful and purposeful life in society: *"Believers fear Allah (ittaqu Allah) as He should be feared and see that you do not die save in submission to Allah"* (Al 'Imran, 3: 102). The wilful observance of one's social responsibilities and the rights of Allah (*huquq Allah*) is the essence of *taqwa*. Therefore, the more one yearns for *taqwa*, the more one gets closer to Allah which is translated into excellence in observing Allah's directives and commands. *"So, hold Allah in awe (fa'ttaqu Allah mastata'tum) as much as you can, and listen and obey and do infaq"* (al-Taghabun, 64: 16).

Wherever it is mentioned in the Qur'an, *taqwa* is often followed by one or another act of goodness, benefit and welfare which raises the status of the believer to become from among those who are conscious of Allah. This is why we consider it a tangible behavioural category.

> ### A Point of Reflection
>
> This elaboration of who the Allah-conscious (*muttaqi*) are, by the Book itself, synergizes faith, worship, and social responsibility. *Taqwa*, therefore, is not a metaphysical, intan-gible concept. It can be measured through one's regularity in prayers, giving of *zakah*, *sadaqah*, spending on one's parents, spouse, children, other relatives as well as on the needy in society. Particularly, *taqwa* is manifested in helping out and liberating people who are enslaved politically, culturally, economically, and intellectually. It also includes other measurable behaviours such as keeping one's promises, contracts, and pledges, belief in the Unseen (*al-ghayb*) or Suprasensible Reality.

Al-ghayb is another central theme in the Qur'an which is dealt with from an ethical perspective. It simply means believing in matters of the Unseen (*ghayb*), that is to say, what lies beyond human sensory experience and perception. The term has its roots in *ghaba* which means to be absent, hidden, invisible or concealed. But whatever is concealed or hidden or invisible does not mean that it is non-existent. Therefore, it is unscientific and irrational to deny its presence because the realm of science does not extend to what is non-empirical.

The realm of *ghayb* also relates to matters which are normally difficult and not possible within human reach, or to experience physically, such as the person of Allah. Yet Allah's existence and presence are a reality. Angels cannot be seen by the human eye, yet they exist and have delivered Allah's message to all Prophets of

Allah. Paradise and Hell do exist, but no common human being can perceive them. Having said that, the Prophet ﷺ in his *isra' wal Mi'raj*, journey of ascension, was shown a glimpse of the life in the other world, so that he could give an eyewitness account of things which normal human beings cannot perceive.

The nature of the Unseen (*ghayb*) and its knowledge is essentially Allah's domain. The arriving of the Day of Judgement is an article of faith and a recurring theme in the Qur'an. Justice demands to have a day of recompense for those who suffered in this world due to their truthfulness, honesty and following Allah's commands: *"So whoever does an atom's weight of good shall see it, and whoever does an atom's weight of evil shall see it"* (al-Zilzal, 99: 7-8). Therefore, a fair evidence-based ethical judgement is not only a common article of faith in the Abrahamic traditions but also a logical and ethical necessity.

Thus, the angels, Paradise, and Hell also become an ethical necessity. In the famous tradition of Jibril, faith in the Unseen is clearly illustrated when the archangel Jibril appeared in human form and not in his original appearance. In his conversation with the Prophet ﷺ, it was apparent that even Jibril does not have full knowledge of some matters of the Unseen. It is Allah alone Who knows all of the Unseen: *"He has the keys to the realm of the non-perceptible; That no one knows but He. And He knows what is on earth and in sea. Not a leaf does fall but with His knowledge"* (al-An'am, 6: 59). That the Prophets of Allah too have no access to the Unseen except that which Allah tells them about is evidenced in the Qur'an: *"Say, I do not say to you that I have the treasures of Allah, nor do I have knowledge of what is beyond the reach of perception nor do I say to you I am an angel. I only follow what is revealed to me"* (al-An'am, 6: 50).

Since human life in this world and particularly human ethical conduct in all possible activities, is directly linked to the Afterlife–which is not perceivable by an ordinary person, belief in the Unseen is an integral part of faith in Islam, Judaism and Christianity.

After referring to belief in the Unseen, as a prerequisite for benefiting from the Book, the verse mentions that those who are Allah-conscious establish the prayer (*salah*), spend of what Allah has given them (*infaq fi sabil Allah*), believe in the earlier revelations which Allah sent down to His Messengers and also in the Hereafter; those are the ones successful (*muflihun*) in the Hereafter.

The Real Success (*Falah*)

Success (*falah*), as a theme, is related to people's ultimate achievement and destiny in the Hereafter. The root *falaha* means to split/cleave, hence, to plough and cultivate. The word for a farmer in Arabic is *fallah*. A farmer ploughs and puts seeds in the land which grow and yield agricultural products. Similarly, the world we live in is like a farm in which we either plant good seeds which produce good fruit or bad seeds which give a poor yield. Ethical conduct and behaviour are like good seeds but whose fruits are not always seen in this world. In the Qur'an, the word *falah* is generally used for success and salvation in the Hereafter. All good deeds done in this world result in a pleasing success in the Hereafter. Another word used in the Qur'an which has a similar sense is *fawz*.

Falah in the Qur'an is linked with sincere self-improvement: "*He who purified himself shall prosper*" (al-A'la, 87: 14). Success, salvation and the ultimate achievement of the believers in the Hereafter are directly connected to ethical conduct and behaviour in this world. No good deed can go unnoticed or unrewarded in the Hereafter: "*The believers have indeed attained true success; those* who in their prayers, humble themselves; who avoid whatever is vain and frivolous; who observe zakah; who strictly guard their private parts; save from their wives or those whom their right hands possess, for with regard to them they are free from blame; as for those who seek beyond that, they are transgressors; who are true to their trusts and their covenants, and who guard their prayers; such are the inheritors, that shall inherit Paradise and in it they shall abide forever"* (al-Mu'minun, 23: 1-11).

Although revealed in Madinah, the verse uses the word *infaq* instead of *zakah*. *Infaq* covers a wider category while *zakah* is specific to what is obligated on the believers. The threshold (*nisab*), conditions and eligible recipients of *zakah* are fixed by the Qur'an and the Prophet ﷺ, while *infaq* has no minimum or maximum limits.

The Culture of *Infaq*

The root word *nafaqa* means to sell well and to finish something, therefore *infaq* means spending. As a recurring theme, spending in the way of Allah (*infaq fi sabil Allah*) stands for spending one's money and property, rather than investing it for personal gain alone in order to please Allah: *"The example of those who spend to please Allah is that of a garden on a high ground, if a heavy rain smites it, it brings forth its fruits twofold, and if there is no heavy rain, even a light shower suffices it. Allah sees all that you do"* (al-Baqarah, 2: 265). The Qur'an puts great emphasis on *infaq*: *"Those who spend their wealth by night and by day secretly and publicly, will find that their reward is secure with their Lord and that there is no reason for them to entertain any fear or grief"* (al-Baqarah, 2: 274). Yet Allah wants to make things easy (*yusr*) for His servants: *"Whoever has abundant means let him spend out of what Allah has given him. Allah does not* burden any human being beyond the means that He has bestowed upon him. Possibly Allah will grant ease after hardship" (al-Talaq, 65: 7). Knowing well the nature of human beings, the Qur'an cautions that *infaq* is to be done without any intention of showing off (*riya'*): *"The example of those who spend their wealth in the way of Allah is like that of a grain of corn that sprouts seven ears, and in every ear there are a hundred grains. Thus, Allah multiplies the action of whomsoever He wills. Allah is Munificent, All-Knowing"* (al-Baqarah, 2: 261).

The culture of *infaq* thus created makes the Muslim community socially engaged, responsible and cohesive. It helps in transforming a self-centred and individualistic personality into a socially responsive and involved personality, well-connected in the community. It also helps in overcoming greed, and self-centredness. *Infaq fi sabil Allah* helps in building a personality trait reflective of *taqwa* and *iman*.

Similarly, Allah states in the Quran: *"And hasten to the forgiveness of your Lord and to a Paradise as vast as the Heaven and the earth, prepared for the Allah-fearing, who spend (yunfiqun) in the way of Allah both in affluence and hardship, who restrain their anger and forgive others. Allah loves such good-doers"* (Al 'Imran, 3: 133-134).

Affluence and comfortable living often make one forget about one's social obligations. Fully aware of this human nature, the Qur'an advises: *"Believers let your possessions and your offspring not make you negligent of Allah's remembrance. For whoever does that they will be losers. And spend of what Allah has granted you by way of sustenance before death should come to any one of you and he should say: Lord why did you not defer my return for a while so that I might give sadaqah and be among the righteous"* (al-Munafiqun 63: 9-10)

Basic Themes in the First Five Verses of *al-Baqarah*

The first five verses of *al-Baqarah* touch on several basic themes and social issues. First and foremost, the Divine character of the Qur'an is confirmed: that this Book is from Allah and contains nothing but the Truth. Second, only those who believe in the Unseen (*ghayb*) [such as the existence of Paradise, Hell and the angels] are most likely to accept and follow the teachings of the Qur'an. Third, they confirm their faith by establishing the prayer (*salah*). Fourth, they spend in the way of Allah (*infaq*). Fifth, they believe in the earlier revelations sent by Allah to other nations. Sixth, their target in all their worldly endeavours is success in the life Hereafter.

Two Types of Human Conduct and Behaviour: Disbelief (*Kufr*) and Hypocrisy (*Nifaq*)

"As for those who have rejected (these truths) it is all the same whether or not you warn them for they will not believe. Allah has sealed their hearts and their hearing, and a covering has fallen over their eyes. They deserve severe chastisement" (al-Baqarah, 2: 6-7). After a brief description of those who seek *taqwa*, have firm belief in the Unseen (*ghayb*), and establish a system of *salah* and *infaq*, now reference is made in the above and next fifteen ayahs (6-20) to those who knowingly reject the Divine *hidayah* and are therefore qualitatively called *Kuffar*.

Kufr, the root word *k f r* means to cover or to hide. It also carries the sense of denial of something. *Kufr* is used as an opposite of *iman* which means affirmation and belief. *Kufr* is also used as an opposite of gratitude (*shukr*). *Kafir* (pl. *kuffar, Kafirun*) means someone who wilfully and knowingly denies the truth and Allah's guidance. *Kufr* may assume different forms. One very obvious form is atheism, or the total denial of a transcendent Deity, the Supreme Being or Lord of the Universe and of human beings. In some cases, *kufr* or polytheism (*shirk*) stands for accepting others beside one God, as in the case of Hinduism, all such forms of associationism (plurality of gods) are called *shirk* by the Qur'an. *Kufr* implies the denial of the One and Only God as the *Ilah*, and Creator, as well as the denial of His Messengers, angels, and the Day of Judgement. It is also *kufr* to believe in the Prophethood of anyone after the final Messenger ﷺ or any guidance after that of Allah's final Book, the Qur'an.

Kafir also refers to the person who follows blindly the traditions of their forefathers, disregards the demands of reason and knowingly rejects Allah's guidance. The Qur'an mentions the behaviour pattern of *kufr* as a recurring phenomenon in the history of mankind. Messengers of Allah were oppressed, ridiculed, insulted, and even killed by such arrogant people who blindly followed the ways of their forefathers. *Kufr*, or wilful denial and insensitivity to the call to righteousness, hardens their hearts which then become as insensitive as a rock. They listen to the beautiful recitations of the Qur'an but never try to grasp its message and meaning. They watch with their own eyes the excellent exemplary conduct of the Prophet ﷺ of Allah, but they never welcome his message.

This attitude of loyalty to local customs, ideologies and culture is not confined to the past. In the modern age of information technology and artificial intelligence, the followers of materialism think they can do whatever they wish through technology and there is no place for God in their worldview. Secularism does not necessarily deny the existence of God, but it restricts the domain of religion to personal life. This dualism of secularism, i.e. one day in the week for worshipping God (Sunday, Saturday or Friday), and the rest of the week for serving material benefits and personal desires, is also a form of *shirk* because it divides life into two exclusive domains, a secular domain and a sacred one. The followers of *shirk* and *kufr* are warned here of a horrible punishment in the Hereafter. The Qur'an repeatedly invites both the disbelievers and polytheists to use their faculties of observation and reason to discover the real Designer, Creator and Sustainer of life and the universe. They are invited to reflect on the beautiful ethical teachings of the Qur'an and come out of their blind following of the customs of old in order to embrace a life of real peace, blessings and success.

The Muslims in Makkah were subjected to oppression and torture by the disbelievers and idolaters just like the followers of the earlier Messengers of Allah were by the disbelievers of their time. The disbelievers and idolaters were their open enemies. But after the migration (*hijrah*) to Madinah, they encountered a new type of denier of the truth, namely, the hypocrites (*munafiqun*) who professed Islam outwardly but actually hated it totally in their hearts.

The Meaning of Hypocrisy (*Nifaq*)

In the following verse, the Qur'an further elaborates on the notions of unbelief and hypocrisy. The latter is defined by the Qur'an as a disease of the heart. The hypocrite (*munafiq*, pl. *munafiqun*) refers to the person who appears and acts like a Muslim, may even come half-heartedly to pray in the mosque, but lacks sincerity and may intend to harm Islam. In this context, the Qur'an refers to *masjid al-dirar* which was built by the hypocrites who were conspiring to harm the Muslim community from within.

In the newly established polity of Madinah, the hypocrites represented a third behavioural pattern. This was prominent among the Jewish converts, who had their old settlements around Madinah. They had their historical alliances with the major tribes of Madinah namely Aws and Khazraj. They used deceptive ways of declaring Islam as their faith in the morning but by the evening withdrew and, dissociated, in order to confuse the Muslim community of Madinah, who considered them, as People of the Book, knowledgeable in religious matters. The Qur'an calls them *munafiqun* or hypocrites. The sincere and true believers always responded to the Prophetic directives by saying: "we believe and testify to the truth of what we hear" (*amanna wa-saddaqna*) while the hypocrites were duplicitous in their conduct and behaviour and lacked sincerity (*ikhlas*) and loyalty. The hypocrites posed a serious threat to the newly established society and state of Madinah. The problem they presented was that they could not be trusted but, at the same time, they could not be treated like disbelievers or idolaters.

The Qur'an exposes them thus: *"Whenever they are told: do not spread mischief on earth, they say: why, we indeed are the ones who set things right. They are mischief makers, but they do not realize it. Whenever they are told: Believe as others believe, they answer: Shall we believe as the fools have believed? Indeed, it is they who are the fools, but they are not aware of it. When they meet believers, they say we believe, but when they meet their evil companions in privacy, they say surely, we are with you, we were merely jesting. Allah jests with them, leaving them to wander blindly in their rebellion. These are the ones who have purchased error in exchange for guidance"* (al-Baqarah, 2: 11-16).

The Qur'an helps us understand the meaning of hypocrisy: *"These hypocrites watch you closely: if victory is granted to you by Allah, they will say "Were we not with you". And were the unbelievers to gain the upper hand, they will say "Did we not have mastery over you, and yet we protected you from the believers? It is Allah who will judge between you on the Day of Resurrection and He will not allow the unbelievers, in any way, to gain advantage over the believers"* (al-Nisa', 4: 141).

Hypocrisy, as mentioned earlier, is a disease of the heart, and the Prophet ﷺ had to face the threat posed by the hypocrites with wisdom and deep insight. The hypocrites of Madinah and the surrounding Jewish tribes were continuously in communication with the Makkan idolaters and they worked together to harm the interests of the Muslims.

Ultimately, the hypocrites could not fully hide their hypocrisy, and the Prophet ﷺ and the Prophet's Companions could identify them due to their behaviour. One of the signs of their hypocrisy was their lax attitude towards the five daily obligated prayers and their avoidance of participation in *jihad*: *"When they rise to prayers, they rise reluctantly and only to be seen by people. They remember Allah but little"* (al-Nisa', 4: 142). Their dislike of and unwillingness to participate in *jihad* is mentioned in the Qur'an: *"What befell you on the day when the two hosts met, was by the leave of Allah and in order that He might mark out those who believe from those who are hypocrites. And when these hypocrites were asked to come and fight in the way of Allah, or defend yourself, they answered: if we but knew that there would be fighting, we would certainly have followed. They were then nearer to infidelity than to faith. They utter from their mouths what is not in their hearts. Allah knows very well what they conceal"* (Al 'Imran, 3: 166-167).

A common tactic used by the hypocrites among the Jews was to publicly declare their Islam and later announce their dissatisfaction with it and revert to their original faith. Consequently, innocent Muslims, who had great regard for the Jews as People of the Book, were confused by this phenomenon. It is stated in the Quran: *"People of the Book! Why do you confound the Truth with falsehood and why do you conceal the Truth knowingly? A party of the People of the Book said: Believe in the morning what has been revealed to those who believe and then deny it in the evening that they may retract"* (Al 'Imran, 3: 71-72).

They were tolerated by the Prophet ﷺ because they claimed to be Muslims and they were so outwardly. But after the Battle of *Ahzab*, in the 5th year of the *hijrah*, the Qur'an directed the Prophet ﷺ and the believers to fight them just like they fought the idolaters: *"O Prophet ﷺ strive against the unbelievers and the hypocrites and be severe to them. Hell shall be their abode, what an evil destination"* (al-Tawbah, 9: 73). Elsewhere, the Qur'an further states, *"Surely, the hypocrite shall be in the lowest depth of the Fire and you shall find none to come to their help"* (al-Nisa', 4: 145).

The hypocrites, the Qur'an points out, are extremely short-sighted. They opt for immediate gains and refuse to face any hardships in the cause of truth and justice. They want to accumulate worldly benefits from the Muslim community as well as from the enemies of Islam, to whom they owe their real allegiance.

Even though the hypocrites of Madinah were few in number, their presence was a matter of concern. The Qur'an warns them about their ultimate destination, which is the lowest level of Hell. Nevertheless, the Qur'an also keeps reminding them about Allah's ongoing favours on them in this world, despite their rebellious conduct that perhaps they realize their ungratefulness to Allah and, thus, return to Him: *"O mankind serve your Lord Who has created you as well as those before you; do so that you are saved. It is He Who has made the earth a resting place for you, and the sky a canopy, and sent down water from above with which He brought forth fruit for your sustenance. Do not, then, set up rivals to Allah when you know (the Truth)"* (al-Baqarah, 2: 21-23).

Hypocrisy enters a person's heart secretly and often one fails to discover it. It is therefore necessary to keep on seeking Allah's refuge from such strikes of Satan, who is always looking for an opportunity to misguide a believer.

The Inimitability of the Qur'an

In the following verse, *"If you are in any doubt whether it is We Who have revealed this Book to Our servant, then produce just a surah like it, and call all your supporters and seek in it the support of all the others save Allah. Accomplish this if you are truthful. But if you fail to do this and you will most certainly fail then have fear of the fire whose fuel are men and stones and which has been prepared for those who deny the truth"* (al-Baqarah, 2: 23-24), the Qur'an puts forward a challenge to all those who considered themselves men of learning, that if they think the Qur'an is the product of a human mind, then let them collect all the experts of the Arabic language and literature and jointly produce a *surah* like the *surah*s of the Qur'an. Here, the Qur'an responds to the objection of the idolaters that it is not a Divine Revelation but a sort of poetic magical spell, created by the Prophet ﷺ, and this is why they described him as a poet or as a *majnun*, one possessed. Elsewhere, the Qur'an invites all those who are proud and confident of their poetic and literary prowess to produce only ten *surahs* like those of the Qur'an. A single *surah* can be short, consisting of a minimum of three verses, or very long and consisting of up to 286 verses, as is the case with *al-Baqarah*: *"Do they say: He has invented this Book himself? Say: If that is so, bring ten surahs the like of it of your composition, and call upon all that you can to your help other than Allah. Do so if you are truthful"* (Hud, 11: 13). In *Surah Yunus*, the challenge is reduced to producing just one *surah*: *"Do they say that the Messenger has himself composed the Qur'an? Say, in that case bring forth just one surah like it and call on all whom you can, except Allah to help you if you are truthful"* (Yunus, 10: 38). Here, in *al-Baqarah*, the same challenge is repeated: *"If you are in any doubt whether it is We Who have revealed this Book to Our servant, then produce just a surah like it ..."* (al-Baqarah, 2: 23). The Qur'an goes further and in *Surah al-Tur*, the challenge is made into a general one: *"Do they say: He has himself fabricated the Qur'an. No, the truth is that they are altogether averse to believing (if they are truthful to this) then let them produce a discourse of similar splendour"* (al-Tur, 52: 33-34).

The Wisdom (*Hikmah*) in the Challenge to Produce Something Like the Qur'an

Why does the Qur'an touch on this important aspect at the beginning of *al-Baqarah*? Obviously, because it is a unique Book with its own structure which is unlike other books written by human beings. It addresses existential issues but from a transcendent perspective. There are at least three reasons why the Qur'an raises this issue at the beginning of this *surah*. Firstly, no human mind has the capacity to produce guidance that transcends the finitude of time and space. All the world classics produced by human beings are subject to time and space while everything in the Qur'an is Divine and not particular to a specific time, place or people. Secondly, it is revealed in an explicit Arabic language devoid of any unnecessary abstractions and complexities, yet it carries high literary value. The Arabs were particularly proud of their literary excellence and command over poetry. This is why the Qur'an invites them to produce something like it since they think it is not Divine but the work of the Prophet ﷺ. Their inability to produce something similar to the Qur'an exposed the falseness of their objection and also validated the Divine nature of the Qur'anic revelation. Thirdly, when it asks them to produce a discourse like it, the Qur'an extends the challenge to the whole of humankind.

This verse is an extension of the first two verses where it was said that this is the Book of guidance for those believers who are Allah-conscious (*muttaqin*) and that its principles are universal, unlike the books produced by human beings which require periodic updating, editing, revising and re-issuing. The Qur'an is the universal and holistic guidance for all of humanity and these two verses of *Surah al-Baqarah,* refer to the inimitability (*i'jaz*) or miracle of the Qur'an.

The uniqueness of the Qur'anic revelation also lies in the fact that no other religious Scripture claims to be an uncorrupted version of the original Revelation. In Christianity, for example, most of the texts carry the name of their scribes like The Gospel according to St. Mathew, St. Mark, St. Luke, and St. John which simply means four different human versions of the Scripture. None of these four respected scribes ever met, or received directly the Gospels from Prophet Jesus, consequently none of them can be accepted as first-hand reports.

By contrast, the Qur'an as we have it today is the direct revelation, communicated to the Prophet Muhammad ﷺ word for word by the archangel Jibril, who then communicated it to his Companions without any gap or break, who committed it to writing and at the same time memorized it in its proper sequence as the Prophet ﷺ instructed. This unbroken chain of communication of the Qur'anic revelation and its preservation in two authentic forms (its memorization by tens of thousands of people and its writing down) is unique only to the Qur'an. The Qur'an is essentially a Book of glad tidings (*bisharat*) and hope which makes life in this world successful (*sa'adah*) and in the Hereafter, rewarding. It ensures Allah's mercy (*rahmah*) for those who obey and follow His guidance and directives (2: 25).

Comprehensiveness of the *Din*

The Qur'an makes use of appropriate parables and similes to make it easy for the common person to understand it. The unbelievers often questioned this aspect of the Qur'an because, in their minds, a Divine Scripture was not supposed to use such mundane and commonplace examples. While the Qur'anic arguments are put forward to guide people, they are not meant only for a selected group–theologians, priests, intellectuals, philosophers or scientists who alone have the capability to decipher and understand it–but rather offer explanations that can be understood even by ordinary people. The Qur'an is a guidance for both the highly sophisticated mind as well as the mind of the common, less educated or even un-educated person: *"On hearing these parables the believers know that it is the truth from their Lord"* (al-Baqarah, 2: 26). Consequently, those who recognize this guidance reconfirm the pledge which was made immemorially by the souls of all human beings who were yet to be born, that they bear witness that Allah alone is their Lord. In other words, those who reject this guidance *not* only act against their consciences but also violate the covenant made by their souls before coming into this world. This is further elaborated by the Qur'an in *Surah al-A'raf*:

"*And recall, (O Prophet ﷺ) when your Lord brought forth descendants from the loins of the sons of Adam, and made them witness against their own selves, asking them: Am I not your Lord, They said: Yes we do testify...*" (al-A'raf, 7: 172). Therefore, according to the Qur'an, those who act against this immemorial pledge and the demands of reason shall be in utter loss on the Day of Judgement. They are called the transgressors, while those who accept the Qur'an and the Prophet ﷺ as their guide and make a firm commitment to follow them in their daily life are given glad tidings. Servitude (*'ubudiyyah*), therefore, does not mean the mere observance of certain rituals but includes conducting all personal, social, economic, political, educational, and cultural activities under the guidance of only the Qur'an and the Prophetic Practice.

Accepting the Qur'an as the Book means that one has made a covenant to obey every directive of the Qur'an while accepting the final Messenger ﷺ means following his noble example in all aspects of one's life. It is naive to think that worshipping idols made of stone alone is transgression, worshipping gods of colour, race, ethnicity, and power equally harm one's *iman* and conflicts with *'ubudiyyah* of Allah. Similarly, a person who may be regular in making prayers but then takes no care of elderly parents and blood relations, makes a serious violation of the covenant they made. For example, when someone hears the call for prayer but remains busy watching a TV talk show or a cricket or a football match, according to this *ayah*, it is a breach of the covenant. When a bill is presented in a parliament contrary to the directions of the Qur'an on a financial, cultural, social or legal issue it too is a sort of transgression. An obvious example of this breach of trust and covenant is given by the Qur'an when rights and obligations towards kith and kin are not observed i.e. instead of *sila rahmi* (observing the rights and obligations toward blood relations), *qata' rahmi* is done. Same is the case with reference to social and cultural matters e.g. a person who makes *hajj* and *'umrah* every few years but observes mythical ceremonies from other religions and cultures in the marriage of his son or daughter unknowingly makes a breach of his *'ahd* or *'aqd* with Allah to accept Him alone as his Master and Lord. *Tawhid* requires that one observes one and the same principle in all spheres of life and has a unified and consistent personality. The person who bows down to Allah in the mosque but also practises mythological rites and superstitions in the name of local culture, festivals, and celebrations, makes a deviation from *tawhid*.

Therefore, the Qur'an states that the godless among people (*al-fasiqun*) are the real losers because they are the ones: *"Who break the covenant of Allah after its firm binding and cut asunder what Allah has commanded to be joined and spread mischief on earth. They are the utter losers"* (al-Baqarah, 2: 27). Godlessness is a manifestation of ungratefulness towards Allah despite His countless favours. A simple example may help in further elaboration: If a medical doctor who is employed by a hospital, is paid a high salary, provided with a modern OT and the necessary support staff, but doesn't come to work on time, doesn't attend to their patients with due care, can such a person qualify to get an award on his performance? Can we call it an attitude of gratefulness to his employer? If, out of His Bounty and Mercy, Allah provides for the needs of every person, is it not fair to expect extreme gratefulness towards Allah through observing the acts of worship which He has made incumbent on Himself towards his servants: *"How can you be ungrateful to Allah Who bestowed life upon you when you were lifeless? Then He will cause you to die and will again bring you back to life so that you will be returned to Him. It is He who created for you all that is on earth* and then turned above and fashioned it into seven heavens, He knows all things" (al-Baqarah, 2: 28-29).

Fasaqa means to go astray from the straight path, leaving the practice of good and indulging in wrong. In Qur'anic terminology *fasiq*, deviant, sinful, with its roots in *fisq* (*fasiqun, fussaq* pl.) has a wider connotation. It may refer to any act of deviation as well as to the commitment of gross sin like the use of liquor or sexual immorality. Although reprehensible legally, nevertheless, wrongdoers (*fasiq*) and hypocrites (*munafiq*) are counted as Muslims and not treated like idolaters or openly rebellious unbelievers.

The Qur'an uses the term *fisq* as the opposite of *iman*: "*Would a true believer be like him who was an evildoer (fasaqa)? Surely, they are not equal*" (al-Sajdah, 32: 18). Like hypocrisy, it is also a disease of the heart: "*O my people why do you torment me when you know well that I am Allah's Messenger to you. So, when they deviated Allah made their hearts deviate. Allah does not direct the evildoers (fasiqin) to the Right Way*" (al-Saff, 61: 5).

Perhaps due to the similarity between the *munafiq* and *the fasiq* the Qur'an refers to the hypocrites as *fasiqun*: "*The hypocrites be they men or women are all alike. They enjoin what is evil and forbid what is good and withhold their hands from doing good. They forgot Allah, so Allah also forgot them. Surely the hypocrites are wicked (al-fasiqun)*" (al-Tawbah, 9: 67). The Prophet ﷺ was advised not to seek forgiveness for the hypocrites: "*It is all the same for them whether you ask forgiveness for them or not for Allah shall never forgive them. Surely Allah does not direct the transgressing folk to the Right Way*" (al-Munafiqun, 63: 6).

Muslims are asked to be careful when dealing with the deviants due to their wickedness: "*Believers when a wicked person (fasiq) brings to you a piece of news, carefully ascertain its truth lest you should hurt a person unwillingly and thereafter repent at what you did"* (al-Hujurat, 49: 6). Similarly, the *fasiqun* are deemed untrustworthy in legal matters: *"Those who accuse honourable women (of unchastity) but do not produce four witnesses flog them with eighty lashes and do not admit their testimony ever after. They are indeed transgressors (fasiqun)"* (al-Nur, 24: 4). The Qur'an also uses this term with reference to the disobedience of Iblis when he was asked to bow down to Prophet Adam ﷺ: *"And recall when We said to the angels 'prostate yourselves before Adam'; all of them fell prostrate except Iblis. He was of the jinn and so disobeyed (fafasaqa) the command of his Lord"* (al-Kahf, 18: 50).

Fisq and *nifaq* are two deadly diseases that the believers are not only enjoined to avoid but they are also told to always make supplication that Allah saves them from these traps of Satan. Islamic behaviour and conduct must reflect truthfulness, trustworthiness and servitude as well as the avoidance of wickedness in all its forms.

This simple, direct, and logical approach of the Qur'an invites every reader of the Book to do soul-searching and self-analysis of one's conduct and behavior in everyday life.

REFLECTION
What type of life are we living?

Are we living a life of gratitude, servitude (*'ubudiyyah*), humility and helpfulness or a life of self-aggrandizement, individualism, selfishness and obedience to the self-made gods of power, pleasure, material gain, glamour and showing off? The Qur'an invites all human beings to engage in a critical self-examination in order to live a meaningful life.

Lessons from the Story of Prophet Adam ﷺ

The verses 30 to 39 of *al-Baqarah* provide an authentic narrative on the purpose and role of human creation. Before the creation of Prophet Adam ﷺ Allah, the Lord of Universe said to the angels: *"Lo I am about to place a vicegerent on earth; they said will you place on it one who will spread mischief and shed blood, while we celebrate Your Glory and extol Your Holiness, He said: Surely I know what you do not know"* (al-Baqarah, 2: 30). That the angels knew only what Allah enabled them to know was demonstrated in an illuminating way when Adam was given knowledge of objects and later on, the same objects were shown to angels and they were asked to name them. When they realised this they said: *"Glory to You, we have no knowledge except what You taught us. You, only You, are All-knowing, All-Wise"* (al-Baqarah, 2: 32). This episode indicates that angels, like human beings, have limited knowledge.

When Allah asked the angels to bow down to Adam, all the angels bowed without hesitation. Iblis (a jinn) felt pride in being created out of fire and refused to bow before Adam, who had been made from clay. This act of disobedience led to his expulsion from Paradise while Adam and his wife were allowed to experience life therein. At the same time, they were warned against Iblis. Iblis, like a hurt snake, reacted to his demotion by persuading Adam to taste the fruit of the forbidden tree. His trick worked and Adam approached the forbidden tree. As soon as Adam realized the trap of Iblis, he and his wife sought Allah's forgiveness with words taught to them by the Most Merciful, the Most Forgiving: *"Our Lord we have wronged ourselves if You do not have mercy on us, we shall surely be among the losers"* (al-A'raf, 7: 23). Their repentance was accepted and both were forgiven.

This episode serves as a reminder to humanity and appears to be a pre-launch test; since Adam was designated Allah's *Khalifah*, deputy or vicegerent on earth, he was destined to face ethical situations that would involve making judgements. Adam went through the test and was found to behave just like a normal human being – he was influenced by his emotions and misjudged but did not insist on doing wrong and returned to his Lord with a heart full of regret and repentance while the Lord, out of His enormous Mercy and Kindness, forgave him: *"Indeed, the good deeds drive away the evil deeds; This is a reminder to those who are mindful of Allah"* (Hud, 11: 14).

> ## REFLECTION
>
> How often do we act as male or female chauvinists in our homes and workplaces?
>
> How often do we violate the principles of our faith and give favour or show bias to someone just because he or she belongs to our party, province, linguistic group, or interest group?
>
> How often do we consider ourselves superior to others because of our wealth, status, knowledge or power?
>
> And how often do we humble ourselves to the One Who has given us resources, capacities, skills, and a meaningful life?

Iblis got elevated to the rank of an angel due to his servitude (*'ubudiyyah*) to Allah but lost this status due to pride (*kibr*) and a sense of self-righteousness. Not only did he disobey, he took pride in his disobedience and asked for Allah's permission to try to misguide human beings from the Right Path. Blinded by his arrogance, he did not ask for Allah's forgiveness and repent, rather he preferred to remain in the wrong and tempt human beings and the jinn away from the path of servitude (*'ubudiyyah*). Iblis never thought he did something wrong. Consequently, he was damned forever. These two models are put before human beings in order for them to use their rational and ethical judgement to choose one or the other behavioural pattern: *"And did We not show him the two highroads (of good and evil)"* (al-Balad, 90: 10).

Iblis's Modern Forms of Temptations: Cultural Colonialism and Entrepreneurial Capitalism

The temptation that Iblis used to entice Adam and Eve is not a mere story of the past, as their progeny we are still facing it all the time: the temptation to control the world economy by one super power, or a group of so-called big nations, to determine the direction of the world economy, to make the people of the world dependent on them for food, health, water, defence and education, which is a well-known strategy of entrepreneurial capitalism. Another contemporary trap of Iblis is cultural colonialism, making people subservient intellectually, politically, and economically in the name of modernity. Addiction to drugs and pornography is another trap of Iblis and his legion in the name of post-modernity, humanism, individual freedom and human rights. As are the claims to ownership of one's body and freedom to select gender identity. Addiction to digital games and animations play the same role when the youth particularly become hooked on them.

The fictitious characters created in such animations become their role models to the extent of controlling the way they think and act.

After the repentance of Adam and Eve, Adam was told to move with his wife to their pre-destined station on earth as Allah's vicegerent (*khalifah*). While Iblis was banished from Paradise due to his pride and arrogance and damned forever, he was allowed to use his evil stratagems (*makr*) to tempt human beings, though none of his temptations, he was told, would work on those who are Allah-conscious(*muttaqin*) and righteous (*salih*).

The Qur'an makes it clear that those who live an ethical life in this world shall also succeed in the Hereafter: "*... then whoever will follow My guidance (The Qur'an, Prophetic example) need have no fear, nor shall they grieve. But those who refuse to accept this (guidance) and reject Our Signs as false, are destined for the Fire, where they shall abide forever*" (al-Baqarah, 2: 38-39).

This brief narrative on how human beings were created from clay and then fashioned into ethical beings, who are fully responsible for their actions, rejects all notions about human creation as an outcome of the evolutionary process, or one which had evolved from a previous prototype. As it is sufficient for the Creator to just say "Be!" (*kun*) to create whatever He wants, it is not correct to assume that human creation went through a long evolutionary trial-and-error process. The narrative also tells us clearly that human beings have an ethical role in this worldly life just as it corrects the misconception that Adam and Eve were sent to earth as a punishment, or due to a perpetual sin, which is blamed on Eve. Humans, therefore, should be defined as "ethical beings", not as a social animal, a *homo economicus*, an amalgam of drives and hungers and desires or accidently a purposeless creation. Aspects of this episode are also mentioned in other places in the Qur'an (e.g. al-A'raf 7: 10-27).

The Fourfold Implication of *Khilafah*: What *Khilafah* is and is not

The more one ponders on these verses, the clearer it becomes that the purpose and destination of human beings on earth were decided long before human beings were created. The angels were clearly told that Adam is Allah's designated vicegerent (*khalifah*) on earth who was not supposed to live in Paradise, which was only a temporary abode wherein he had a first-hand experience of Paradise. In other words, Adam and Eve were not banished to earth as a punishment or due to a "sin" initiated by Eve. And since both Adam and Eve were fully forgiven for their forgetfulness, there can be no logical justification for a primordial sin to be removed by sacrificing Prophet 'Isa ﷺ for the redemption of humanity. Elsewhere, the Qur'an totally rejects the crucifixion of Jesus which it considers as a fiction and myth: *"And for their saying, we slew the Messiah, Jesus, son of Mary, the Messenger of Allah ﷺ whereas in fact they had neither slain him nor crucified him, but the matter was made dubious to them..."* (al-Nisa', 4: 157).

Second, the role of *khalifah* on earth was not to act as a pontiff, priest, or holy guide but to follow and implement Divine Guidance, *hidayah* conveyed orally or in the form of a Scripture and delivered to Allah's chosen persons or Messengers. These Messengers were neither mystics nor theologians but practicians who, with the best of their capacity, not only communicated Divine Guidance, but through their own role model educated people on how to live an ethical and moral life so that human beings are not left to depend on individual speculations, trial and error, guesswork or on personal inner experience for making ethical judgements. Because no personal, subjective, esoteric experience, by its very nature, can be objective, ultimate and shared with others as a guidance. Messengers receive

Guidance, implement, and apply it, and as a human role model their conduct and behaviour provides people with a viable ethical model.

Third, Prophet Adam ﷺ was taught the names of things which the angels were unaware of. This empowerment through knowledge was the reason why the angels were asked to bow down to Adam. The bowing down of angels was not to honour Adam but simply in obedience to the command of the Possessor of All Knowledge.

Fourth, the concept of *Khilafah* mentioned here, and in several other places in the Qur'an, has nothing to do with the concept of priesthood or with theocracy. It simply stands for holistic leadership. Since all human beings by their very constitution are fashioned to be Allah's *khulafah* (pl. of *khalifah*) therefore whoever is ethically more competent is qualified to assume the role of leadership. The Qur'an mentions: *"Allah commands you to deliver trusts (amanat) to those worthy (ahliha) of them, and when you judge between people, judge with justice ('adl)"* (al-Nisa', 4: 58). *Khilafah* is neither "holy" nor "profane". Khalifah is neither a king nor ordained priest. *Khilafah* is a system of its own kind, to be understood objectively in its own right and not from the perspective of the Western secular liberal democratic ideals or theocratic claims made by the Christian and other ecclesiastic authorities.

This aspect has been elaborated with the help of the examples of several Messengers of Allah in the Qur'an, Prophet Dawood ﷺ was given *Khilafah* by Allah: *"O Dawood We have appointed you vicegerent (khalifah) on earth. Therefore, rule among people and do not follow (your) desire lest it should lead you astray from Allah's Path..."* (Sad, 38: 26). Similarly the supplication of Prophet Sulayman ﷺ indicates how the political sphere was included in his Prophetic role: *"... My Lord, forgive me and bestow upon me the gift of a kingdom (mulk) such as none other after me will observe"* (Sad, 38: 35).

The same is reflected in the episode of Prophet Yusuf ﷺ who was responsible for the treasury in Egypt. The supplication of Prophet Muhammad ﷺ, reconfirms the integration of the spiritual and material domains: *"And pray: My Lord cause me to enter wherever it be, with Truth, and cause me to exit wherever it be with Truth, and support me with authority (sultan) from yourself"* (Bani Isra'il, 17: 80). All these examples in the Qur'an indicate that there is no separation between the so-called secular and sacred in Islam. The Prophet ﷺ has put this understanding beautifully in a *hadith*: "All this earth is made a mosque for me". In other words, there is no such thing as a secular space or time. Allah's authority is not confined to a purpose-built mosque, temple, synagogue or certain acts of devotion; human life in totality is for serving Allah. It is in this context that the Prophet ﷺ stated: "The honest trader shall be among Prophets (*nabiyyin*), the truthful (*siddiqin*) and the martyrs (*shuhada*)". Trade, agriculture or any other worldly activities are not secular in Islam. Since all human activities are supposed to be inspired by ethical and moral considerations, all human transactions are essentially ethical and volitional acts.

The Leadership Role of Earlier Peoples: The Case of Bani Isra'il

After elaborating on the role of human beings on earth, namely, to act as Allah's vicegerent, or deputy, the Qur'an offers a historical analysis of how the children of Israel (*Bani Isra'il*) behaved when they were given the role of leadership (*Khilafah*) of mankind. They were chosen as custodians of *hidayah*, the Divine guidance which was given to them through their Prophets who were all followers of the *Din* of Prophet Ibrahim ﷺ. A detailed account of this is provided in verses 40-120 of *al-Baqarah*.

The origin of the term, "Children of Israel", can be traced back to Prophet Ya'qub ﷺ (Jacob) who was the son of Prophet Ishaq ﷺ (Isaac) and the grandson of Prophet Ibrahim ﷺ. He was given the title Israel which simply means the *servant* of God. The word Israel or servant of God has the same meaning as the Arabic word 'Abdullah. The word Israel, in the Qur'an, has no relation with the illegitimate existence of the state of Israel as an ethnocentric or racist regime. Apparently the reason why the Qur'an refers, again and again, to Bani Isra'il is that it wants its readers not only to realise how those who follow Allah's commands are rewarded but also how those who use their evil stratagems to play with Allah's commands are made a living example of, and are condemned and punished due to their actions. The Qur'an makes frequent references to towns and valleys on global trade routes which were totally annihilated because of the unethical conduct of their people, like the people of Prophet Lut ﷺ: their city was totally submerged in the sea. The remains of Petra in Jordan are also mentioned as a reminder and a lesson from history. The Qur'an refers to the negative attitude of Bani Isra'il towards Prophet Musa ﷺ. The following ninety verses or so remind the Children of Israel, of Allah's favours and blessings on them and their ungrateful response. To begin with, a reference is made to the covenant made between them and Allah: *"Children of Israel! Recall My favour which I had bestowed on you and fulfil your covenant with Me and I shall fulfil My covenant with you, and fear Me alone: And believe in the Book (i.e. al-Qur'an) which I have revealed and which confirms the Scripture you already have, and be not foremost among its deniers. Do not sell My signs for a trifling gain and beware of My wrath. Do not confound Truth by overlaying it with falsehood, nor knowingly conceal* the Truth. Establish prayer and dispense zakah and bow in worship with those who bow. Do you enjoin righteousness (birr) on people and forget your own selves even though you recite the Scripture? Have you no sense?" (al-Baqarah, 2: 40-44).

The Israelites knew well, as the Qur'an informs us, how their Lord liberated them from the slavery of the Pharaoh, who used to kill their males and spare their females. They are reminded of how they were saved when the sea was made to split for their safe crossing while the Pharaoh and his army were drowned. These tangible favours and miraculous events, which they experienced, should have humbled them and made them thankful servants of Allah. However, when Prophet Musa ﷺ was summoned by his Lord for a period of just forty nights, they took to worshipping a calf during his absence, despite continuous cautioning by his brother Harun. Instead of repenting for their sins, they further told Prophet Musa ﷺ that they would not believe in him unless and until they saw with their own eyes Allah talking to him. They were caught by a tremendous thunderbolt that caused them to die and then they were resurrected miraculously so that they may become thankful. But even this special experience did not change their ungratefulness towards Allah. The detailed accounts of how the Israelites were again and again given an opportunity to make up for their wrong ways indicate Allah's kindness even when a nation has repeatedly violated the covenants it had made with its Lord.

In the Wilderness of Sinai

After their deliverance from captivity in Egypt, they wandered for forty years in the Sinai desert during which an overclouded sky protected them from exposure to the sun. They were served food in the form of *manna* and *quails*. To avoid any dispute over access to water, each of their twelve tribes was provided with a spring of their own. But even then, they did not show their thankfulness and gratitude. They declared that they were tired of the same type of food, even though they got it effortlessly. They wanted to have cucumbers, corn, lentils, garlic, and onions. Consequently, they were told to move to a township with instructions that, when they enter it, they should glorify their Lord and repent. But the wrongdoers among them changed the words refusing to plead for forgiveness, their transgressions had no limits: *"And ignominy and wretchedness were pitched upon them and they were laden with the burden of Allah's wrath. This was because they denied the signs of Allah and slew the Prophets unrightfully. All this because they disobeyed and persistently exceeded the limits"* (al-Baqarah, 2: 61).

The misconduct of the Israelites and their violations of the teachings of their own Scripture became a normal practice. Ahab, the king of Israel, for example, imprisoned Prophet Micah ﷺ and ordered that he should be given only dry bread and water (I Kings 22: 26-27). Prophet Zechariah ﷺ was stoned to death when he criticized idol worship and the moral corruption prevalent in Judah (Chronicles 24: 21). When John the Baptist criticized Herod, the ruler of Judah, he was imprisoned and at the instigation of the wife of Herod's brother, John was beheaded, and his head was presented to her (Mark 6: 17-28). Even with this track record, the Israelites today continue to believe in their theological myth of the "Chosen People". They interpret the Covenant, made between them and Yahweh as binding on Him even when they break it. This ethnocentric and racial superiority has become an integral part of their identity.

The Qur'an questions such an understanding of themselves and reminds them of Allah's continuous kindness, forgiveness, and favours upon them. Even when they failed to fulfil their commitments, Allah did not withdraw His mercy and kindness from them, otherwise they would have been totally annihilated.

The frequent references to how the Israelites treated their own Prophets provided consolation and courage to the Prophet ﷺ and his Companions during the period of tests and trials and the oppression they faced from their own tribesmen because of their embracing Islam.

The Qur'an refers briefly to their history of over four thousand years of continuous negative attitude, unjust conduct and rebellious behaviour and provides evidence of Allah's unlimited Mercy, Who provided them continuously with opportunities to return to His obedience. The Qur'an's frequent reference to Prophet Musa ﷺ and how the Israelites treated him appears an educative method of the Qur'an to teach the Muslim *ummah* not to commit the same mistakes. It also provides evidence of Allah's continuous Mercy, Forgiveness and Kindness towards even those who persistently violated His commands as an ongoing reminder (*tadhkir*) for the wrongdoers. They were given one chance after another to mend their ways and protect themselves from Hell. This leaves no room for the unbelievers, polytheists, the People of the Book, and the defaulters (*fasiqin*) to plead innocence and unawareness of opportunities given to them in order to return to goodness and virtue. At the same time, it reminds the Muslim *ummah* about what is expected of it vis-à-vis Divine guidance, the Qur'an and the Sunnah of the final Messenger ﷺ.

The general principle observed by the Qur'an is the rejection of any ethnic or racial basis for superiority in this world as a basis of reward in the life after death. The ethical approach of the Qur'an offers hope to even Jews, Christians and Sabeans, as long as they do not indulge in idolatry and act ethically while believing in the Unity of Allah and also in the Last Day: *"Whether they are ones who believe in (the Prophet ﷺ) or whether they are Jews, Christians or Sabeans – all who believe in Allah and the Last Day and do righteous deeds – their reward is surely secure with their Lord; they need have no fear, nor shall they grieve"* (al-Baqarah, 2: 62).

Here, *"those who believe"* refers to the Muslims while *al-ladhina hadu* refers to the Israelites. We know during the short absence of Prophet Musa ﷺ, the Israelites started worshipping a calf and, later, some of them regretted what they had done and returned to guidance (*hidayah*); this is why they were called *hud* or *yahud* in the Qur'an. The Arabic words *hād* and *hud* both refer to regret and returning to the right path. The word *nasara* refers to the helpers of Prophet 'Isa ﷺ as mentioned in *Surah al-Saff*: *"Believers become Allah's helpers as Jesus son of Mary said to the disciples 'Who is my helper (ansari) in (calling people) to* Allah?" (al-Saff, 61: 14). Some scholars are of the opinion that *nasara* (sing. *nasrani*) refers to the inhabitants of the Palestinian town of *nasirah* and this is why Jesus was also called *yasu' al-nasiri*. However, the derivation of the term from helpers (*ansari*) seems to be more correct. The term *al-sabi'in* (sing: *sabi'i*) refers to a religious group who concentrated in Harran (Iraq) from where Prophet Ibrahim ﷺ originated. They were originally star worshippers and well aware of Greek metaphysical and mythical thoughts before they adopted Judaism and Christianity. They worshiped in the direction of the North Pole. A group of them who followed the way of Prophet Ibrahim ﷺ was known as *muwahidun*. The Qur'an in this *ayah* refers to these followers of *tawhid*.

Shirk (Associating with Allah) and *Nifaq* (Hypocracy), The Two Major Transgressions that Lead to Helfire

With this brief elaboration on the four groups mentioned in the verse, the core message conveyed by this verse is that there is no basis whatsoever for the Jewish perceptions, or such understandings of any other people, that they are a chosen people and hence destined to Paradise. The final judgement of human beings will not be based on colour, race, ethnicity, or genealogy. The only basis of judgement will be ethical conduct and behaviour performed by a person who believes in Allah's Oneness and the Hereafter. Here, the Qur'an opens the door of Allah's Mercy even for the followers of earlier Prophets as long as they avoid associating others with God, leave polytheistic practices, and also believe in the life to come. Subject to holding firmly to belief in *tawhid* and *Akhirah*, their good deeds will not be lost.

Needless to say, polytheism includes all forms of associations with the Divinity of Allah including attributing any Divine characters to Messengers of Allah. *Shirk*, or association in Allah's Person or Attributes and Authority, as well as *nifaq*, hypocrisy, therefore are two major transgressions that lead a person to Hellfire. The Quran clearly specifies: *"My son! Do not associate others with Allah (in His Divinity). Surely, associating others with Allah is a mighty wrong"* (Luqman, 31: 13); *"Those who disbelieved be they from the People of the Book or among those who associated (mushrikin) others with Allah shall be in Fire and will abide in it"* (al-Bayyinah, 98: 6); *"Surely Allah does not forgive that a partner be associated to Him although He forgives all other sins for whomever He Wills"* (al-Nisa', 4: 48); *"Allah has promised Hell Fire to the hypocrites both men and women and the unbelievers"* (al-Tawbah, 9: 68). Thematically associating others with Allah and hypocrisy appear in the Qur'an as the most hated acts in the sight of Allah: *"Surely the hypocrites shall be in the lowest depth of Fire and you shall find none to come to their help"* (al-Nisa', 4: 145).

The Qur'an elaborates in several places that accepting any person, object or system as the focus of devotion and adoration along with Allah is polytheism. Therefore, even considering land as sacred or an individual, or a system like materialism, or hedonism (pleasure and fun as the goal of life), as one's objective and ultimate goal, is a deviation from *tawhid*. The Qur'an keeps on reminding us that Allah alone is *ilah* or the Ultimate Authority: *"...Is there any god (ilah) associated with Allah?"* (al-Naml, 27: 60).

Realizing *Tawhid* in the Social Sphere

The Qur'anic verse makes it clear that the criterion for success is only good conduct and behaviour and even a believer, despite acts of social service, may not qualify for Paradise if he associate anything with Allah or doubt the reality of the Day of Judgement. Therefore, the claims of some that their religion is 'humanity', and that they work for the welfare of humanity alone, make no sense in the light of this verse. A person who claims to serve humanity without belief in Allah or without intending to serve Him makes a clear departure from serving Allah alone. On the other hand, if one gets involved in the social sphere because Allah wants him to help the needy, the orphans and the oppressed, then this would actually be a translation of *tawhid* in the social sphere. Seeking Allah's pleasure with sincerity cannot be substituted with "serving humanity" as an ultimate goal, which simply means seeking credit as a humanitarian and not as a servant of Allah, who does everything only to please Allah, particularly the delivery of *huquq al-'ibad* (the rights of Allah's servants).

Allah's promise to relieve those in fear or the aggrieved is conditional, for this is promised only to the believers among Muslims and the People of the Book who believe in Allah's Oneness, and in the Day of Judgement and do good deeds. Later on, in *Surah al-Baqarah*, it is further emphasized that faith qualifies for reward (*ajr*) only when it is translated into good deeds *'aml salih*: "*Whoever submits himself completely to the obedience of Allah and does good will find his reward with his Lord*" (al-Baqarah, 2: 112). That final judgement, it is emphasised, is based on each person's own ethical and moral conduct and not on belonging to a family of priests, pious saints, religious or spiritual leaders and Prophets, and is made clear by the Qur'an: "*Those who spend their wealth in the way of Allah and do not follow up their spending by stressing their benevolence and causing hurt will find the reward secure with your Lord. They have no cause for fear and grief*" (al-Baqarah, 2: 262).

Elsewhere in the Qur'an, acts of devotion such as prayer and *zakah* are added as an integral part of good deeds and as a precondition for saving oneself from chastisement: "*Truly the reward of those who believe and do righteous deeds and establish prayers and pay* zakah *is with their Lord; they have no reason to entertain any fear or grief*" (al-Baqarah, 2: 277). Further along in the *surah*, the Qur'an also includes consistency and steadfastness in Allah's obedience and not wavering from the path of Allah as necessary traits in the believers who are spared chastisement: "*Surely those who said our Lord is Allah and then remained steadfast, shall have nothing to fear nor to grieve*" (al-Ahqaf, 46: 13).

The message conveyed here is very simple: in the final judgement what counts is sincerity (*ikhlas*) in faith (*iman*) along with total obedience to Allah (*'ubudiyyah*) alone and excelling in doing good deeds (*'aml salih, 'amal khayr, huquq Allah, huquq al-'ibad*) or observing one's duties towards Allah and His creation. No claims of being a favourite people, or descendants of some pious persons, carry any weight in the scales of Divine Justice.

The Transgressions of the Israelites

The following verse: *"And recall when We made a covenant with you, and caused the Mount Sinai to tower above you, hold fast to the Book that We have given you and remember the directives and commandments in it, that you be pious. Then you turned away from your covenant, and had it not been for Allah's Grace and Mercy upon you, you would have long been utter losers"* (al-Baqarah, 2: 63-64), reminds the Jews of Allah's numerous favours to them which they witnessed with their own eyes. As we mentioned earlier, for example, making a safe passage for them to cross the Red Sea; delivering food from heaven; providing twelve springs of fresh water without any effort on their part; causing them to die and then resurrecting them were more than enough as evidence, explicit enough, to make them submit totally to *tawhid*. But they kept shying away from the right path. Repeated blessings of their Rabb and His direct and miraculous interventions did not convince them to change their behavior and rebellious psyche. Here, they are further reminded of another miracle of Allah when they made an oath of obedience under the shadow of Mount Sinai that they will hold fast to the Torah, desist from their rebellious attitude and adopt the path of *taqwa*, or Allah-consciousness, but they also blatantly violated this oath.

The word used in the Qur'an for the mountain is Tur, which literally means a mount with greenery, i.e. not a barren mountain. The Syriac and Coptic languages have the same word which denotes the same meaning. The Qur'an also informs that Prophet Musa ﷺ was also summoned to one of these mountains to receive commandments from Allah. Even today, these mountains are evidence of Allah's favours and of the deviations and transgressions of the Israelites; they stand as witnesses to their ungratefulness towards Allah's undeniable favours.

Allah's Mercy and the Israelites' Response

The detailed accounts of the Israelites, the Jewish tribes, narrated in the Qur'an indicate that everything they faced, like the diaspora, was partially a punishment and a warning to them. It was again of Allah's Mercy that when they did not act, as they were expected to, they were only removed from the role of leadership they had been given, but still had the chance to improve themselves as true followers of the original teachings of the Torah. For example, the Qur'an informs that it was their own desire to let their Lord determine for them a day dedicated to worship. They were told the Sabbath or Saturday is that day, with instruction that on Saturday they will do nothing but worship in the form of prayers and study and practice of the Torah. They were not supposed to cook, hunt, trade or even travel on that day: "12. And the Lord spoke unto Moses saying: 13. Speak thou also unto the children of Israel saying verily my Sabbaths ye shall keep: for it is a sign between me and you throughout your generations; that ye may know till I am the Lord that doth sanctify you. 14. You shall keep the Sabbath therefore; for it is holy unto you: everyone that defiled it shall surely be put to death: for whosoever doeth any work therein, that soul shall be cut off from among his people. 15. Six days may work be done; but in the seventh is the Sabbath of rest, holy to the Lord; whosoever doeth any work in the Sabbath day, he shall surely be put to death. 16. Wherefore the children of Israel shall keep the Sabbath, to observe the Sabbath throughout their generations, for a perpetual covenant." [Exodus 31: 12-16]

Even with such clear instructions, as a result of their own request, the Children of Israel did not hesitate to violate the sanctity of the Sabbath. The next verse mentions: *"And you know the case of those of you who broke the Sabbath, how We said to them; become apes, despised and hated. And thus We made their end a warning for the people of their own time and for the succeeding generations, and as admonitions to the God-fearing (muttaqin)"* (al-Baqarah, 2: 65). The Qur'an here refers to the Jewish community of Elath in the time of Prophet Dawood ﷺ, (1013-973 BC), the place which is currently known as Aqabah and called Elath in Deuteronomy 2:8. Using their evil stratagem, the Israelites made ponds on the banks of the sea, where the fish got trapped. Thus, without any effort or use of fishing nets, they got fresh fish on the Sabbath. This wilful violation of a clear commandment invited Allah's punishment on them, and they were turned into apes. We are told that, within three days of their metamorphosis the whole community passed away.

This narrative is followed by another episode regarding the murder of a person, a crime that none accepted responsibility for. And so, when Prophet Musa ﷺ informed them that Allah wanted them to sacrifice a cow, they knew well which cow was to be sacrificed, but they kept asking questions about its colour and other details. They kept asking question after question until the specifications of the cow were so clear that they had to comply and slaughter the cow they considered sacred. The message conveyed was clear, if the cow could not save her own life how could she help and protect them? Similarly, when they were commanded *"smite the corpse with a piece of it"* the dead person for a while came back to life and disclosed the name of his murderer. But after witnessing all these miracles they did not change their crooked ways. These events provide living evidence of Allah's enormous and uninterrupted Mercy, Kindness, and Forgiveness towards a people who were given chance after chance to return to the path of obedience. These and several Divine interventions did not make them a grateful people. The Qur'an mentions about their conduct: *"then (even after observing this) your hearts hardened and became like stones, or even harder. For surely there are some stones from which streams burst forth and some that split asunder and water gushes out, and some that crash down for fear of Allah. Allah is not heedless of things that you do"* (al-Baqarah, 2: 74).

A Universal Message: *Tawhid* as the Common Ground

Frequent references in the Qur'an to the encounters of Prophet Musa remind one of the similarity of the message of all of Allah's Prophets and Messengers as well as the resistance, obstruction and insults they had all received from their own people and how patiently and persistently they carried on their mission. The Qur'an also looks objectively at the claims of the Jews and Christians that their religion is the only way of salvation. The Qur'an reminds us that all these Prophets and Messengers, including Prophet 'Isa (Jesus) invited people not to associate anyone with God and direct all their devotions to the One and Only Lord, Allah.

> Needless to say, that *tawhid* is the cornerstone of the message (*da'wah*) of all Messengers from Prophet Ibrahim ﷺ to Prophet Muhammad ﷺ. They all called for the elimination of conflict, duplicity and contradictions in one's life.

There are many similarities between the struggles of Prophet Musa ﷺ and that of the Prophet ﷺ. Both had to migrate from their hometowns due to persecution and safety of their lives and both were ridiculed by their own people as mere magicians or madmen. In critical situations such as wars, those insincere Israelites abstained from fighting, telling Prophet Musa ﷺ to go fight along with his God while they would just sit and wait for the outcome! The hypocrites of Madinah showed the same attitude and behaviour at the Battle of badr and Uhud. The encounters of Prophet Musa ﷺ taught the believers that the difficulties and problems they were facing from the polytheists and hypocrites were not particular to them. Prophet Musa ﷺ and other Israelite Prophets had faced similar or more critical situations. The believers, therefore, had to be strong and steadfast for the sake of creating a just and ethical order.

A general perception of 'religion' is that it is something personal and, therefore, it is confined to certain rituals ceremonies, devotions and festivities, and one is considered 'religious' as long as one adheres to them even if one is unfair to their spouse, parents or children or acquires wealth without considering whether it is lawful or unlawful. Such a concept of religion is totally rejected by all the original teachings of Allah's Prophets and Messengers, the Qur'an refers to supplication of sayyidina Ibrahim: "*Surely my prayer, all my acts of worship and my living and my dying are only for Allah the Lord of the whole Universe. He has no associate. Thus have I been bidden, and I am the foremost of those whose submit themselves (to Allah)*" (al-An'am, 6: 162-164).

> *Tawhid* simply means the prevalence of Allah's Rule, Authority, and Sovereignty in all social, economic, cultural, and legal spheres, including the acts of worship in accordance with the Divine injunctions. There can be no discrimination in the implementation of the Divine injunctions between the poor and the rich, between a person from a noble tribe or a person from an ordinary family.

The core message in the teachings of Prophets Ibrahim, Isma'il, Ishaq, Ya'qub, Yusuf, Musa, Dawood, Sulayman, as well as other Israelite Prophets, is *tawhid*, a unified life in obedience to the One and Only Lord: Allah. A few verses further down in *al-Baqarah* the advice of Prophet Ya'qub ﷺ is narrated: *"Why, were you witnesses when death came to Ya'qub? He asked his children 'Who will you serve after me?' They said we shall serve your God and God of your forefathers Ibrahim, Isma'il, and Ishaq, the One God and unto Him we submit"* (Al-Baqarah, 2: 133). We are further told, in the narrative of the history of the Israelites, how all of Allah's Prophets were opposed, insulted, and even killed by the perpetrators of *kufr, taghut* and *shirk*. Therefore, what the Prophet's Companions such as Bilal, Khabbab and Yasir experienced at the hands of the Makkans, or what the Prophet ﷺ experienced at Taif, was not something new. Not only does this narrative provide confidence and courage to the oppressed Companions of the Prophet ﷺ, it also shows them how to respond to the challenges of *da'wah* with constancy, perseverance, and wisdom. Muslim women, for example, globally, face a similar situation when they are ridiculed, insulted, and physically attacked for wearing a headscarf or, an *abaya* or long and loose shirt which traditionally has been a part of Jewish and Christian women's attire in public places. They are denied their human rights to practice their faith by the so-called liberal democratic pluralistic and enlightened societies of the West.

The Israelites' Practice of Double Standards

The *surah* also informs about the fate of the people who used their evil stratagem to evade the directives and commands of Allah. Several historical events are mentioned in the Qur'an regarding this from verse forty onwards. At the same time, it also refers to the unlimited favours that Allah had bestowed upon them, the most important of which is making them leaders of mankind to establish *tawhid,* peace and justice in society. But even when the Israelites preached obedience to the One and Only Lord, their own conduct contradicted what they preached. They were asked to establish the prayer and pay the *zakah,* but they themselves tried to avoid both: *"Do you enjoin righteousness on people but forget your own selves even though you recite the Scripture"* (al-Baqarah, 2: 44). The continuous advice to establish the prayer (*salah*) and to be steadfast and firm in faith did not help in bringing any inward change in them, whereas *tawhid* demanded the regular performance of the prayer in order to transform their hearts and minds and to have unison of the inner and outer self: *"Establish prayer and dispense zakah and bow in worship with those who bow. Do you enjoin righteousness on people and forget your own selves even though you recite the Scripture: Have you no sense? And resort to patience and prayer for help. Truly prayer is burdensome for all except the devout (khashi'in). Who realize that ultimately they will have to meet their Lord and that to Him they are destined to return"* (al-Baqarah, 2: 43-46). They even stopped offering the prayer in congregation, which resulted in the fact that their individual prayers too became irregular and mechanical. One visible impact of distancing themselves from the remembrance of Allah was that, instead of using fair economic practices, they become globally known as revengeful money lenders, as depicted in the Shakespearean character of Shylock.

They were reminded of Allah's great favour on them of relieving them from the oppression of the Pharaoh who used to kill their male children and spare their females (2: 49). Similarly, when Prophet Musa ﷺ led them out of captivity and the Pharaoh and his army chased them, Allah made for the Israelites a safe passage in the Red Sea so they could cross it safely. The Children of Israel witnessed the drowning of the Pharaoh and his army in broad daylight, as a living miracle of Allah but even this did not make them a thankful people. The believers are reminded to self-assess their own actions and behaviour in light of the blessings that Allah bestows on them. Are they grateful to Him, and therefore punctual in *'ibadah* and observing kindness, love and fairness toward their own family and members of society?

The Negative Effects of the Israelites' Cultural Assimilation in Egypt

The Qur'an also tackles the Israelites' cultural and religious assimilation during their captivity in Egypt. Influenced by the old cult of cow worship, they also started regarding cows with certain features as sacred. When Prophet Musa ﷺ went to Mount Sinai for a forty-day retreat, they made a heifer of gold and started worshipping it. To liberate them from this cultural baggage, Prophet Musa ﷺ was asked to tell them to sacrifice a cow. They raised a series of questions in order to avoid slaughtering a cow. But with each question they raised, Allah made the circle around them tighter.

The Qur'an refers to this episode in the following words: *"And then recall when Musa said to his people, 'Behold Allah commands you to slaughter a cow' They said: 'Are you jesting with us?' Musa answered: 'I seek refuge in Allah that I should behave in the manner of the ignorant.' They said: 'Pray to your Lord that He make clear to us what she is like.' Musa answered: 'He says she is a cow neither old nor immature, but of an age in between the two. Do then what you have been commanded.' They said: 'Pray to your Lord that He make clear to us of what colour she is?' Musa answered: 'He says she is a yellow cow with a bright colour which is pleasing to those who see.' They said: 'Pray to your Lord that He make clear to us what cow she is, cows seem much alike to us, and if Allah wills, we shall be guided'. Musa answered: 'Lo! He says she is a cow unyoked to plough the earth or to water the tillage one that has been kept secure, with no blemish on her!' Thereupon they cried out 'Now you have come forth with the information that will direct us right. And they slaughtered her, although they scarcely seemed to do so'"* (al-Baqarah, 2: 67-71). This single incident shows the mischievous attitude and psyche of the Israelites toward Allah's commands and directives given through Prophet Musa ﷺ.

The Response of the Jewish Community in Madinah

In the newly established community of the believers in Madinah there were Prophet's Companions of Jewish background who were fully committed and sincere to the Prophet ﷺ and the Islamic worldview. But there were also others who behaved in the same way their forefathers had behaved with the Prophets sent to the Israelites, and they used their evil designs to confuse and misguide the believers.

The materialistic streak in the Israelites coupled with their conviction that the last Prophet ﷺ would appear only from amongst the descendants of Prophets Ishaq and Yaq'ub encouraged them to persist in their awful behaviour even though a prediction was made in their own Scripture about the coming of a redeemer of the Israelites from the progeny of Isma'il. The Qur'an does not approve of this racist approach, which is based on genetics, for all the Prophets of Allah were truth-bearers and this is an integral part of Islamic belief.

In view of their track record and endless violations of Scripture, the Prophet ﷺ as well as the believers are advised by the Qur'an: "*Do you hope that these people will believe in the message you are preaching, even though a party of them has been wont to listen to the words of Allah and after they had fully grasped it knowingly distorted it*" (al-Baqarah, 2: 75). The reason for their frivolous attitude and behaviour, as the Qur'an informs, is the hardening of their hearts which made them unreceptive to the message of Truth: "*Then (even after observing this) your hearts hardened and became like stones, or even harder. For surely there are some stones from which streams burst forth and some that split asunder and water issues out, and some that crash down for fear of Allah. Allah is not heedless of the things you do*" (al-Baqarah, 2: 74).

While pointing out the deviations that the Israelites introduced in their system of worship, business dealings and the concept of the final judgement and life after death, the Qur'an questions the role of their religious leaders who used to mix their own views with the revealed directives of God. One of their innovative views was that even if they were condemned to Hellfire, they would be chastised therein only for a short while because they are descendants of Messengers of Allah: "*Woe then, to those who write out the Scripture with their own hands and then, in order to make a trifling gain claim: This is from Allah. Woe to them for what their hands have written and woe to them for what they thus earn. They say, 'The fire will certainly not touch us except for a limited number of days,' say to them have you received a promise from Allah, – for Allah never breaks His promise – or do you attribute to Allah something about which you have no knowledge? Those who earn evil and are encompassed by their sinfulness are the people of the fire and there will they abide. Those who believe and do righteous deeds are the People of the Garden and there will they abide"* (al-Baqarah, 2: 79-82).

Immediacy Instead of Ultimacy

The call of the Qur'an (*da'wah*) to the People of the Book (the Jews, Christians and others) is based on two fundamentals: the first is *Tawhid*, the uncompromising unity of Allah and denial of any deity besides Him; while the second is conviction in life after death preceded by the Day of Judgement. Belief in life after death (*Akhirah*) has been an established principle in the teachings of all the Prophets of Allah. *Tawhid*, at a practical level, gets rid of contradiction in one's attitude and behaviour as well as of hypocrisy and obedience to speculative gods, including the gods of ethnicity, language, colour, wealth, power, and pleasure. Life after death provides an ethical foundation for human conduct and behaviour. It prevents a person from becoming self-centred, egocentric, seeking short-term material gains or embracing pure materialism. It builds an ethical censor in the behaviour which helps one choose between what is ethically lawful, hence loved by Allah and rewarded in the Hereafter, and what is ethically unlawful, hence condemned, and punishable in the life Hereafter.

> # REFLECTION
> ## *Akhirah* an existential reality
>
> The Afterlife (*Akhirah*) is not simply a matter of belief. It directly impacts the believer's nature and quality of life in this world. It also guides the believer on how to lead this present life in view of the outcomes he or she expects in the Hereafter. The Qur'an has explicitly indicated how an ethical management of this worldly life can result in a permanent life of bliss, pleasure, and satisfaction.

Tawhid and *Akhirah* are the two fundamental keys to a balanced, moderate, peaceful, and unified life. Shortcomings in either one causes imbalance and unfairness in one's way of life in this world. The acceptance of these two basic principles has a direct impact on the ultimate destiny of human beings. However, if a person wants to risk the ultimate reward of *Akhirah* for some fleeting gain, the Qur'an does not deny them the freedom of such a choice.

Apparently, the reason behind preferring this worldly pleasure over success in the Hereafter is caused by a lack of faith and trust in life after death. In the final analysis, greed, jealousy, hatred, injustice, and exploitation of others have their roots in the love of short-term gains and desires (immediacy). Those who prefer immediate gain can go to any length to grab power and wealth as goals of their lives. Power struggles at individual, national, and global levels, and yearning for economic and political hegemony are manifestations of such immediacy. By contrast, belief in *Akhirah* entails that one does one's best to achieve justice, respect for human life and the welfare of others even at the cost of personal suffering in this world, in order to seek Allah's pleasure in the Hereafter.

Most of the man-made ideologies and systems of thought claim to take care of the immediate needs of people while Islam offers a universal ethical code in life that takes care of the immediate and natural needs of people and also helps them in attaining the good pleasure of Allah in *Akhirah*. The dominant trend in the case of the Israelites seems to be immediacy. Unlike Judaism, Christianity considers worldly gains and pleasures as sinful, and hence it calls for the denial of the world and monasticism became its ideal.

The Qur'an and the Sunnah of the Prophet ﷺ offer a middle-of-the-road solution, i.e. the adoption of an ethical way of life or seeking good in this world and good in *Akhirah*.

The frequent reference to the history of the Israelites invites them as well as the Muslims to understand the benefits of living a life of thankfulness to Allah through serving Him alone in all matters of life. Worldly attractions and desires often make people forget about the real purpose of life and their role in the realization of peace, justice, the dignity of human beings and security in society

The inclination of the Israelites toward material gains and prosperity was coupled with their conviction that Messengers and Prophets shall appear only from the progeny of Prophet Ishaq ﷺ. As the Qur'an points out, both Prophets Isma'il and Ishaq were the children of Prophet Ibrahim ﷺ which means that the ethnic approach of the Jews was illogical. Furthermore, Islam was the faith of all the Prophets and Messengers of Allah. All of them called their people to follow only the Creator, The Lord of the Universe and work for success in the Hereafter. The Qur'an confirms the original teachings of all earlier Messengers without any discrimination between them:

"The Messenger believes and so do the believers, in the guidance sent down upon him from His Lord: each one believes in Allah, and in His angels, and in His books, and in His Messengers. They say: we make no distinction between any of His Messengers we hear and obey our Lord Grant us Your Forgiveness, to You we are destined to return" (al-Baqarah, 2: 285).

But why do human beings, sometimes, act in an unethical way? The Qur'an states: *"These are the ones who have bought the present life in exchange for the world to come, their chastisement shall not be light and, nor shall they be helped"* (al-Baqarah, 2: 86).

It is this psyche of acquiring immediate worldly gains, not necessarily always by ethical means, but by any means, which deters people from welcoming ethical guidance sent in the form of the Qur'an. The Qur'an further states that such a psyche is not new. The earlier Messengers of Allah faced similar situations: *"Surely, we gave Moses the Scripture and caused a train of Messengers to follow him and then sent Jesus, the son of Mary, with clear proofs, and supported him with the Spirit of Holiness. But is it not true that every time a Messenger brought to you something that was not to your liking, you acted arrogantly, you called some Messengers liars and killed others?"* (al-Baqarah, 2: 87).

The verse also comments on the way the Israelites (and for that matter, any other people who do not welcome truth from their Lord) react: *"They say our hearts are well protected. No, the fact is Allah has cursed them because of their denying the truth. So scarcely do they believe"* (al-Baqarah 2: 88) This twisted approach of the unbelievers leads them to oppose the Prophet ﷺ and create obstacles in the way of *da'wah*: *"And now that there has come to them a Book from Allah, how are they treating it? Even though it confirms the Truth already in their possession and even though they had prayed for victory against the* unbelievers, and yet when that Book came to them and they recognized it – they refused to acknowledge its truth. Allah's curse be upon the unbelievers"* (al-Baqarah, 2: 89).

One very obvious reason for their condemnation by Allah is their arrogance and stubbornness. Even after having known the truth, they said: *"we hear but disobey"* (al-Baqarah, 2: 93). Those who claimed they were necessarily bound for Paradise because they were the descendants of Prophet Dawood ﷺ are asked by the Qur'an to pray for their own death, if they really believe this, to see whether they are bound for Paradise: *"Say to them if indeed the Last Abode with Allah is yours, in exclusion of other people, then long for death if you are truthful. But they shall never long for it because of the evil deeds they have committed; Allah is well aware of the wrongdoers, you will certainly find them most eager to cling on to life, indeed even more eager than those who associate others with Allah. Each one of them wishes to live a thousand years although the bestowal of long life cannot remove him from chastisement. Allah sees whatever they do"* (al-Baqarah, 2: 94-96). This hostile attitude of the unbelievers is also reflected in their dislike for Jibril, the angel who brought Divine Revelations to all Allah's Messengers, including the final Messenger of Allah ﷺ: *"Say whoever is an enemy of Gabriel (should know that) he revealed this (Qur'an) to your heart by Allah's leave: it confirms the Scriptures revealed before it and is a guidance and good tiding to the people of faith"* (al-Baqarah, 2: 97).

The Dialogical Approach

Notwithstanding the ethnocentric approach of the People of the Book, the Qur'an uses an optimistic and positive *da'wah* approach which consists of an ongoing dialogue, not only with the People of the Book but with all of humanity. The Qur'an invites all humankind to cooperate on the basis of a common ethical and moral vision of life. Nowhere does it define Islam as a new or Arabian faith. Since the Qur'an is undisputedly fully preserved in written form as well as in the memories of millions of believers, the People of the Book and others are repeatedly invited to study it objectively and without any preconceived ideas. One will find in the Qur'an the same message delivered by all the earlier Messengers of Allah: *"We surely sent down to you clear verses that elucidate the truth, which only transgressors reject as false"* (al-Baqarah, 2: 99). The Qur'an questions the negative mindset of the Israelite religious scholars and others who were convinced that the Qur'an contains true guidance, yet they vehemently opposed it publicly. The Qur'an also questions their baseless allegations against their own Prophets: *"And then followed what the evil ones falsely attributed to the Kingdom of Sulayman, even though Sulayman had never disbelieved; It is the evil ones who disbelieved, teaching people magic. And they followed what had been revealed to the two angels in Babylon, Harut and Marut, although the two never taught it to anyone without first declaring: 'We are merely a means of testing people so do not engage in unbelief.' And yet they learn from them what might cause division between a man and his wife. They could not cause harm to anyone except by the leave of Allah and still they learned what harmed rather than profited them, knowing well that he who bought it will have no share in the World to Come. Evil indeed is what they sold themselves for. Had they but known'"* (al-Baqarah, 2: 102).

> **REFLECTION**
>
> ► To what extent does pride in ethnic superiority rather arrogance due to knowledge make one desist from accepting the truth?
> ► Was it belief in racial supremacy and pride as People of the Book which prevented them from accepting Islam?

The Qur'an makes it clear that Harut and Marut did not teach any magic. They taught them how to undo evil spells. Still the evildoers of Bani Isra'il indulged in magic and attributed it wrongly to the angels.

With reference to the Israelites, the Qur'an points out that dodging the truth became more or less their habit due to their continuous disobedience of the instructions given in their Scripture. Therefore, their resistance to the Islamic message was not really surprising. They knew well that the Qur'an is true and genuinely from Allah, but their pride and arrogance prevented them from accepting Islam. Their long history shows that they behaved with the same arrogance towards their own Prophets.

One example of their behaviour towards the Prophet ﷺ is mentioned by the Qur'an: "*O you who believe do not say (to the Prophet ﷺ) ra'ina (lend ear to us) but say unzurna (favour us with your attention), and pay heed (to him). A painful chastisement awaits the unbelievers*" (al-Baqarah, 2: 104). The Qur'an, at this point also refers to the hypocrisy of the Jewish people living around Madinah: "*And when they meet those who believe (in the Prophet ﷺ) they say: we too believe in him. But in their intimate meetings they say to one *another how foolish, why should you intimate to them what Allah has revealed to you, for they will use it as argument against you before your Lord; are they unaware that Allah knows all that they hide and all that they disclose"* (al-Baqarah, 2: 76-77).

The Jewish community living around Madinah resisted the Islamic *da'wah* and kept conspiring against the Prophet ﷺ and the believers even after having signed the covenant known as the *Mithaq Madinah* or the Madinan Covenant. Their rabbis knew that the Qur'an is the word of Allah and that the Prophet ﷺ is His final Messenger, yet they were not prepared to change their ways and accept the faith which was basically no different from the faith of Prophets Ibrahim, Musa, 'Isa and other Prophets of Allah.

A dialogue between two known Jewish scholars of Madinah, Huyayy ibn Akhtab and his brother Abu Yasir, is documented by Ibn Ishaq's *Sirah* of the Prophet ﷺ. The Mother of the Believers Safiyyah, the daughter of Huyayy ibn Akhtab and the niece of Abu Yasir, reported, that when the Prophet ﷺ came to Madinah, her father Huyayy ibn Akhtab and uncle, Abu Yasir went to meet him and had a discussion with him. When they returned home, she overheard their conversation:

Uncle: Is it him? Do you recognize him, and can you be sure?
Father: Yes (by God).
Uncle: And what do you feel about him?
Father: By God, I shall be his enemy as long as I live.

This attitude of knowingly denying the truth, the Qur'an states, is taken by some of them as a matter of pride: *"But is it not true that every time a Messenger brought to you something that was not to your liking, you acted arrogantly: you called some Messengers liars and killed others. They say: our hearts are well protected. No, the fact is Allah has cursed them because of their denying the truth"* (al-Baqarah, 2: 87-88).

The long list of continuous transgressions and wilful violations by the Jewish tribes of Madinah is clear proof of their attitude of ungratefulness, arrogance, pride, and self-righteousness. The repeated warnings and punishments which were inflicted on them, in their past history, did not change them at all. Despite all this, Allah out of His love and Compassion did not annihilate them entirely and only withdrew His favour from them by demoting them from the leadership of mankind.

Implications of the Covenant: Serving Allah Through *Salah* and *Zakah*

The Qur'an reminds the Israelites about the covenant they made with their Lord Yahweh. First and foremost, the covenant (the Ten Commandments) begins with unqualified obedience to the Creator: *"You shall serve none but Allah"* (al-Baqarah, 2: 83). As discussed earlier servanthood (*'ubudiyyah*) is a comprehensive term in the Qur'an and in earlier revelations. The most frequently mentioned acts of worship in the Revelations sent to the Israelites and Muslims are *salah* and *zakah*. *Salah* represents the believer's thankfulness to Allah by bowing down, prostrating to Him and requesting Him several times a day to grant them guidance, protection and success in their endeavours. *Zakah* helps in cleansing the heart of selfishness and the love of wealth.

> **REFLECTION**
> *Zakah* is an Act of Worship, not a Tax
>
> As an act of worship, *zakah* makes one realize that whatever wealth believers have, it does not really belong to them. The real Owner and Provider is Allah. One is only a partial beneficiary because of one's endeavours to get it but whatever one acquires has in it a share, as the right, of the needy, the orphan, the indebted, the incarcerated and for spending in the way of Allah. *Zakah* therefore is essentially an act of worship, not a tax, which creates financial sustainability in an Islamic society.

Zakah is made obligatory along with a clearly defined system of its distribution. Every believer who has the means, i.e. enough yearly savings that reach a certain threshold, has to pay *zakah* in order to alleviate poverty, remove insecurity, the gap between the rich and the poor, and violation of human rights from society. If the system of its collection and distribution is properly organized by a Muslim society or the state, within a short period, it brings prosperity, dignity, and self-reliance for the members of society. Unfortunately, the Israelites did not maintain either acts of worship. They abandoned the congregational *salah* and the payment of *zakah*, and this was a violation of the covenant they had with their Lord.

Serving Parents as a Demand of *Tawhid*

The covenant refers to matters of faith, rituals, dealings, and transactions with family members as well as society at large. After touching on *tawhid* (Oneness of Allah), the covenant talks about *salah*, *zakah* and serving one's parents in the most dignified and respectful manner, particularly when they reach old age. Unfortunately, the so-called civilized world today, proudly claims to have set homes for senior citizens in order to take care of the elderly's health and welfare. The Jewish Scripture and the Qur'an approach this issue differently as they both enjoin providing for one's parents and grandparents all possible comforts at home, not as a favour but as an obligation. Parents and grandparents are supposed to live with their children and grandchildren and not sent to care homes: *"Your Lord has decreed: Do not worship any but Him; Be good to your parents; and should one of them attain old age with you do not say to them even 'fie', neither chide them but speak to them with respect, and be humble and tender to them, and say: Lord show mercy to them as they nurtured me when I was small"* (Banu Isra'il, 17: 23-24).

The wordings of the above verse clearly indicate that parents are an integral part of the family and, even when their children have their own living arrangements, they have an obligation to personally take care of them. Even when they become adults and get married, they should listen to them and obey them, take care of their welfare, spend on them and treat them with dignity, respect and honour. Never should parents and grandparents be considered a burden or sent to care homes. The ethical dimension highlighted here is: parents did their best to nurture and raise, care for and feed children who were totally dependent on them, and now, in their old age it becomes the children's ethical and legal obligation to do their best to comfort them and this is a manifestation of *tawhid*.

The primacy of *tawhid* is also fully reflected in the covenant that the Israelites made with their Lord. The first point that this covenant underscores is *tawhid*: *"You shall serve none but Allah and do good to parents, kinsmen, orphans and the needy, you shall speak kindly to people and establish prayer and give zakah. And yet except for a few of you, you turned back on this covenant and you are still backsliders"* (al-Baqarah, 2: 83).

REFLECTION
The Primacy of *Tawhid* as Reflected in the Covenant of the Israelites

According to this covenant, *tawhid* is not merely a theological construct, rather, it determines the whole behaviour of a person. *Tawhid* has to be realized at four levels: first, a *tawhidic* personality on an individual level, reflected in serving Allah alone in conduct and behaviour. Second, the translation of *tawhid* in full obedience to parents in *ma'ruf*. Third, the development of compassion (*rahmah*) towards relatives and fellow human beings. Fourth, the fulfillment of social responsibility by paying *zakah* to those who deserve it, and excellence in spending wealth on the needy in order to alleviate poverty and letting people achieve self-reliance in economic and financial matters. *Zakah* as an institution also helps the state in keeping peace in society.

This covenant has direct relevance to the followers of Islam. *Tawhid* is the foundational principle of Islam and an integral part of the message of all the earlier Prophets of Allah. As mentioned earlier, *tawhid* is not a theological concept, rather, it determines the whole behaviour of a believer. The realization of *tawhid* at the individual level means one's liberation from a dualistic concept of life (secular and sacred) and also the denial of all the gods of colour, race, nationalism, language or ethnicity. At a family level, it prescribes ethical conduct and behaviour towards one's parents, spouse, children and other members of the extended family. At the social level, one has to fulfil one's obligations towards one's neighbours, the needy, the orphans and the downtrodden i.e. *huquq al 'ibad*.

The Qur'anic Model of Extended Family

The concept of the extended family, as elaborated in *Surah al-Nur*, includes not just one's parents, brothers, and sisters but also one's grandparents, uncles, aunts and cousins, from both the paternal and maternal sides. One has to spend on them not as a favour but as an obligation. The objective is to build a caring and cohesive extended family as the building block of a responsible and fair (*'adil*) society, as opposed to an individualistic society in which one's major concern is one's individual self. It replaces the concept of 'me' with a culture of 'we' in society. The Qur'anic sociology advocates a cohesive, unified and ethically responsible social order.

The moral social order, the Qur'an wants to realize not only demands the respect and honouring of parents but also focuses on the dignity and value of human life. The covenant declares sanctity of human life as a universal Divine commandment for the Israelites as well as for the Muslims: *"And recall when We made a covenant with you, that you shall not shed one another's blood and shall not turn out one another from your homelands; you confirmed it, and you yourselves are a witness to it. And here you are killing one another, turning out a party of your own from their homelands, aiding one another against them in sin and enmity, and if they come to you as captives you ransom them although the very act of expelling them (from their habitation) was unlawful to you. Do you believe in a part of the Scripture and reject the rest? What else, then, could be the retribution of those among you who do this than that they should live in degradation in the present life, and that on the Day of Resurrection they should be sent to the severest chastisement? Allah is not heedless of what you do"* (al-Baqarah, 2: 84-85).

To sum up, the directives of the covenant remind the Israelites about the pledge they made to their Lord to respect human life, and to avoid the violation of human property and freedom. Though addressed to the Children of Israel, the text of the covenant is equally binding on the Muslims until the Day of Judgement. The commonly known objectives of *Shari'ah* include protection of life, property, and religious freedom which are not particular to the Muslims. These are universal rights granted by the Qur'an and the Sunnah of the final Messenger ﷺ. The violation of any of these three objectives of the *Shari'ah* is also a violation of the concept of *tawhid*. In other words, tenets of faith and behaviour cannot be separated. Human behaviour in social, economic and political governance, whether in times of war or peace, should be fully aligned with *tawhid*.

The following verse informs the believers of the possible reasons that drove the Israelites to disregard the pledge they made to God: *"These are the ones who have bought the present life in exchange for the world to come. Their chastisement shall not be lightened nor shall they be helped"* (al-Baqarah, 2: 86).

The covenant made by the Israelites, as said earlier, has equal relevance for the followers of Islam. If the Muslims break their covenant with Allah, i.e. to serve Him alone, and disregard the *Shari'ah*, Allah's justice requires that they are treated no different than how the Israelites were treated. Respect for human life, honour, property, faith and reason, the five objectives of *Shari'ah*, therefore, are universal principles to be followed by the Muslims and actually by the whole of humankind.

The Rights of the Marginalized: The Culture of *Ihsan*

The Qur'anic universal ethical order makes the rights of the needy and the poor an integral part of the moral and legal obligations imposed on those who have means and resources. Social mobility, the alleviation of poverty, the removal of ignorance, diseases and insecurity are major concerns of the Qur'anic ethical order. The Qur'an demands to create an Islamic welfare society wherein virtue prevails while greed, oppression, exploitation and injustice are minimized.

Doing good (*ihsan*) to parents is an obligation that has no limits. The word *ihsan* has its roots in *husn*, which means loveliness, seemliness and agreeableness. *Ihsan* refers to the tendency to excel at something and make it beautiful. It also refers to qualities like benevolence, politeness, sympathy, generosity, tolerance, and consideration. Fairness (*'adl*) while doing something is not the same as doing it with *ihsan*. Fairness entails giving someone or something what one deserves while *ihsan* entails going above and beyond, more than fairness.

The Qur'an also recommends a caring and dignified attitude

towards kinsfolk (*al-aqriba'*). Islam does not conceive of family as a nuclear unit but rather as an extended family which plays a crucial, constructive, and educational role in the transfer of values, culture, and ethical and moral behaviour. The family plays a central role in the establishment of social equity and when family is marginalized, society's values and culture get forgotten and lost.

The Ethics of Communication

The Qur'an advises the believers to communicate with people with politeness and kindness: *"You shall speak kindly to people"* (al-Baqarah, 2: 83). This ethics of communication is deemed desirable by the Qur'an even when addressing those who may be proud, arrogant and rebellious. Prophet Musa ﷺ and his brother Prophet Harun ﷺ were advised to approach the Pharaoh, the tyrant of his age, but politely: *"Go both of you to Pharaoh, for he has transgressed all bounds, and speak to him gently (qawlan layyinan), perhaps he may take heed or fear (Allah)"* (Ta-Ha, 20: 43-44). The message conveyed is simple, the ones who call to Allah (*da'iyah*) should control their emotions and behave politely but firmly in all situations. The Prophetic practice is to talk with others moderately. Communication with even those who may be stubborn has to be polite or else depart from them in a friendly manner: *"and when the foolish ones address them, they simply say: Peace to you"* (al-Furqan, 25: 63).

Polite and kind speech does not mean weakness rather it shows confidence and strength of character because keeping one's emotions under control is an attribute of true believers, the Qur'an mentions: *"Who spend in the way of Allah both in affluence and hardship, who restrain their anger (al-kazimin al-ghayz) and forgive others. Allah loves such gooddoers"* (Al 'Imran, 3: 134). The Prophets of Allah were advised to invite people towards His path in the most beautiful way: *"Call to the way of Your Lord with wisdom and goodly exhortation and reason with them in the best manner possible"* (al-Nahl, 16: 125).

The violations made by the Israelites of their covenant and Scriptural instructions are repeated in modern history in the form of the violation of the rights of the native Muslims of Palestine and also of the Muslims in other parts of the world. Having talked about the respect for life and the freedom of people, the Qur'an questions the claim of those who commit oppression and follow other than Allah. Can it be that they deserve respect in this world and in the Hereafter just because they are descendants of great Prophets of Allah?

With this background in mind, when one reads again the following verses, their freshness and relevance to the whole of humanity becomes self-evident: *"And recall when We made a covenant with the children of Israel you shall serve none but Allah and do good to parents, kinsmen, orphan and the needy you shall speak kindly to people and establish prayer and give zakah. And yet, except for a few of you, you turned back on this covenant with you, and you are still backsliders. And recall when We made a covenant with you that you shall not shed one another's blood and shall not turn out one another from your homelands: you confirmed it, and you yourselves were witness to it. And here you are killing one another, turning out a party of your own from their homelands and aiding one another against them in sin and enmity, and if they come to you as captives you ransom them although the very act of expelling them was unlawful to you. Do you believe in a part of Scripture and reject the rest? What else then could be retribution of those among you who do this than that they should live in degradation in the present life and that on the Day of Resurrection they should be sent to the severest chastisement? Allah is not heedless of what you do. These are the ones who have brought the present life in exchange for the world to come. Their Chastisement shall not be lightened nor shall they be helped"* (al-Baqarah, 2: 84-86).

The following verse further mentions the unfair attitude of the Israelites toward their benefactor, Prophet Musa ﷺ, who liberated them from their captivity in Egypt. We are told that the Israelites made their own personal interests and gains their ultimate concern and virtually their gods. They accepted only that part of the teachings of their Prophets which accrued benefit for them. They proudly rejected some of their Prophets, accusing them of being liars and even killing some of them. This ingratitude of the Israelites and their belief that they were the Chosen People, and that God shall always be on their side, made them haughty and arrogant. They knew through their own Scripture about the coming of a Prophet ﷺ as their redeemer. But when the Prophet ﷺ arrived in Madinah, they strongly opposed him. This arrogance became their second nature. The Qur'an states: *"And now that there has come to them a Book (al-Qur'an) from Allah how are they treating it? Even though it confirms the Truth already in their possession and even though they had prayed for victory against the non-believers and yet when that Book came to them, and they recognized it, they refused to acknowledge its Truth. Allah's curse be upon the unbelievers. Evil indeed is what they console themselves with. They deny the guidance revealed by Allah, grudging that He chose to bestow His gracious bounty on some of His servants whom He willed"* (al-Baqarah, 2: 89-90).

The negative response of the Jews to Islam did not frustrate the Prophet ﷺ though they tried their best to confuse new Muslims. The next few verses expose the insincerity of the Jews vis-à-vis Islam. Their disobedience was also reflected in their selection of the words they used when they spoke with the Prophet ﷺ. They always showed disrespect to the Prophet ﷺ and Jibril, because he brought the Qur'anic Revelation to the Prophet ﷺ. The Qur'an states: *"Say whoever is an enemy of Gabriel, (should know that) he revealed this (Qur'an) to your heart by Allah's leave. It confirms the Scripture revealed before it and is a guidance and good tiding to the people of faith, whoever is an enemy of Allah, His Angels, and His Messengers and to Gabriel and Michael will surely find Allah as enemy to such unbelievers"* (al-Baqarah, 2: 97-98).

The Culture of Using Communication in a Dignified Way

The negativity of the Jewish community in Madinah was reflected in their conversations and communication with the Prophet ﷺ. It was a common practice to seek the Prophet's attention by using the expression *unzurna* (favour us with your attention). But the Jews intentionally used an expression that had a double meaning to cause insult to the Prophet ﷺ and so, instead of using *unzurna,* they used the word *ra'ina* which, in Arabic, meant lend us your ear but, in Hebrew, it meant, "Listen, may you become deaf!" The Qur'an guides the believers to observe total respect when addressing the Prophet ﷺ and to talk to him in the most dignified manner.

The culture that the Qur'an wants to establish demands respect for Allah's angels and the Messenger of Allah ﷺ. Believers are advised to pay due respect to the Prophet ﷺ: *"Verily those who cause annoyance to Allah and His Messenger - Allah has cursed them in this world and the Hereafter and has prepared for them a humiliating chastisement"* (al-Ahzab, 33: 37). Elsewhere it states: *"Believers do not advance before Allah and His Messenger, and fear Allah. Verily Allah is*

All-Hearing, All-Knowing. Believers do not raise your voices above the voice of the Prophet ﷺ and when speaking to him do not speak aloud, as you speak aloud to one another, lest all your deeds are reduced to nothing without your even realizing it. The ones who lower their voices in the presence of the Messenger of Allah ﷺ are those whose hearts Allah has tested for taqwa (Allah-consciousness). Theirs shall be forgiveness and a great reward" (al-Hujurat, 49: 1-3). Showing the slightest signs of disrespect to the Prophet ﷺ by the Jews or the hypocrites could have easily led to a serious internal clash or conflict in the community. This is why the Qur'an instructed the believers to address the Prophet ﷺ in a dignified and respectful way.

The *ayah* implies that in an Islamic society whoever is placed in a leadership position should be respected. The social norm, the Qur'an wants to inculcate is the practice of civility and dignified speech, but at the same time no hero worship.

The Status of Earlier Sacred Laws

One of the questions raised by the Jewish scholars and others was, if Allah was knowledgeable, why certain Divine Revelations superseded the earlier ones, and why are the commands given in earlier Scriptures set aside in favour of a later Revelation. The Qur'an responds in a simple but convincing way? First, people are reminded that no doubt Allah is All-knowing, but He is also All-powerful and absolute authority belongs to Him alone, hence He can always modify a time-specific legislation with a permanent command. Second, Allah invites those who question these to compare what is modified by the Qur'an and contrast it with what was prescribed earlier. Under the rule of 'qualification' some Quranic ayahs qualify others; an obvious example of qualification (*naskh*) is the Qur'anic verse: *"They ask you about wine and games of chance. Say in both of these there is great evil, even though there is some benefit for people, but their evil is greater than their benefit"* (al-Baqarah, 2: 219). The verse conveys a clear message that intoxicants and gambling are both harmful and need to be avoided. The message is further reinforced when it is stated: *"Believers Do not draw near to prayer while you are intoxicated until you know what you are saying"* (al-Nisa', 4: 43). But here intoxicants are not clearly declared to be prohibited. This gradualism is a general principle in the Qur'anic legislation, for it allows ease, *yusr*, as in the case of making up the days of fast missed in Ramadan due to a legitimate reason. Sometimes the principle of *tadrij* or gradual legislation allows for some degree of adjustment before a matter is closed, like here in the case of intoxicants. Finally, the verse which prohibited intoxicants came with a clear injunction: *"Believers! Intoxication, games of chance, idolatrous sacrifices at altars and divining arrows are all abominations, the handiwork of Satan. So, turn wholly away from it that you may attain to true success"* (al-Ma'idah, 5: 90). The example given above fully answers the objections of the People of the Book and others. The Arabian culture was a hedonistic culture in which liquor was an integral part of life, just like it is nowadays in parts of the world. Allah knew well how to unhook people from intoxicants in a gradual way. If it was done through one single command, it would have created hardship for a lot of Muslims who were used to consuming intoxicants for years. But when it was finally declared that intoxicants were prohibited, people instantly complied and poured out their stocks of intoxicants in the streets of Madinah.

Abrogation (*naskh*) literally means substitution, supersession, and making something void but the Qur'an uses it mostly in the sense of a modification or qualification of a legal ruling by another legal ruling: *"For whatever verse We abrogate or consign to oblivion, We bring a better one or the like of it. Are you not aware that Allah is All-Powerful? Are you not aware that the dominion of the heavens and the earth belongs to Allah and that none apart from Allah is your Protector or Helper?"* (al-Baqarah, 2: 106-107).

Raising unnecessary questions on topics, such as abrogation, was a favourite practice of the hypocrites and the People of the Book. The Qur'an refers to this in a historical context: *"Or would you ask your Messenger in the manner Moses was asked before? And whoever exchanges faith for unbelief has surely strayed from the Right Way"* (al-Baqarah, 2: 108).

The purpose of asking unnecessary questions by the People of the Book was to confuse and create doubt in the minds of newly converted Muslims and other members of the Muslim community in Madinah: *"Out of sheer envy many people of the Book would be glad to turn you back into unbelievers after you have become believers even though the truth has become clear to them"* (al-Baqarah, 2: 109).

Solidarity of the newly created *ummah* required the discarding of minor issues, as much as possible, while remaining firm as far as the fundamentals were concerned. The Prophet's response to the uncouth and bad manners of the People of the Book was considerate, kind and forgiving, which shows his unequalled forbearance, tolerance and fortitude, as pointed out in the Qur'an: *"We have sent you forth as nothing but mercy to people of the whole world"* (al-Anbiya', 21: 107). His ethical excellence, forgiving nature and kindness were exemplary, the Qur'an observes: *"And you are certainly on the most exalted standard of moral excellence"* (al-Qalam, 68: 4). Being a mortal who may show signs of irritation and annoyance vis-à-vis the conduct of the hypocrites, the Prophet ﷺ is further advised to be steadfast and keep acting with kindness: *"Nevertheless, forgive and be indulgent towards them until Allah brings forth His decision. Surely Allah is All-Powerful"* (al-Baqarah, 2: 109).

In order to keep their faith strong, the Qur'an reminds the believers to seek help through *salah* and *zakah*. The *salah* (prayer) is not simply a matter of individual devotion to Allah, its performance in congregation, besides its role in building brotherhood, helps in the consolidation of the *ummah*. The mosque, as the place of congregation for the believers five times a day, creates a sense of belonging, one vision and purpose of life, and obeying together the commands of the One and true God. Similarly, *zakah*, as mentioned earlier, is not a charity but a social obligation to uplift the downtrodden, the poor and the needy to make them self-reliant and to help liberate people who are denied their human rights. Therefore, the Qur'an states: *"Establish prayer and dispense zakah. Whatever good deeds you send forth for your own good, you will find them with Allah. Surely Allah sees all that you do"* (al-Baqarah, 2: 110).

REFLECTION

To deserve Paradise, one has to submit fully to Allah as well as obey the Prophet ﷺ, and this obedience must be reflected in one's personal, social, and professional conduct and behaviour and also in one's observation of Divine commands. Blood relationship or intercession are of no avail when it comes to entering Paradise.

The Qur'an looks critically at the claims of the Israelites and Christians regarding Paradise. The Israelites thought that their genealogical relation with their Prophets was enough for them to enter Paradise while the Christians believed that the intercession of Prophet 'Isa ﷺ was enough for their salvation. The Qur'an stresses that only those who take Allah Alone as their Lord, not associating anyone or anything with Him, observe Allah's Divine commands and act virtuously deserve to enter Paradise.

The believers are encouraged to develop these attributes to deserve entering Paradise. What matters in terms of reward is ethical conduct and behaviour and the observance of Divine commands, as mentioned later in *Surah al-Ma'idah*: "*Then we revealed the Book to you (O Muhammad) with truth, confirming whatever of the Book was revealed before, and protecting and guarding over it. Judge then in the affairs of men in accordance with the law that Allah has revealed and do not follow their desires in disregard of the truth which has come to you. For each of you We have appointed a law (Shari'ah) and a way of life and had Allah so willed, He would surely have made you one single community, instead, in order to test you by what He gave you. Vie then, with one another in good works*" (al-Ma'idah, 5: 48). In other words, excellence in observing Allah's commands, the *Shari'ah*, is the key to success in the Hereafter while genealogical pride cannot save anyone.

Who is a Muslim?

A Muslim is someone who wilfully accepts the supremacy of Allah's commands and follows the practice of His final Messenger Muhammad ﷺ, and performs good deeds with sincerity as best as possible. Paradise is attained only by those who excel in their Islamic ethical conduct and behaviour irrespective of their colour, race, language or geographic origin. Such practising Muslims are also called *muhsinin* by the Qur'an. The root of the word *muhsin*, (pl. *muhsinin*) is *h s n* which means a good, agreeable or desirable act or thing. *Ihsan* refers to worshipping Allah as though one sees Him, for if one does not see Him, He nevertheless sees one.

Allah makes clear: *"They say: none shall enter the Gardens unless he be a Jew or (according to the Christians) a Christian. These are their vain desires. Say 'Bring your proof if you are speaking the truth' (none has any special claim upon reward from Allah). Whoever submits himself completely to the obedience of Allah and does good, will find his reward with his Lord. No fear shall come upon them nor shall they grieve. The Jews say: The Christians, have no basis for their belief and Christians say the Jews have no base for their beliefs. They say so even though they read the Scripture. The claim of those who have no knowledge (of the Scripture) is similar. Allah will judge between them concerning their differences on the Day of Resurrection"* (al-Baqarah, 2: 111-113).

Religious Pluralism and the Right to Worship in an Islamic Polity

The creedal differences between the Jewish and Christian communities created a gulf between them to the extent that each of these two communities destroyed the places of worship of the other. The Qur'an makes a general observation that irrespective of creed, a place of worship must be honoured. The context of this Qur'anic statement is the objectionable behaviour of the Makkans who stopped the Muslims from visiting the House of Allah, in Makkah, but the injunction is not specific to one place of worship, it is rather a general principle applicable to any place of worship.

The Muslims are, therefore, enjoined to protect, not just their own mosques, but also the churches, synagogues and temples which happen to be within the boundaries of an Islamic polity. Moreover, the followers of other faiths should not encounter any hardship when trying to visit their places of worship. The verse also provides guidance regarding common places of religious significance such as al-Aqsa Mosque. The Qur'anic principle is to give control of such places to those who are tolerant and fair. The Muslims alone qualify on this count for the custodianship of the Holy mosque of Jerusalem: *"Who is more iniquitous than he who bars Allah's places of worship that His name be mentioned there and seeks their destruction? It does not behove such people to enter them, and should they enter, they should enter in fear. There is degradation for them in this world and a mighty chastisement in the Next"* (al-Baqarah, 2: 114). Here, the Qur'an is referring to the intolerance of the Jews and Christians towards other's places of worship. Islam goes a step further and the Qur'an grants, as citizens, the right to worship to even the disbelievers (*kuffar*): *"Say, O unbelievers I do not worship those that you worship, neither do you worship Him Whom I worship, nor will I worship those whom you have worshipped, nor are you going to worship Him Whom I worship, to you is your religion and to me my way of life"* (al-Kafirun, 109: 1-6).

The Qur'an advocates religious and cultural co-existence and pluralism and provides a set of universal standards of human conduct. These objectives and standards are generally discussed in legal literature under the title of the major objectives of the Sacred Law. However, these are not confined to purely legal matters but are also applicable to all possible human interventions, whether at the personal, collective, national, or international levels.

To ensure the right to visit places of worship, irrespective of one's religious denomination, is an objective of *Shari'ah*. The Qur'an is the only Divine Revelation that has used words like monasteries (*sawami'*), churches (*biya'un*), synagogues (*salawatun*) and mosques (*masajid*), with specific instructions to protect all of them and make them easy to access: *"Those who were unjustly expelled from their homes for no other reason than their saying: Allah is Our Lord. If Allah were not to repel some through others (through jihad), monasteries (sawami') and churches (biya'un) and synagogue (salawatun) and mosques (masajid) wherein the name of Allah is much mentioned would certainly have been pulled down..."* (al-Hajj, 22: 40).

For the Muslims, the verse instructs that mosques belong to Allah and no one can claim their ownership. The idolaters, like the people of Makkah at the time of the Prophet ﷺ, therefore, had no legal or social right to claim ownership or custodianship of the House of Allah. Similarly, in a Muslim community, the mosques must remain open for all Muslims irrespective of their legal school of thought.

Similarity of and Constancy in the Message (*Da'wah*) of all the Prophets

The Qur'an repeatedly reminds the Israelites about the message of *tawhid* delivered by their own Prophets, in the lineage of Prophet Ya'qub ﷺ (Jacob), delivered to them, which is partially preserved in the Scripture they have today. It invites them to follow Allah's commands unconditionally and totally. It also invites them to think about how unreasonable they are with the Qur'an and the final Messenger ﷺ who has endorsed the original message brought by Prophets Ibrahim, Isma'il, Ishaq, Ya'qub and others. Except for a few of them, a majority of the Jews never paid any serious attention to the Qur'an or even to their own Scripture. Instead, the Israelites wanted the Muslims to follow their deviant ways: *"Never will the Jews be pleased with you nor the Christians until you follow their way. Say: Surely Allah's guidance is the true guidance. Should you follow their desires disregarding the knowledge that has come to you, you shall have no protector or helper against Allah"* (al-Baqarah, 2: 120).

The Qur'an also corrects the confusion in the minds of the Israelites about their *qiblah* (towards which they offer their prayer). It reminds them of the historical fact that the first place of worship was built by Prophets Ibrahim and Isma'il in Makkah. The forefathers of the Israelites also prayed towards the Kaaba in Makkah until Prophet Sulayman ﷺ built the Temple in Palestine.

The verse also elaborates on the leadership role, that only those descendants of Prophets and Messengers deserve it who meet the requisite qualification for it, through devotion and commitment to the cause. Therefore, their claim to leadership due to a blood relationship with Prophet Ya'qub ﷺ had no scriptural basis.

Before declaring the change of leadership and making an announcement to the Muslim *ummah* that it is a witness to mankind, the Qur'an validates the centrality of the Sacred Mosque in Makkah as the original *qiblah* of Prophets Ibrahim and Isma'il: *"Recall when Abraham's Lord tested him in certain matters and when he successfully stood the test. He said: Indeed I am going to appoint you a leader (Imam) of all people. When Abraham asked: And is this covenant also for my descendants? The Lord responded: My covenant does not embrace the wrongdoers. And when We made this House (Kaaba) a resort for mankind and place of security, commanding people: Take the station of Abraham as a permanent place for prayer, and enjoined Abraham and Ishmael: Purify My House for those who make tawaf (walk around it) and those who abide in devotion ('akifin) and those who bow and who prostrate themselves (in prayer). And when Abraham prayed: O my Lord! Make this a place of security and provide those of its people that believe in Allah and the Last Day with fruits for sustenance. Allah answered: And I shall still grant him who disbelieves the enjoyment of his provision, for this short life, and then I shall drive him to the chastisement of fire, that is an evil end. Recall when Abraham and Ishmael raised the foundations of the House praying: Our Lord! Accept this from us; You are All-Hearing, All-Knowing. Our Lord Make us submissive (muslimin) to You and make out of our descendants a community that submits itself to You, and show us the ways of Your worship and turn to us in mercy, You are Much-Relenting, Most-Compassionate, Our Lord Raise up in the midst of our offspring a Messenger from among them who shall recite to them Your verses, and instruct them in the Book and in Wisdom and purify their lives. Verily You are the Most-Mighty, the Most-Wise"* (al-Baqarah, 2: 126-129).

The Conferment of Leadership on Prophet Ibrahim ﷺ

After the original prayer made by Prophets Ibrahim and Isma'il, the Qur'an informs that the leadership of humankind was conferred on Prophet Ibrahim ﷺ, due to his total submission to Allah and his success in all trials and difficulties he faced with steadfastness (*istiqamah*). It also explains that this honour was personally merited due to his outstanding obedience and is not automatically transferable to his progeny. It also shows that ultimately, as a result of the supplication made by both Prophets Ibrahim and Isma'il, the final Messenger was destined to be from the descendants of Prophet Isma'il ﷺ according to Allah's plan. Anyone who reads these verses can easily understand the irrationality of the Israelites' claim of leadership on a genealogical basis. In other words, the Muslims too cannot claim leadership (*imamah*) on the basis of lineage. It is against the Sunnah of Allah.

We also learn that the original House of Allah was built by Prophets Ibrahim and Isma'il, hence the change of *qiblah* from Jerusalem to Makkah was not a deviation. Similarly, since Prophet Ibrahim ﷺ was neither a Jew nor a Christian but a true servant of Allah, the source of the Qur'anic message essentially originates in the faith of Prophets Ibrahim and Isma'il. The Qur'an refers to this beautiful aspect of Prophet Ibrahim ﷺ: *"And who but a fool would be averse to the way of Abraham? For it is We who chose Abraham for Our mission in the world and surely in the World to Come, he shall be reckoned among the righteous. Such was Abraham that when his Lord said to him: "Submit (aslim) he said I have submitted (aslamtu) to the Lord of the Universe". And Abraham enjoined the same upon his children, and so did Jacob: "My Children behold, Allah has chosen this din (way of life) for you. Remain till death in submission (muslimun). Why were you witnesses when death came to Jacob? He asked his children who will you serve after me? They said: we shall serve your God, the God of your forefathers, Abraham, Ishmail and Isaac, the One God and unto Him do we submit (wa nahnu lahu muslimun)"* (al-Baqarah, 2: 130-133).

In these beautiful words, the Qur'an builds a historical argument regarding Prophet Ibrahim's faith as the common source and origin of the faith of the three *tawhidic* faith traditions: Islam, Judaism and Christianity. It establishes not only a common ground for inter-faith communication, but also proves that *tawhid* was the original faith of the Jews and Christians. They were asked to stay firm on *tawhid*. Unfortunately, Judaism developed into an ethnocentric faith while Christianity turned into Trinitarian theology. Islam, as the *din*, came to revive the pristine faith of Prophets Ibrahim, Musa and 'Isa. Both the Old and New Testaments partially confirm that *tawhid* was their original faith. Islam is essentially an invitation to all human beings to embrace the faith of Prophet Ibrahim, unadulterated *tawhid*, Allah's Sovereignty and Authority, and deny all man-made gods and goddesses of power, glamour, pleasure and nationalism.

A Dialogue Based on the Abrahamic Faith

After providing a solid common basis for meaningful dialogue, the Qur'an makes a general comment that the progeny of Prophet Ya'qub ﷺ will be judged by Allah on the basis of their deeds and compliance with the ethical teachings of their Messengers and not on the basis of their lineage: *"They say: Be Jews or be Christian, then you will be rightly guided. Say to them "No, follow exclusively the Way of Abraham who was not one of those who associate others with Allah in His Divinity. Say we believe in Allah and in what has been revealed to us and to Abraham, Ishmael, Isaac, and Jacob and the descendants and in what was given to Moses and Jesus and in what the other Prophets received from their Lord. We make no distinction between any of them and we are those who submit to Allah. And then if they come to believe as you believe, they are on right guidance; and if they turn away, then quite obviously they have merely fallen into opposition to the Truth. Allah will suffice you for protection against them. He is All-Hearing, All-knowing"* (al-Baqarah, 2: 135-137).

The Qur'an also makes an observation on certain religious rites and ceremonies. In most religions other than Islam, initiation rites often include the use of certain symbols and colours. In some African religions, for example, each tribe has its own way of making an initiation scar on the initiated person's face or arm which becomes his identification with the tribe. In Hinduism, saffron lines are applied on the forehead while in Christianity baptism with oil or the use of the cross are well known.

Sibghat Allah: From Physical Identity to Ideological Identity and from Symbolic Colours and Signs of Devotion to Substantial Transformation and Exemplary Conduct

The Qur'an raises a question: what is better, a temporary symbolic colour, a mark on the body of the believer or a permanent attitude, conduct and behaviour as an indication of total acceptance and submission to Allah? This shift from a physical identity to an ideological identity actually transforms the particularity of faith into a universalized faith identity. Ethical actions, moral conduct and kind behaviour toward the poor, the needy, the orphan, and the old with humility and servitude to Allah makes more sense than the use of a colour bar on the face of the believer. Actions should speak for what one believes: *"Say take on Allah's colour (Sibghatullah), And whose colour is better than Allah's? It is Him that we serve"* (al-Baqarah, 2: 138).

Allah's Colour

The most obvious and outstanding sign of devotion to Allah is not a symbolic colour, initiation rite or wearing a thread or a cross or a robe, it is rather one's exemplary conduct, following of the Prophetic behaviour in personal, social, economic, political, legal and cultural matters. This is what amounts to adopting "Allah's colour" or total obedience to Him. This Qur'anic call is universal. Everyone is invited to join in the universal community of those who immerse themselves in the obedience of Allah and liberate themselves from narrow attachment to soil, language, race, colour or nationalism.

The Qur'an extends its dialogical discourse of adopting the original Message of Prophet Ibrahim ؑ and all the Israelite Prophets, namely *tawhid* (pure Oneness of Allah), observing Allah's directives and commands in all human activities.

The Qur'an invites the People of Book to nothing more than following and implementing *tawhid* in their lives: *"Say (O Prophet ﷺ) will you then dispute with us concerning Allah when*

He is our Lord and your Lord? Our deeds are for us and your deeds are for you. And it is Him that we serve exclusively. Or do you claim that Abraham and Ishmael, Isaac and Jacob and the descendants (of Jacob) were 'Jews' or 'Christians'. Say who has greater knowledge, you or Allah? Who does greater wrong than he who conceals a testimony he has received from Allah? Allah is not heedless of the things you do" (al-Baqarah, 2: 139-140).

The historical fact to which the Qur'an refers here is that the title "Israel", which means the servant of Allah, was given to Prophet Yaqʻub ﷺ, and this means that by submitting to Allah alone, he practised pure *tawhid*, and advised his descendants to do the same. This simply means that the faith of Prophets Jacob, Solomon, and David was not Judaism but submission to Allah alone or *tawhid*.

The Islamic *daʻwah* is essentially a call to go back to the original faith of the great Prophets of Allah: Ibrahim, Ishaq, Yaʻqub, Musa and ʻIsa. Islam (acceptance of the One and Only true Lord) is not a new "religion" but the original and common faith of the whole of humanity.

The Leadership Role of the Muslim *Ummah*

The Qur'an refers to the historic fact that the Sacred Mosque in Makkah, which houses the Kaaba, was built by Prophets Ibrahim and Ismaʻil hundreds of years before Prophet Sulayman ﷺ built the Temple in Jerusalem. A pertinent observation is made at this point on the change of the *qiblah* from Jerusalem to the Kaaba in Makkah. While in Makkah the Prophet ﷺ used to pray in the *Haram* in a way that he was facing both the Kaaba and Jerusalem because the Kaaba was in the centre of the circular structure of the mosque.

When the Prophet ﷺ moved to Madinah, he kept praying toward Jerusalem for around sixteen months but in his heart of hearts, the Prophet ﷺ desired to pray facing toward the *qiblah* of his forefathers Isma'il and Ibrahim. The change of the *qiblah* was also a test to measure the believers' degree of sincerity and commitment to their *din*. Before announcing the change of the *qiblah,* the Qur'an states that what makes a particular direction significant is not its being the north or south but its specification by the Lord of the Universe.

> It resolves the issue in a unique way, for it states that all the directions (north, south, east, and west) belong to Allah who is not confined by time and space. Therefore, the debate about which direction is the correct one is not an issue. What matters is the command of Allah. He knows what is best for His people, for soon He was going to confer on the Muslim *ummah* the role of the leadership of humankind, and it was appropriate to symbolically shift the centre of *da'wah* to its original place and declare the *maqam Ibrahim* as the *musalla*.

This *ayah,* which was revealed before the *ayah* of the change (*tahwil*) of *qiblah,* pre-empted what would be the reaction of the Jews and also the *munafiqun* who were still not sincere to Islam. The message conveyed is simple: no direction is sacred in itself, and all the directions belong to Allah. What matters is not a geographic direction but Allah's command (*hukm*) which must be obeyed. Therefore, while performing the *'Asr* prayer, when the Companions heard the announcement during the *salah,* they changed their direction from facing north to south towards the direction of Kaaba.

Conferment of the Leadership Role of the Muslim *Ummah*

After providing enough evidence about the unfair and extreme attitude of the Jews and Christians toward Allah and His Prophets, the Qur'an announces a change in the leadership of humanity from the Children of Israel to the Children of Isma'il. The Muslim *ummah* is now selected to communicate God's guidance to the whole of humankind. The reason for this is also given by the Qur'an which states that the Muslim *ummah* is a middlemost and moderate nation: *"And it is thus that We appointed you to be the community of the middle way so that you might be witnesses to all mankind and the Messenger might be a witness to you"* (al-Baqarah, 2: 143).

This leadership role is organically linked with the globalization of the message of Prophet Ibrahim ﷺ who invited people to the absolute obedience of Allah (*tawhid*) over a vast expanse from Iraq to Arabia. The change of the *qiblah* from Jerusalem to Makkah indicated the revival of the global Abrahamic tradition: *"We see you oft turning your face towards the sky; now We are turning you to the direction that will satisfy you. Turn your face towards the Holy Mosque; and wherever you are turn your faces toward it in prayers. Those who have been granted the Scripture certainly know that this (injunction to change the direction of prayer) is right and is from their Lord. Allah is not heedless of what they do. And yet no matter what proofs you bring before the People of the Book they will not follow your direction of prayer nor will you follow their direction of prayer. None is prepared to follow the other's direction of prayer. Were you to follow their desire in disregard of the knowledge which has come to you, you will surely be reckoned among the wrongdoers. Those to whom We have given the Scripture recognize the place (towards which one must turn in prayer)* as fully as they recognize their own sons, this even though a group of them knowingly conceals the Truth. This is a definite Truth from your Lord; be not then among the doubters" (al-Baqarah, 2: 144-147).

> ## REFLECTION
> ### Facing Towards the *Qiblah*
>
> Facing toward the *qiblah* for prayers means submission to Allah's directives in all strategic matters, whether these are economic, social, political, legal, or cultural in their nature. It would be ridiculous to face towards the Kaaba in *salah* while facing towards trade capitals of the world for guidance in economy and trade, or looking towards politically and militarily powerful countries for protection and security. It would also be illogical to face the Kaaba in prayer but continue to follow the social and cultural practices of the so-called advanced and civilized world in the name of the "best practices". It would be against reason to pray facing the Kaaba while following godless educational, legal, and political systems in which personal interest, power, and glamour are worshipped as gods. The change of *qiblah*, therefore, means the adoption of Allah's colour (*sibghat Allah*), i.e. total *tawhid* in all human endeavours, initiatives, research and development strategies.

The Qur'an also predicts that the truth of the Islamic message is evident, yet the People of the Book would remain adamant about its rejection just as they did in the past with their Prophets. In other words, the role of the Muslim *ummah*, as a middlemost community, lies in continually presenting the message as the Prophet ﷺ did without worrying about the outcome of the efforts. *Da'wah* must be given with *istiqamah*, with consistence and persistence and the outcome should be left to Allah, He alone shows guidance to whomsoever He likes: *"Allah guides whoever He wills onto a Straight Way"* (al-Baqarah, 2: 213).

The *Ummah* as a Model of Justice (*'Adl*) and Moderation (*Wasatiyyah*)

The Qur'anic expressions *ummatan wasatan* (middlemost nation) and *khayra ummah* (the best of nations) not only indicate the balance, beauty and moderation of the Islamic message, they also show that this message, which is a way of life, is not discovered by trial and error, rather it is provided by the Most-Kind, All-Knowing and Loving Lord of humankind. Its teachings protect people from taking extremes in matters of life. The responsibility to communicate this universal message of Islam of justice and moderation to all humankind is threefold. First, one must internalize the message and become deserving to belong to the *khayra ummah* as a role model of *da'wah* through one's practice: *"Believers why do you profess that which you do not practice? It is most loathsome in the sight of Allah that you should profess what you do not practice"* (al-Saff, 61: 2). Second, one must use the most effective, appropriate and modern means of *da'wah* to communicate this message: *"(O Prophet ﷺ) call to the way of your Lord with wisdom (hikmah) and most beautiful exhortation (al-maw'izah al-hasanah) and reason with them in the best manner possible"* (al-Nahl, 16: 125). And third, one must make one's best efforts to achieve a fair, equitable and peaceful order so that people see for themselves how the Islamic teachings transform society, the economy, culture, education as well as the state: *"And fight (struggle) against them until the mischief (fitnah) ends and the way (din) prescribed by Allah - the whole of it - prevails"* (al-Anfal, 8: 39).

The responsibility to create peace and order, and eliminate injustice, exploitation, oppression and the violation of human rights cannot be discharged fully unless there is a socio-political order that operates according to the Divine principles of moderation and fairness. Therefore, the concept of *iqamah* of *din* and observing the Islamic way of life, include the transformation of individuals, and society as well as the social, cultural, economic, and political order.

REFLECTION
The Responsibility of Being Witnesses unto Mankind (*shuhada 'ala al-nas*)

To discharge the responsibility of being witnesses unto mankind, the *ummah* has to take some concrete steps:

1. It has to internalize the Qur'anic message in order to become a living role model.
2. It has to use the most effective, appropriate and modern means of da'wah communication.
3. It has to make the best efforts in order to achieve a fair, equitable and peaceful order for people to see for themselves how the Islamic teachings transform society, the economy, culture as well as the state.

The Qur'an elsewhere further elaborates on the role of the Muslim *ummah* in the restoration of peace and order and human rights: *"How is it that you do not fight in the way of Allah and in support of the helpless - men, women and children - who pray 'Our Lord bring us out of this land whose people are oppressors and appoint for us from Yourself a protector and appoint for us from Yourself a helper (to liberate from this bondage)"* (al-Nisa', 4: 75).

The expression *shuhada' 'ala al-nas* places an individual and collective responsibility on the Muslim *ummah* to strive for achieving peace, security liberation and the wellbeing of oppressed people regardless of colour, race or faith. The above verse is not confined to the restoration of human rights for Muslims but includes all the oppressed people of the world, as an ethical obligation of the Muslim *ummah*.

The responsibility to present the Islamic message is clearly defined and placed on every individual believer as well as on the whole Muslim *ummah*: *"And it is thus that We appointed you to be the community of the middle way so that you might be witness to all mankind and the Messenger might be a witness to you"* (al-Baqarah, 2: 143). To be a witness unto the whole of humanity means that every Muslim is individually and collectively responsible for presenting a model for observing *tawhid* and the Prophetic Sunnah, as well as to use the best possible ways for the communication of the Islamic message. Every believer is responsible and accountable for it in front of Allah on the Day of Judgement. In his last sermon, the Messenger of Allah, making Allah his witness, asked the pilgrims very specifically whether he had appropriately conveyed to them the Islamic message. In other words, after him, each and every Muslim has to play this role of conveying the Islamic message in its totality.

In each age, therefore, the task of being witnesses unto humankind is to be performed with the most appropriate means and methodology. The age of information technology makes the task much easier. The Islamic message of peace, love, balance and moderation (*'adl*) and realization of *ma'ruf* and eradication of vice, evil (*munkar*), oppression (*taghut*) and injustice (*zulm*) can be conveniently made available to millions of human beings through electronic and digital means of communication. While focusing on this collective responsibility of the *ummah* the Qur'an further elaborates that while the whole of the *ummah* may not be discharging its responsibility for some reason, at least a group of people must take up this task and make an organized and coordinated effort, striving for *amr bi al-ma'ruf*, realization of ethical behaviour and conduct in transactions and avoidance of *munkar*, all that is unethical, immoral and obscene: "*There must be one group (ummatun) among you, who invites to good (khayr), and enjoins the good and right (ma'ruf) and forbids the wrong (al-munkar)*" (Al 'Imran, 3: 104).

REFLECTION

Ma'ruf refers to the Divinely guided principles of good and virtue which have a universal applicability, such as fairness, trustworthiness, steadfastness and perseverance, to stand for the truth and so on. These universal Islamic values are not particular to any specific time, space, territory or people. These are not social constructs. As Divine universal values, they transform any society and social behaviour due to their universal applicability and relevance.

The universality of Islamic teachings is also reflected in the directive to face towards the Kaaba, whenever and from wherever a believer is going to make the five daily prescribed prayers. This consolidates and unifies the *ummah* and serves as a reminder, to obey and serve the One and Only God; follow guidance from only one Book and take only the final Prophet ﷺ as the role model, in order to belong to the Muslim *ummah*.

This Qur'anic directive to make the best effort to locate the direction of the Kaaba also drives the Muslim scholars to exercise *ijtihad*, not only to find the correct direction of the *qiblah* but also to find legal solutions to emerging socio-economic, political, legal, cultural and developmental issues.

The Obligations of the Leadership of Mankind

While elaborating on the wisdom behind determining one single direction for prayer, the Qur'an reminds the believers about the obligations of leadership at a global level. The role of leadership is fourfold. First and foremost, it includes learning how to approach read and recite the text of the Qur'an correctly and share it with others. Second, it includes building an Islamic character through the purification of the heart, mind and self (*tazkiyah*), which is a prerequisite for progress and development in this world and success in the life to come. Third, it includes the elaboration *ta'lim al-kitab*, and implementation of the teachings contained in the Book in all walks of life. Fourth, it also includes learning from the practice, hikmah, of the Prophet ﷺ, as a role model, in order to find solutions to existential issues and problems faced by human beings. This fourfold task can only be properly performed when the believers seek continuous help through prayer and steadfastness. Prayer in Islam is not limited to a ritual enacted five times a day, but as an intellectual and spiritual re-confirmation of Allah's authority in all matters. It is a direct ongoing request to Him for guidance and to keep one on the Straight Path and, with His support, to disseminate the message without failure, fear or doubt:

"Just as when We sent among you a Messenger of yourselves, who recites to you Our verses, purifies your lives, instructs you in the Book and in Wisdom and instructs you what you did not know. So, remember Me and I shall remember you; give thanks to Me and do not be ungrateful to Me for My favours. Believers! Seek help in perseverance and in prayer. Allah is with those that are patient" (al-Baqarah, 2: 151-153).

The Culture of Gratitude, Perseverance and Remembrance

The desire of Islam to see the culture of gratitude embedded in its followers means that it desires of them the use of reason and critical thinking in the appreciation of the favours and blessings of Allah. The most obvious favours are the capacities given to human beings to think, see, walk, talk and act coherently. Even a temporary loss of any of Allah's blessings makes a person incapacitated, helpless and frustrated unless one is steadfast.

The Qur'an, again and again, reminds its readers about the enormity of Allah's blessings and favours which call for excelling in serving Him in the way He wants: *"So remember Me and I shall remember you, give thanks to Me and do not be ungrateful to Me for My favours"* (al-Baqarah, 2: 152).

Remembrance (*dhikr*, pl. *adhkar*) comes from the verb *dhakara* which means to remember, recall and recollect. *Dhikr* does not mean remembering Allah's blessings only at a particular time or place. Remembering Allah at all times is the primary step toward the adoption of the colour of Allah (*sibghat Allah*).

The word *dhikr* has been used in the Qur'an with reference to the Qur'an itself: *"As for the admonition (al-dhikr) indeed it is We who have revealed it and it is indeed We who are its Guardian"* (al-Hijr, 15: 9). At another place it is said: *"What We recite to you consists of signs (ayat) and wise admonition (al-dhikr al-hakim)"* (Al 'Imran, 3: 58). Similarly the word is used for the Message of the Qur'an: *"And We have sent down this Reminder (al-dhikra) upon you that you may elucidate to people the teachings that have been sent down for them"* (al-Nahl, 16: 44). The *dhikr* of Allah is closely associated with the functions of the heart and mind. Just as with every heartbeat, the heart purifies the blood and pumps out clean blood in the body, and thus every heartbeat conveys the message of life; similarly, Allah's *dhikr* has to become the heartbeat of the believer: *"And remember (O Prophet ﷺ) your Lord in your heart (wa'dhkur) with humility and fear and without raising your voice, remember Him in the morning and evening and do not become of those who are negligent"* (al-A'raf, 7: 205).

The true believers are those who remember Allah at all times: *"...the men who remember Allah much (al-dhakirin) and the women who remember Allah much (al-dhakirat) for them has Allah prepared forgiveness and a mighty reward"* (al-Ahzab, 33: 35).

When we think about *dhikr*, in our imagination, we usually visualize a *tasbih* made from rounded beads, used for counting the names of Allah. The Qur'an and Sunnah provide a different vision. The most perfect form and way of *dhikr* is *salah*: *"He who purified himself shall prosper, remembering (wa dhakara) his Lord's name and praying"* (al-A'la, 87: 14-15); *"(O Prophet ﷺ) recite the Book that* has been revealed to you and establish prayer. Surely prayer forbids indecency and evil. And Allah's remembrance (dhikrullah) is of even greater merit. Allah knows all that you do"* (al-'Ankabut, 29: 45).

Elaborating further on the prayer as the most appropriate form of Allah's *dhikr*, the Qur'an mentions: *"Believers when the call for prayers is made on Friday hasten to the remembrance of Allah (dhikr Allah) and give up all trading. This is better for you, if you only knew. But when the prayer is ended, disperse in the land and seek Allah's Bounty (fadl) and remember Allah much (wa'dhkuru Allaha kathiran) so that you may prosper"* (al-Jumu'ah, 62: 9-10).

Here two dimensions of *dhikr* are made crystal clear. The first is remembrance of Allah in prayer, so when the call is made for the Friday prayer, the believers have to abandon all activities and head to the mosque for *dhikr*, because it is this *dhikr* which protects the believers from immorality and evil. But when the prayer is over, *dhikr* of Allah's Greatness, Authority and Sovereignty, must continue when the believers return to their business and other activities, they rather increase in their remembrance of Allah.

This integration of *dhikr* in trade and all other activities clearly means that the believers have to be not only dutiful to Allah but be honest, truthful and observant of the exact standards and measures, in delivery of products, and in fulfilling their contracts. In brief, they have to observe the same servitude (*'ubudiyyah*) and the same fear of Allah that they experienced in prayer.

Friday, for Muslims, is not a Sabbath nor is it a day for rest or just worship. All the days of the week must be permeated with the remembrance of Allah in all human transactions. This makes *dhikr* an integral part of all the believer's transactions. Allah's *dhikr* in trade and industry means a conscious adoption of ethical and moral ways of earning and spending in the way of Allah.

Thus, *dhikr* should not be confined to the sanctuary of the heart or mind but must be visible in all human dealings and transactions. This does not minimize in any way the importance and obligation of doing *dhikr* in prayer.

This ongoing *dhikr* in prayer as well as in other activities is mentioned in different places in the Qur'an: *"Those who remember (yadhkuruna) Allah while standing and sitting or (reclining) on their backs and reflect on the creation of the heavens and the earth (saying) our Lord You have not created this is vain. Glory to You, save us then from the chastisement of the fire"* (Al 'Imran, 3: 191).

In other words, *dhikr* whether in the prayer or other activities, must be coupled with meditation, reflection, thinking critically and trying to understand the implications of every single word of the Qur'an.

The Culture of Ethical Intelligence and Striving (*Jihad*)

The next three verses contain a forceful message for the believers to seek help through steadfastness and prayer, for Allah is always with those who are steadfast and do their utmost with their resources and life to achieve peace and order in society. The Qur'an considers highly those who have given their lives in the way of Allah: *"Believers! Seek help in patience and in prayer, Allah is with those who are patient. And do not say of those who are killed in the way of Allah that they are dead, they are alive even though you have no knowledge of their life"* (al-Baqarah, 2: 153).

Prayer and steadfastness are shields which protect the believers and the whole community from frustration, depression, disappointment and hopelessness. Prayer is essentially a direct communication between the believers and the Lord of the Universe. The believers can converse with Allah as if they see Him, for if they do not see Him, He nevertheless sees them. Hence, prayer is a source of solace, inner peace and strength for the believers, as individuals or as a community, whenever a calamity visits them. The consolation, comfort, solace and satisfaction one gets from *salah*, in a crisis situation, reinforce a person with enormous strength. It is in this sense that when Allah tests His obedient servant in a situation of fear, economic crisis, loss of a dear one or loss of wealth, in all such cases when a person makes *salah*, they experience consolation, inner peace, strength and contentment.

The other source of consolation and solace is steadfastness which makes ethical considerations prevail over emotional considerations. Ordinarily, when people are insulted, they immediately respond with an insult. The Qur'an guides the believers to do differently. One should not allow emotions to prevail or retaliate to a situation in a reflexive way, emotions must be managed through an ethical filter. The Qur'an teaches the believers to repel what is wrong with what is good: *"Indeed, the good deeds drive away the evil deeds"* (Hud, 11: 114). This training of the mind and heart is done through prayer. Once the grievance, or the problem is presented by a believer in front of Allah, he feels relieved: *sabr*, perseverance now requires a believer to wait and see how the Lord resolves the issue and when. The nearest meaning of steadfastness (*sabr*) therefore, can be perseverance, persistence, and constancy; not to withdraw but to make an effort, more intensively, with full trust in Allah.

The response of the believers in crises is to approach Allah through remembrance, seeking forgiveness, offering gratitude and giving thanks. The Qur'an teaches the believers to say: *"Verily we belong to Allah and it is to Him that we are destined to return"* (al-Baqarah, 2: 156), in all situations. These are not mere words, but rather an expression of total reliance on and trust in Allah. A close look at the above verses reveals a thematic link between remembrance, prayer and steadfastness, these most oft-repeated Qur'anic words which stand for remembrance of Allah praying to Him and following the path of truth, servitude, thankfulness, and perseverance for the sake of Allah. After underscoring the significance of gratitude and (*dhikr*) remembrance, the Qur'an advises the believers to seek help through (*sabr*) steadfastness and *salah*, as an act of gratitude towards Allah alone. In the same vein, the Qur'an enjoins the believers to be persistently steadfast in the way of Allah and sacrifice their lives in the cause of the *din* and truth.

The Qur'an maintains very clearly that those who sacrificed their lives in the way of Allah should not be considered dead. Allah has His own ways of favouring His servants. Sometimes He tests the patience of His servants through the loss of property, life or health.

The Qur'an refers to such situations and shows how the believers are supposed to respond: *"We shall certainly test you by afflicting you with fear, hunger, loss of properties and lives, and fruits. Give glad tidings, then, to those who remain patient. Those who when any afflictions smite them they say: 'Verily we belong to Allah and it is to Him that we are destined to return; upon them will be the blessings and mercy of their Lord, and it is they who are rightly guided"* (al-Baqarah, 2: 155-157).

Continuity and Change in the *Shari'ah*

The underlying principle in all the Qur'anic legislation is benefit (*naf'*), easiness and relief (*yusr*) for the believers. There is no hardship in the *Shari'ah*. *Shari'ah* actually relieves and removes difficulties faced by the believer. The principles of the *Shari'ah* are one and the same for earlier nations like the Israelites as well as for the followers of the final *din* of Allah. However, since the followers of earlier sacred laws corrupted the Revelations sent to them, the Qur'an was revealed to correct them. This is why, Islam retained those practices which were not corrupted as a whole. And substituted those which were not in conformity with the Divine principles.

The greater and smaller Pilgrimages (*hajj* and *'umrah*), were introduced by Prophets Ibrahim and Isma'il, but with the passage of time, several deviant practices were added to them. For example, the *sunnah* of Hajar, of running between the two mountains near the Kaaba namely Safa and Marwah, to seek help from Allah, was corrupted by placing idols of Asaf on Safa and Na'ilah on Marwah and they were kissed by them during *sa'i*. After the conquest of Makkah when the first *hajj* was made under the leadership of Abu Bakr ﷺ, the idols were removed and the *sahabah* made *sa'i* between these two mountains.

Similarly, while making *tawaf* of the Kaaba the pre-Islamic Arabs considered doing *tawaf* without any clothes as more pleasing to their God. Islam, due to the principle of *haya,* condemned it and substituted it by covering the body with two white sheets, easily available at all times and everywhere in the world, to cover the upper and lower parts of the body.

The Qur'an calls Safa and Marwah *Sha'air* or signs, fixed by Allah as a reminder of the state of extreme anxiety experienced by Hajar when she and her son Isma'il were left alone in the desert. The mountains as such have no sacredness. Since Allah declared them His *sha'air* they carry significance otherwise these are just mountains. *Sha'air* is the plural of *sha'irah* which refers to something that symbolically reminds one of Allah's blessing and favours. This could refer to a place, an action, or an object such as the Kaaba, 'Arafat, Safa, Marwah, Ramadan, 'Eid al-Fitr and 'Eid al-Adha. These are all *sha'air* of Allah and their observance is a reflection of a believer's faith and practice.

And since the religion of Islam as *din*, is meant as a revival of the original Abrahamic faith and of the practice of Prophet Isma'il ﷺ, the moving between Safa and Marwah was made part of *'umrah* and *hajj* as taught by them. When, at a later stage, polytheism spread among the Arabs, they placed the idols they called Asaf on Safa and Na'ilah on Marwah. Once the idols were removed from Safa and Marwah as well as from the House of Allah, the original practice of Prophet Isma'il ﷺ was restored. Still, due to past memory, the *sahabah* felt uncomfortable in doing *sa'i*. The matter was settled by the Qur'an once and for all: *"Surely, Safa and Marwah are the symbols of Allah. Hence whoever performs hajj to the House or makes 'umrah will find that it is no sin for him to ambulate between the two. And whoever does a good work voluntarily should know that Allah is Appreciative, All-Knowing"* (al-Baqarah, 2: 158).

The use of the expression *"fala junaha"*, "it is no sin", does not mean one may or may not perform the rotation between Safa and Marwah but it is rather mandatory in the manner that Prophets Ibrahim and Isma'il did. Similarly, in the matter of the prohibition of liquor the word *hurrima* is not used and the word *fajtanibuhu* ("turn away from it" 5:91), is used. Avoidance here does not mean it is subject to one's like or dislike to avoid or not to avoid. Though the word *hurrima* is not used, *fajtanibu* is an absolute command of prohibition of intoxicants of any sort, therefore *haram*. In brief, the Islamic *Shari'ah* kept those practices which were originally prescribed by earlier Prophets, such as circumambulation around the Kaaba, touching or kissing the Black Stone or the *sa'i* between Safa and Marwah.

The Unreasonableness of the People of the Book

The Jewish scholars in Madinah knew well about the prophecy of the appearance of a final Messenger of Allah, but they concealed this information in order to maintain their religious leadership. In Islam, there is no concept of an immune formal clergy. Every believer, male or female, can seek guidance directly from the Qur'an and the Prophetic Sunnah (Practice). However, the believers are enjoined to develop a deep knowledge (*tafaqquh*) of the *din*. Allah's mercy is limitless, therefore even those who deliberately create confusion among the believers are told to seek His forgiveness because He is the Most-Kind, the Most-Forgiving. At the same time, those who wilfully reject the Truth and refuse the message of Islam, i.e. the disbelievers (*kuffar*) are warned of a momentous chastisement and punishment in the Hereafter:

"Those who conceal anything of the clear teachings and true guidance which We have sent down even though We have made them clear in Our Book, Allah curses such people and so do all the cursers, except those who repent and make amends and openly declare (what they had concealed). Such shall I pardon for I am Much Relenting, Most Compassionate. As for those who disbelieved and died disbelieving surely the curse of Allah and of the angels and of all men is on them. Thus, shall they abide, and their chastisement shall not be lightened nor shall they be given respite" (al-Baqarah, 2: 159-162).

The Culture of Research, Reason, and Introspection

Islam's most outstanding feature is the principle of uncompromising *tawhid*. The purpose of all the acts of worship (*'ibadat*) is to confirm, through devotion, Allah's Supremacy, Uniqueness and Transcendence, for He alone deserves worship and praise. The Qur'an invites all human beings to make the best use of their faculties of observation, audition and introspection to distinguish between what is true and what is false, what is right and what is wrong and also man's purpose and role in this world.

The Qur'an invites human beings to search for satisfactory answers not only through contemplation, which is the basis of all philosophical and mathematical thinking, but more importantly seek guidance from Allah's revealed directives. Anyone with the capacity to observe cannot fail to appreciate the beauty of the sky with its galaxies and, stars, sun and moon. The Qur'an wants people to ponder on nature as well as on their own existence and think: Are all the variations and changes that happen in the universe caused by some random blind forces? Or is there an order, a regulator and a planner behind it? Moreover, are there diverse powers that cause these changes in the universe or is there just One Almighty, Only Authority who synchronizes the apparently opposing forces? Also, what is the desired outcome of any cosmic movement or changes? A thunderstorm may cause a flood in a particular area, but it also provides much needed water, which is the source of life, to human beings, animals, and land. It is also possible that this storm hits a town and washes away homes, roads, disrupts electric and power supply systems and causes huge casualties. Are these natural phenomena random and accidental events or a moral consequence of the behaviour of people and, hence, appropriately planned and executed by the One and Only Allah who controls everything? Reason dictates that such coordination and synergy are only possible when there is only "One and Single Command", otherwise perpetual clash and collision are inevitable.

Qur'anic Pointers

If one critically uses one's faculty of reason (*'aql*) to observe the alternation of day and night and its physical and psychological effects on humans, animals, the environment and ecology, one can realise that these signs of Allah provide ample evidence of His Control, Command and Authority, all while demonstrating His Kindness, Love and Compassion for His creation. Had there been only one long extended night, or just one long extended day, the whole cycle of life would have to be re-oriented. If one reflects on the oceans, seas and rivers, which provide fish for consumption, freshwater and also waterways for ships to travel and transport merchandise, one discovers a purpose as well as a great wisdom and benefits in all these creations. Can all these act on their own? Are they self-created or has someone planned and placed them in a cosmic scheme which universally synergizes with ecology? Is all this a self-automated mechanical phenomenon or has it been fashioned by a Designer Who caused all this according to a purpose, objective and a destined end?

The Qur'an invites human beings to use their observation, rational capacity and critical thinking to find evidence-based answers to all such questions: *"Is there any god associated with Allah (a'ilahun ma'a Allah)"* (al-Naml, 27: 60-63). The more one thinks about these questions in an unbiased fashion, the more one is convinced about the supremacy and authority of Allah.

In other words, the basic principle in the universe is not multiplicity and plurality but *tawhid*, i.e. the existence of a unified command, design, purpose, and end. The universe is not blind and *tawhid* is the operational principle in the whole universe and is observed by everything that is created.

And it is only Allah alone Who can create all this, it follows that

Allah alone must be the Lord of all animate and inanimate beings. This understanding of *tawhid* has been the core teaching of all the Messengers of Allah. The Qur'an touches on this again and again: "*We raised a Messenger in every community (to tell them): serve Allah and shun all oppressors*" (al-Nahl, 16: 36). The Qur'an invites human beings to use their faculties of reason and introspection to discover the Truth. It also informs us about objects and persons who were falsely taken as gods but all these shall, on the Day of Judgement, dissociate themselves from those who took them to be gods. Consequently, their followers who always thought their religious leaders will intercede for them shall only regret over their ignorance:

"*Your God is One God, there is no God but He; the Most Merciful, the Most Compassionate. (To guide) those who use their reason, there are many Signs in the structure of the heavens and the earth, in the constant alternation of night and day, in the vessels which speed across the sea carrying goods that are of profit to people, in the water which Allah sends down from the sky and thereby quickens the earth after it was dead and disperse over it all manner of animals, and in the changing course of the winds and the clouds pressed into service between heaven and earth. Yet there are some who take others as equals to Allah and love them as Allah alone should be loved but those who truly believe they love Allah more than all else. If only the wrongdoers were to perceive now, as they will perceive when they will see the chastisement, that all power belongs to Allah alone and that Allah is severe in chastisement. At that moment those who have been followed will disown their followers and they will see the chastisement and their resources will be cut asunder. And the followers will then say 'Oh if only we might return again, we would disown them as they have disowned us.' Then Allah will show them their works in a manner causing them bitter regrets. Never will they come out of the fire*" (al-Baqarah, 2: 163-167).

Is Religion a Personal Matter?

A popular view about "religion" is that it is a personal matter between a believer and his God and has nothing to do with other spheres of life. Islam looks at human life holistically and provides guidance and directives not only regarding acts of worship but also regarding a host of other things ranging from table manners to business ethical behaviour. While in captivity in Egypt, the Israelites deviated from the original Abrahamic way of life. Islam revived the Abrahamic faith and culture based on the principle that all pure (*tayyib*) and lawful (*halal*) things are permissible. In a cross-cultural context, certain things are repulsive irrespective of a person's faith and background. Islam replaced people's relative likes and dislikes with the principle of *halal* (permissible), *haram* (prohibited), disliked (*makruh*) and indifferent (*mubah*). In principle, everything that is permissible and pure is allowed: *"O people eat of the lawful (halal) and pure (tayyib) things in the earth and follow not in the footsteps of Satan"* (al-Baqarah, 2: 168). It is on the basis of this principle that Islam prohibits blood, swine, the meat of strangled animals, non-slaughtered animals, carrions and all intoxicants. Moreover, all the things that were prohibited in the original teachings of Prophet Ibrahim ﷺ have also been prohibited in Islam. Due to its uncompromising *tawhid*, Islam prohibits the consumption of anything that is prepared as an offering to any idol. It allows only that which is prepared in the name of Allah.

Along with the general principle that whatever is pure and lawful can be consumed by believers, the Qur'an also places certain limits: *"They ask you what has been made lawful to them. Say that all clean (tayyib) things have been made lawful to you and such hunting animals as you teach, training them to hunt, teaching them the knowledge Allah has given you – you may eat what they catch for you – but invoke the* name of Allah on it. Have fear of Allah (in violating His law) Allah is swift in His reckoning" (al-Ma'idah, 5: 4); It further elaborates: *"Do not eat of (the animal) over which the name of Allah has not been pronounced (at the time of its slaughtering), for that is a transgression (fisq)"* (al-An'am, 6: 121).

Nevertheless, the sanctity of the life of human beings is a major concern of the Qur'an. In situations in which a believer can find nothing to save his life but that which is unlawful, the Qur'an allows to eat from what is unlawful but only to the extent which allows to save life: *"Believers! Eat of the pure things wherewith We have provided you for sustenance and give thanks to Allah if it is Him that you serve. He has made unlawful to you only carrion and blood and the flesh of swine and that over which there has been pronounced the name of anyone other than Allah's. But he who is constrained (to eat of them) – and he neither covets them nor exceeds the indispensable limit, incurs no sin. Allah is All-Forgiving, All-Compassionate. Those who conceal anything of the Book revealed by Allah and sell it away for a trifling gain are surely filling their bellies with Fire. Allah will neither address them on the Day of Resurrection nor shall He pronounce them pure. A painful chastisement lies in store for them"* (al-Baqarah, 2: 172-174).

The Culture of Righteousness, Piety, and Allah-consciousness: The *ayat al-Birr*

Al-Baqarah begins with a simple statement that this Book is guidance (*hidayah*) for the Allah-conscious (*muttaqin*). The (*ayat al-birr*) *Birr* verse is the longest verse in *Surah al-Baqarah*, it explains the implications of Allah-consciousness (*taqwa*), the foundations of faith, the importance of the acts of worship, social obligations, ethical behaviour in human transactions and the meaning of truthfulness (*sidq*) and Allah-consciousness (*taqwa*).

The word *birr* in Arabic means to fulfil and discharge in the most appropriate manner, the rights of someone, the rights of Allah or those of His creation. The verse appears in the context of an ongoing debate in Madinah about the change of the *qiblah*. It puts an end to this debate and channels the discourse towards personal and social ethical engagements and obligations.

The Jews traditionally prayed toward Jerusalem, which was also the *qiblah* for Muslims for the first sixteen months after the Prophet ﷺ migrated to Madinah. When the direction of the *qiblah* was changed towards the Kaaba, the Jews caused a furor. Both Judaism and Christianity associated themselves to a fixed direction, i.e. Jerusalem. The change of the *qiblah* towards Makkah gave a clear message that though all four directions belong to Allah, He is Ever-Present and is everywhere, therefore confining Him to the east or the west conflicts with the basic understanding of Allah's Power. The believers were asked to face towards the House of Allah in Makkah wherever they may be in the world. But the more important message conveyed by the change of *qiblah* was the transfer of leadership from the Israelites to the Muslim *ummah*.

As for the meaning of *ayat al-birr*, first and foremost, the verse underscores that virtue and piety are not confined to offering prayer while facing towards the East or West. Virtue includes the performance of acts of worship, correct beliefs as well as having socially-responsible conduct. Virtue is directly associated with Allah's good pleasure, and it ceases to have any meaning when done by a person who does not firmly believe in Allah, the Hereafter, the Angels, the revealed Books, and all the Prophets sent by Allah. Faith in Islam is more than a verbal confession. When the Qur'an talks, for example, about the life to come, it simply means to advise the believers to live in this world with an ever-present sense of accountability vis-à-vis Allah and to observe the highest standards of morality at the personal, social, economic, political and cultural levels. Similarly, belief in the angels re-validates the authenticity of the revealed Books, particularly the Qur'an, and its delivery to Allah's Messengers through the archangel Jibril. The verse also mentions that virtue and piety are linked with belief in the truthfulness of all the Messengers of Allah.

The full implications of this verse need to be further explored. After elaborating on how faith in Allah's power and authority, in angels, the revealed Books and all Messengers is interlinked, the focus shifts to social ethical behaviour, the rights of relatives and other social obligations. It is mentioned that the wealth and resources one gains through lawful means are Allah's blessings to begin with, and as such one should not think one's wealth is the result of one's efforts alone. Similarly, a common understanding is that a person who performs frequent *'umrahs,* pays regular *zakah* and observes the five daily prayers is a religious person. Of course, all these deeds are good and enjoined by Islam, but the real virtue (*birr*) is not limited to observing the obligatory acts of devotion. Rather, real virtue and piety lie in spending one's wealth generously on one's relatives, the orphans, the needy, those who ask for help, and those who are in debt or short of means while travelling. If one concentrates on this part of the verse, one notices that it underscores that social responsibility is an integral part of faith, piety, Allah-consciousness and virtue. When spending of one's wealth, one must start with one's own relatives. In fact, a *hadith* further elaborates that it is preferable to spend even on those needy relatives with whom one may not be on good terms because whatever is being spent for the love of Allah is not done for winning people or favouring them but to please the Real Owner of everything in the universe.

The verse also makes it a social obligation to take care of the needy and orphans. Those who have resources have an obligation to create a system which provides the best education, healthcare, character building and personality development of the orphans, so that they become confident, dynamic, and productive members of society. The needy in the verse refers to even those who may have some resources but are temporarily deprived of them. The social responsibility of a believer also includes the use of their resource to free those who are oppressed. Islam aims for the total elimination of slavery, not through a command but through persuasion and the permanent institutional framework of *zakah* and spending for the liberation of the oppressed – those who are subject to political oppression, denied freedom of belief, or are culturally colonialized and are intellectually subjugated.

Doing all these good deeds (*khayr, ma'ruf*) does not reduce the importance of *salah* and *zakah* as *'ibadah* and an obligation; and nor can a social good substitute for an *'ibadah*. *Salah* and *zakah* are essential *'ibadat* (it is incorrect to think that *zakah* is a tax, it is an obligatory *'ibadah*), in view of its importance, no social work can relieve a person from observing punctually this regular *'ibadah*. It is also important to understand that, while Islam makes social welfare an obligation, everything a person does should have only one objective i.e. to please Allah alone. Islam does not identify with the concept of serving humanity for the sake of humanity. Islam wants every believer to do their utmost to relieve the suffering of people, regardless of their colour, race, nationality or faith. The believer helps others only for the sake of pleasing Allah and not for any worldly recognition as a champion of humanitarianism. Serving humanity for the sake of humanity directly conflicts with *tawhid*. While serving human beings in order to please Allah and to obey Him makes it a virtue or *'aml khayr*.

Virtue and piety are further elaborated in terms of facing situations of test and trial with steadfastness, perseverance, trust in Allah's help (*nusrah*) and without any fear, or weakness. Those who reflect virtue, piety and Allah-consciousness in their behaviour, attitude and actions are called the truthful (*sadiqun*) and Allah-conscious (*muttaqun*) in the Qur'an.

In the final analysis, *birr* and *taqwa* are manifested in tangible ethical behaviour as key performance indicators because *taqwa* is not abstract. Ethical conduct re-confirms one's conviction in *tawhid*, the life to come, and the rights of Allah as well as those of His creation. This one single verse summarizes several major features of Islam as *din*, or the way of life:

"Righteousness does not consist in turning your faces towards the East or towards the West, true righteousness consists in believing in Allah and the Last Day, the Angels, the Books and the Prophets, and in giving away one's property in love of Him to one's kinsmen, the orphans, the poor and the wayfarer, and to those who ask for help, and in freeing the necks of slaves, and in establishing prayer, and dispensing the zakah. (True righteousness is attained by those) who are faithful to their promise once they have made it and by those who remain steadfast in adversity and affliction and at the time of battle (between Truth and falsehood). Such are the truthful ones (sadaqu) such are the Allah-fearing (muttaqun)" (al-Baqarah, 2: 177).

The Sanctity of Life and Legal Equality: The Principle of Justice (*'Adl*) and Excellence (*Ihsan*)

Achieving peace, security, justice and fairness in society is an integral objective of the *Shari'ah*. The Qur'an, as *al-Huda* (the

Guidance), does not confine itself to personal salvation, morality, and spirituality as desired by some world religions. According to the Qur'an all Messengers and Books in their original teachings, provided guidelines for the personal, social, economic, and cultural matters of their people. They did not divide life into material and spiritual, sacred, and profane. Social justice, in this context has been a common theme in all earlier Divine legislations (*Shara'iy*): *"Indeed, We sent our Messengers with clear Signs and sent down with them the Book and the Balance that people may uphold justice"* (al-Hadid, 57: 25).

The Qur'an therefore commands the believers to observe justice in all matters: *"Allah commands justice ('adl) and doing good and compassion (ihsan) to kith and kin, and He forbids all shameful deeds (fahsha') and wickedness (munkar) and rebellion (baghy). He instructs you that you may receive admonition"* (al-Nahl, 16: 90). Justice must encompass human life in its entirety. It is an Islamic obligation to be just not only to one's own self, one's family members, friends, neighbours and business partners, but even to one's own enemies. Fairness and justice are to be observed in their full measure and without any discrimination or bias in personal, social, economic, legal, political, and cultural matters: *"And give full measure and weigh with justice (bi'l-qist). We do not burden anyone beyond his capacity"* (al-An'am, 6: 152).

The protection, preservation and promotion of human life, regardless of religion, colour, race or nationality, are major objectives of the *Shari'ah*. The Qur'an declares that killing one person unjustly is the same as killing all humankind: *"Therefore, We ordained for the Children of Israel that he who slays a soul unless it be (in punishment) for murder or spreading mischief on earth shall be as if he had slain all mankind; and he who saves a life shall be as if he had given life to all mankind"* (al-Ma'idah, 5: 34). What was prescribed for the Israelites is also made obligatory on the Muslims. The fact of the matter is, this command of the *Shari'ah* has universal benefit for the whole human race. In that sense *Shari'ah* is not particular to the Muslims. Also by implication *Shari'ah* commands, too, are essentially universal and beneficial for the whole of humanity. *Shari'ah* is not a monopoly of the Muslims.

While establishing the sanctity of human life, the Qur'an also legislates punishment for murder: *"Believers! Retribution (qisas) is prescribed for you in cases of killing: If a free man is guilty then the free man; if a slave is guilty then the slave; if a female is guilty, then the female. But if something of a murderer's guilt is remitted by his brothers this should be adhered to in fairness, and payment may be made in a goodly manner. This is an alleviation and a mercy from your Lord and for him who commits excess after that there is a painful chastisement. People of understanding, there is life for you in retribution that you may guard yourselves against violating the law"* (al-Baqarah, 2: 178-179).

The word *qisas* (retribution) is from the root *qasas* which means to follow in the footsteps of someone, in search of a person. *Qisas*, therefore, means evidence-based, verified investigation leading to the identification of a particular person for retribution. The words used in the Qur'an enumerate several important social, psychological, ethical, and legal dimensions. This command leads one to understand aspects of Islamic social justice. The Qur'anic principle of *qisas*, too, has a universal application because the Qur'an clearly explains that: *"People of understanding, there is life for you in retribution that you may guard yourselves against violating the laws"* (al-Baqarah, 2: 179), which acts as a strong deterrent against murder and bloodshed in any human society.

Implications of the Qur'anic Ordinance: The Principle of Legal Equality

The first important legal principle therefore is the observance of justice. If a male has killed a male then retribution is to be taken only from that male who, after proper investigation, is established as the murderer. The pre-Islamic tradition was to substitute a slave or a female from the tribe of the accused instead of the murderer. Similarly, in some situations the aggrieved family took the law into their own hands and killed several persons in retribution.

The Qur'anic principle of equal treatment of all human beings, irrespective of their gender, status or religion was a revolutionary step and a departure from the pre-Islamic conventions, tradition, and practices. The Qur'an upholds the sanctity of life and human dignity and honour disregarding gender, colour, race or faith of a person. It wants justice for all human beings.

Social Justice

The Qur'an considers manslaughter a crime against society and humanity, therefore, its punishment must be done publicly to deter people from harming the lives of others. Islamic law takes a very serious view on the loss of life, sexual offences, theft, and public disturbance (*fitnah* and *fasad*) which disrupts public safety and trade routes. It enjoins severe public punishments for all these crimes. The objective is to prevent and discourage people from committing these offences. Consequently, there had been a low crime rate in Muslim societies where the *Shari'ah* injunctions were implemented. The psychological impact of these strict punishments guarantees security and protection of the honour and property of Muslim and non-Muslim citizens alike. This again indicates that the *Shari'ah* by nature is not specific to Muslims. Wherever these laws are applied, citizen shall experience protection of life, honour, and property.

Since murder, sexual offences and theft are social crimes, no individual is allowed to take the law into one's own hands, inflict punishment or pardon the culprit. An aggrieved family cannot take the law into its hands even though it has the right to pursue retribution or accept blood-money (*diyyah*). At the same time, it has the option to forgive the culprit, which is commended by Islam, in order to consolidate brotherhood and a culture of forgiveness (*'afw* and *ihsan*). In determining a financial penalty, the amount is to be decided according to the norms of society (*ma'ruf*). But in both situations, i.e. retribution or accepting blood-money, it is the state alone that adjudicates the matter. However, the state has no authority to forgive a criminal or convert a death sentence into a minor penalty.

The Supremacy of Law and the State

This and other Qur'anic injunctions require the establishment of a strong independent legal system and governance. In Islam, no religious scholar (*'alim*) or individual is allowed to carry out punishments or execute the *hudud* sentences. Religious scholars can give their advice (*fatwa*) on matters of law and order, but they have no authority to implement any penalties. The state and the legal authority alone have the right to investigate, verify and order any execution of an order.

> ### A Point of Reflection
>
> While the media delights in the projection of instances of the takeover of governance by 'Mullahs' or 'Maulvis' as a depiction of an Islamic state, it is no more than a fiction based on disinformation. Only the state can, after a proper and transparent procedure, decide and execute punishments in all criminal, civil, commercial, or international legal disputes. In other words, the Qur'anic teachings can be appropriately implemented only when an Islamic political and legal order exists.

There is no separation between "religion" and state in Islam. The Qur'an emphasises this aspect and refers to Prophets Dawood, Sulayman and Yusuf who had a political role while, at the same time, were also "religious" and "spiritual" leaders. The concept of an Islamic state is not new but goes back to the establishment of political orders by Prophets Sulayman, Dawood, Yusuf and the final Messenger ﷺ. The Prophet ﷺ guided the believers in spiritual, economic, social, political and security matters. He did not only lead the prayers, he also led the army and decided legal matters. Kingship and theocracy have no place in Islam. Religion and politics are not exclusive. Ethics and law belong to one single totality.

It may also be said that, in Islamic *Shari'ah*, punishments are essentially deterrents and discourage people from doing unlawful acts. The word used in the Qur'an in reference to punishments is *nakal* which means make exemplary or as a deterrent: *"As for the thief – male or female – cut off the hands of both. This is a response for what they have done, and an exemplary punishment from Allah. Allah is All-Mighty, All-Wise"* (al-Ma'idah, 5: 38).

Exemplary public punishments have a deep psychological impact on society. Their severity prevents others from committing the same and acts as a hindrance and deterrent against violation of ethical measures. It cautions society about the unavoidable consequences of any unethical activity.

Social and Legal Fairness

The Qur'an in matters of legal penalties and punishments does not discriminate on the basis of gender. In the above verse, the nature of crime determines the severity of punishment, irrespective of gender, social status or economic or political status. This legal equality afforded to women was given by the Qur'an fifteen centuries ago while, in most so-called democratic countries, women were deprived of their basic human rights until the middle of the twentieth century.

Besides legal matters, the Qur'an also provides guidance on social issues such as marriage, divorce, nursing babies, business transactions, the congregational prayers, the status of those who sacrifice their property and life in the way of Allah as well as how to write a will with fairness and according to Islamic law. Islam wants *'adl* to be observed in all matters and tries to avoid unfairness.

It is human nature that in a family, due to any reason, some persons may be loved more than others. A person on his death bed, influenced by attachment or dislike of a person may deprive the heir or heiress of some of their share. Preempting all such situations, Islam rejects the idea of the elder son inheriting a major part of the leftover property. It provides a Divine scheme of distribution of the property which cannot be altered by even a law court. Therefore, the Qur'an directs to observe *'adl* while writing the will. It also reminds the person who records the will to be aware of his responsibility in front of Allah: *"It is decreed that when death approaches, those of you who leave behind property shall bequeath equitably to parents and kinsmen. This is an obligation on the God-fearing. Then if anyone alters the will after hearing it, this sin shall be upon them who alter. Surely Allah is All-Hearing, All-Knowing. He who suspects that the testator has committed an error or injustice and then brings about a settlement among the parties concerned incurs no sin. Surely Allah is Much-Forgiving, Most-Compassionate"* (al-Baqarah, 2: 180-182).

The later revelations in *Surah al-Nisa'*, regarding the Divine law of inheritance (al-Nisa', 4: 11-12 and 4: 176), qualify how a will or testament (*wasiyyah*) can be made. *Al-Nisa'* elaborates on the distribution of whatever is left to posterity (property, cash, any assets) by a deceased person, and this verse of *al-Baqarah* on the will must be understood in light of *al-Nisa'* and the Prophetic *hadith* which specifies that a person cannot leave in his will more than a third of what he owns in favour of those who are not legal inheritors, such as distant relations, needy people or charitable institutions which are not covered in the Divine command mentioned in *Surah al-Nisa'*. No will can be made in favour of legal heirs according to the command of the Prophet ﷺ. While still alive, a person has every right to give his wealth to whomever he desires, but this should be done with fairness and not with the intention of depriving any heir of inheriting a legal share, after his death. Distribution of one's property even in one's lifetime must be done justly and with the fear of Allah in mind.

The wisdom behind the legislations of the Qur'an on social issues seems to be to protect and promote love and trust within the family, which is the building block of an ethical social order. Disputes on wealth distribution and inheritance often lead to litigations and even physical violence. The Qur'an pre-empts all these human behaviours and provides a code of law which protects the sanctity of the family and mutual respect, love and solidarity within it and also allows a certain margin of benefit for those who may not be legal heirs.

The Dimensions of Piety

Piety, Allah-consciousness, doing good and serving none but Allah (*tawhid*) are recurring themes in the Qur'an, and they are often interconnected with one another. Right from the beginning of this *surah*, piety and Allah-consciousness are elaborated as the characteristics of those who sincerely follow the ethical teachings of the Qur'an as a blessing for themselves and mankind. This attitude of piety is not confined to a particular activity. Spending one's wealth for the good pleasure of Allah was mentioned earlier as an indication of piety, but the latter also includes fighting against oppression, injustice, and violation of human rights just as it includes honouring and respecting one's parents. Performing acts of worship with sincerity and humility is also an indication of piety. All acts of devotion and worship are supposed to make the believer more Allah-conscious and careful in their dealings and transactions.

Fasting the month of Ramadan is an obligatory act of worship which is meant to increase the believer's piety. Like several other practices, fasting as a theme is a common practice in most of the world religions. The difference lies in the concept as well as in the form. In some religions fasting for spiritual elevation requires denial of the material urges like food and rest. Therefore, total abstention from food, sex, sleep, and socialization is made and celibacy and self-mortification become instrumental in achieving piety and spirituality. In some other religions partial avoidance of certain things is considered fasting like taking no solids but only liquids or abstention from talking for a specific duration.

Fasting (*Sawm* or *siyam* in Arabic) literally means to desist from something or to leave something but in legal parlance it refers to abstention from food, drink, and sex from dawn to sunset. *Saim* is used in Arabic for a horse who is not fed on grass but on special nutrients to keep the horse slim but full of energy.

> ### The Meaning of Fasting
>
> Fasting removes the burden of sins, strengthens *iman*, and makes the believer fit to strive for truth, honesty, peace, and fairness in society.

Fasting and the Inculcation of Allah-Consciousness

Taqwa, Allah-consciousness, is a major theme in the Qur'an, that keeps on appearing in different contexts. The main purpose of fasting or *sawm*, according to the Qur'an specifically is the inculcation of Allah-consciousness or *taqwa*. Fasting is unique in the sense that while other rituals, *salah*, *zakah* and *hajj* have a visible physical form, no one except Allah or the person who is fasting knows whether a person is fasting or not. This builds a special bond of *'ubudiyah*, servitude, between Allah ﷻ and His servant. The believer cannot see Allah physically, but may feel Him around, watching his activities, feelings, and thoughts. It builds a moral and ethical filter which pre-judges all human actions. A whole month of constant punctuality in congregational prayers, spending one's wealth in the name of Allah, offering food and hospitality to fellow believers, making an extra effort to be polite, truthful, honest, forgiving while suppressing anger and other negative emotions, and avoiding vain talk help to inculcate in the believers all that is good which leads to the transformation of their behaviour and personality. It is like four weeks of intensive ethical and moral therapy. Normally even the best of therapies do not bring results instantly, it takes time to produce effects. Several sessions in a sequence are needed for an effective therapy. But in the month of Ramadan, change of behaviour starts from day one. And a whole month's practice makes this change part of one's personality.

The way in which fasting is made mandatory itself carries great wisdom. The Qur'an states that fasting has been made obligatory for a short duration, i.e. one lunar month. But if one happens to be ill or travelling, one can skip the fast and make up the days in which one has not fasted after Ramadan. Those who are terminally ill or too old to fast, can offer an expiation (*fidyah*) i.e. for each day of missed fast, they have to feed a poor person because Allah wants ease (*yusr*) and not hardship (*'usr*) for the believers.

The month of Ramadan, the 9th month of the lunar calendar, is mentioned again in a unique context, that of the revelation of the Qur'an in this month:

"During the month of Ramadan the Qur'an was sent down as a guidance to the people with clear Signs of the True Guidance (al-Huda) and as the Criterion (al-furqan), between right and wrong. So those of you who live to see this month should fast in it and whoever is sick or on a journey should fast the same number of other days instead.

Allah wants ease (yusr) and not hardship ('usr) for you so that you may complete the number of days required, magnify Allah for what He has guided you to, and give thanks to Him" (al-Baqarah, 2: 185). Several important aspects are elaborated in this *ayah*. First, it establishes that, historically, the Qur'an was revealed during the month of Ramadan.

The Qur'an further specifies that the revelation took place on a blessed night (al-Dukhan, 44: 2). It is further narrowed down to: *"Behold We revealed this (al-Qur'an) in the night of power"* (al-Qadr, 97: 1). According to authentic Prophetic traditions, this was one of the odd nights in the last ten days of Ramadan, i.e. the 21st, 23rd, 25th, 27th or 29th. Most probably it is the twenty-fifth or twenty-seventh night. No other Scripture of the world's religions provides such historical precision about its delivery. Scriptures of other religions are recorded by scribes who were not even the first-hand reporters or recipients of the Scripture, The New Testament is a perfect example of it. In some other religions, Scriptures remained in oral tradition for centuries and then were recalled and recollected not even in the language in which they were originally revealed, as is the case of the Christian and Buddhist Scriptures.

The Qur'an is the only Scripture that was committed to memory as well as in written form in its original language, from day one. This is why the revelation calls itself al-Qur'an (that which is recited, collected together) and *al-Kitab* or the Book (a written record): *"That this indeed is a noble Qur'an, inscribed in a well-guarded Book, which non but the pure (mutahharun) may touch"* (al-Waqi'ah, 56: 77-79). This establishes the fact that even in the early Makkan period, segments of the Qur'an were already written down and physically touched only when in a state of purity. The well-known account of 'Umar embracing Islam in the sixth year of the Prophethood, in Makkah, is an evidence of it (details are provided in the books of *sirah*).

The command, "fasting is prescribed upon you" (*kutiba 'alaykum*), while indicating that it is obligatory on all believers, also refers to exceptions such as those who are sick, travelling, or senior in age. Persons who are sick or in travel or too old are allowed to defer the fasts and make up the missed days later. Here, a legal maxim (*qa'idah fiqhiyyah*) is also provided, namely that the Lawgiver does not like to burden His servants with more than they can bear. The operating principle in the *Shari'ah*, therefore, is known as *yusr* or easiness and not *'usr* or hardship. Instead of fasting, an option is provided to, those who have fragile health and do not have the capacity to fast. They can feed a person with two wholesome meals, for every fast they missed. The count of thirty fasts is to be completed in any case.

When a believer realizes how kind and compassionate is the Lord toward him/her, the only response is to glorify Him (*tukabbirullah*) on His blessing and Guidance (*hidayah*) and opportunity (*tawfiq*).

During Ramadan, the believer develops an intimate relationship with the Qur'an, listening every evening to a portion of the Qur'an during the late night prayer of *tarawih*, and striving to perform all the daily prayers in congregation in a *masjid*.

Fasting in the month of Ramadan brings a tangible behavioural change in the believers. The believers are trained in this blessed month in self-control which empowers them ethically and morally to do good and avoid all temptations. The believers are told that while fasting they are not allowed to take any food or liquid, nor can they have sex. At the same time taking food or enjoying sex, as such is not declared bad or sinful, it on the contrary is a blessing. When the fast is over, i.e. after sunset, the prohibitions on food, drink and sex are lifted. Living a balanced family life is the desired behaviour and practice of the blessed Prophet ﷺ in Islam: *"It has been made lawful for you to go into your wives during the night of the fast. They are your garment and you are theirs. Allah knows that you used to betray yourselves and He Mercifully relented and pardoned you. So you may now associate intimately with your wives and benefit from the enjoyment Allah has made lawful for you, and eat and drink at night until you can discover the white streak of dawn against the blackness of the night; then (give up all that eating) complete your fasting until night sets in"* (al-Baqarah, 2: 187).

The simile of "garment" used by the Qur'an beautifully summarizes the whole philosophy of an ideal family life in Islam. It indicates that a husband and a wife are to protect each other like a garment protects its wearer from the heat and cold. It also shows they have to guard their secrets and not divulge them to others. They support each other with dignity and honour and just as a garment compliments the good appearance of a person, similarly spouses should add to each other's dignity, honour, beauty and build a balanced and cohesive family life. Hence, against this backdrop, piety and *taqwa* do not mean world rejection but involvement in social, political, and cultural life in an ethical way. This also removes a misgiving that it is not easy for a common person to follow the *Shari'ah*. It shows that the *Shari'ah* does not make things difficult but rather makes them easy for the believers: *"Believers! Fasting is enjoined upon you, as it was enjoined upon those before you, that you become God-fearing. Fasting is for a fixed number of days, and if one of you be sick, or if one of you be on a journey, you will fast the same number of other days later on. For those who are capable of fasting (but still do not fast) there is a redemption: feeding a needy man for each day missed. Whoever voluntarily does more good than is required, will find it better for him; and that you should fast is better for you, if you only know.*

"During the month of Ramadan, the Qur'an was sent down as a guidance to the people with Clear Signs of the true guidance and as

the Criterion (between right and wrong). So those of you who live to see that month should fast it, and whoever is sick or on a journey should fast the same number of other days instead. Allah wants ease and not hardship for you so that you may complete the number of days required, magnify Allah for what He has guided you to, and give thanks to Him. (O Muhammad), when My servants ask you about Me, tell them I am quite near. I hear and answer the call of the caller whenever he calls Me. Let them listen to My call and believe in Me; perhaps they will be guided aright" (al-Baqarah, 2: 183-186).

The Culture of *Tazkiyah* in Financial, Trade and Economic Transactions

Trade, commerce, finance, and economic matters, in Islam, are not secular, worldly, or materialistic because Allah likes those who earn a lawful income (through ethical means) and spend out of it on the needy and those in debt. Therefore, the Qur'an provides an elaborate ethical code in all financial matters. Two general principles are given in the following verse: *"Do not usurp one another's possessions by false means nor proffer your possessions to the authorities (in bribe) so that you may sinfully and knowingly usurp a portion of another's possessions"* (al-Baqarah, 2: 188).

After discussing how fasting helps in self-purification (*tazkiyat al-nafs*), the Qur'an now refers to *tazkiyat al-mal*, how to earn and spend ethically. First and foremost, it prohibits the usurpation of what belongs to others. This short and simple statement strikes at the roots of financial corruption in any society. Often near blood relations and business partners are driven by greed to make false claims on the property of others. In doing so, the authorities are sometimes approached through people who can influence their judgement or even bribe them in kind or with favours. The Qur'an pre-empts this social evil and, with the force of the law, tries to remove this evil from society.

This one single verse prohibits all forms of bribes, under-the-table dealings, commissions, usurpations, unlawful possessions, theft, games of chance, interest or usury, and brings all economic and commercial matters under the *Shari'ah*.

Self-discipline or purification of the heart (*tazkiyat al-nafs*) is a comprehensive term. *Zaka*, the root from which *tazkiyah* is taken, means to grow, to increase as well as to cleanse and purify. In the context of wealth, it purifies only that wealth which does not contain any unlawful element.

The Messengers of Allah are sent to purify the conduct and behaviour of people, at four levels:
1. Individual faith (*iman*), conduct and behaviour;
2. Family and social life;
3. Economic, commercial, political and cultural life;
4. Ethical and moral uplift of human beings at an international level.

Liberation from Superstitions

Mythical thinking and superstition are a common heritage of human civilizations. Even in the so-called modern scientific age in the trade capitals of the world in Europe and America level 13 is skipped in high-rise buildings. The pre-Islamic Arabs had some customs, such as when returning from a journey or during the prescribed days of the *hajj* season, they would not enter their homes from the main entrance but from a back door or a specially made window.

The Qur'an liberates people from all such superstitions. The Qur'an creates a direct link between the believer and their Lord for guidance. It instructs the believers to call directly on Allah for help, guidance and support, for He hears and responds to the call of every sincere seeker of help: "*People question you concerning the phases of the moon say: they are signs to determine time for the sake of people and for the pilgrimage. Also tell them: True righteousness is not that you enter your houses from the back, righteousness lies in fearing Allah. So, enter your houses by their doors, and fear Allah that you might attain true success*" (al-Baqarah, 2: 189).

War Ethics

In the second year of the *hijrah*, the Muslims were allowed for the first time to wage war against the (*mushrikin*) idolaters of Makkah: "*Fight in the way of Allah against those who fight against you but do not transgress, for Allah does not like transgression. Kill them wherever you confront them and drive them out from where they drove you out. (For though killing is sinful) wrongful persecution is even worse than killing. Do not fight against them near the Holy Mosque unless they fight against you; but if they fight against you, kill them, for that is the reward of such unbelievers. Then if they desist, know well that Allah is Ever Forgiving, Most Compassionate, keep on fighting against them until mischief ends and the way prescribed by Allah prevails. But if they desist, then know that hostility is directed only against the wrongdoers. The sacred month for the sacred month; sanctities should be respected alike (by all concerned). Thus, if someone has attacked you attack him just as he attacked you and fear a lot and remain conscious that Allah is with those who guard violating the bounds set by Him"* (al-Baqarah, 2: 190-194).

Three important aspects of war ethics against (*mushrikin*) idolaters and non-believers are highlighted here. First, killing other human beings as such is not desirable, but if the polytheists attack the Muslims, the latter must retaliate. Even when the (*mushrikin*) idolaters fight against Muslims in the area of the *Haram*, Sacred Precinct, the Muslims should fight them back to protect themselves and restore peace in the area.

Second, the purpose of war is to eliminate oppression and injustice, and restore peace and security to allow the believers to carry out their acts of devotion without any fear or obstruction. Third, war is not waged to convert (*mushrikin*) idolaters to Islam but rather to establish justice and peace. The polytheists have a right to follow their beliefs, but they cannot be allowed to create corruption, lawlessness or insecurity in the area surrounding the Holy Mosque. Once peace and order are restored, the believers are advised not to exceed the norms of fairness in their retaliation against any troublemakers. All such excessive acts are against the principle of *taqwa* or Allah-consciousness. The Qur'an wants the believers to observe manners and *taqwa* even when they confront their bitter enemies.

The believers are prompted to participate in *jihad* physically as well as financially. Therefore, the believers are asked to contribute generously in the facilitation of *jihad*. There is ample evidence from the Companions who participated in *jihad* and also spent whatever they possessed in the way of Allah.

The war ethics touched on in these verses allows the believers to retaliate when the unbelievers attack them even during the sacred months (Rajab, Sha'ban, Dhu'l-qi'dah and Dhu'l-Hijjah) because the protection of life and honour is one of the main objectives of the *Shari'ah* and were the Muslims not to retaliate to protect themselves, these principles would be violated.

The believers are instructed to respond adequately but not to exceed the limits even when retaliating. It is also highlighted that killing others in war is unavoidable but *fitnah* (transgression), lawlessness, and oppression are worse than killing. Hence, to eliminate a bigger evil, the killing of those who instigate lawlessness is permissible. Here, the Qur'an refers to another principle of the *Shari'ah*, namely that of the bigger and lesser evils. The Qur'an upholds the sacrosanctness of the Sacred Mosque, and to uphold its sanctity it allows them to retaliate against those who violate the sanctity of the Mosque. The Qur'an allows the Muslims to wage war only until oppression and lawlessness are eliminated, law and order restored, or Allah's *din* prevails. At any stage, during such wars, if the enemy withdraws, the Muslims are advised to stop fighting.

The Prohibition of Self-infliction of Harm

Before starting a detailed discourse on *hajj*, an important comment is made on voluntary contributions in the cause of Allah. The believers are directed to spend of their wealth (i.e. other than the obligatory *zakah*) as much as they can afford in the struggle for peace and the realization of the *din*. They are also warned that they should not indulge in harming themselves with their own hands.

The verse: *"...And do not cast yourselves into destruction with your own hands"* (al-Baqarah, 2: 195) has much wider implications. An apparent meaning is that love of wealth and selfishness may hinder a person from *infaq*, spending in the way of Allah, which may deprive them of great reward. Therefore, one should be generous with one's wealth for spending it for the sake of Allah saves one from chastisement in this life and after one's death.

Another dimension of this verse is that inflicting harm on oneself, like suicide is totally prohibited. Similarly use of chemicals that harm life or smoking fall in the category of harmful things to life. A third implication is that harm is mostly caused by one's own actions, Allah never desires harm for His servants. Therefore, when one faces a calamity, one needs to find, through soul searching, the wrong one has done which ultimately harmed. The believers are urged to make use of Allah's given blessings and resources to establish an ethical Islamic order, and avoid indulging in things that harm quality of life.

The Globalisation of *Da'wah* and Islamic Brotherhood

The Qur'an and the Prophetic sayings emphasize the theme of brotherhood, fraternity, and unity: *"Surely the believers are none but brothers unto one another, so set things right between your brothers"* (al-Hujurat, 49: 10). *Hajj*, as one of the pillars of faith, helps greatly in building brotherhood at a global level.

Generally speaking, the Qur'an does not go into details when speaking about the acts of worship, for these were amply demonstrated by the Prophet ﷺ through his own conduct and practice. It touches on salient features of *hajj* as the practice of Prophets Ibrahim and Isma'il, because its purpose and objective were distorted with the passage of time. The Qur'an revives the spirit of *hajj* and the original practice of Prophet Ibrahim ﷺ (*sunnata abikum Ibrahim*).

Hajj is one of the five pillars of Islam. It is an obligation on all those who have the means to undertake it and can afford to perform it.

The believers who have the means to perform this obligation and do not do so are warned of a grave consequence on the Day of Judgement as explained by some Prophetic traditions. *Hajj* is performed in the twelfth month of the lunar calendar, Dhu'l-Hijjah.

As soon as the *hajj* season begins, believers from all over the world start arriving to the Sacred House as Allah's guests: *"And publicly proclaim pilgrimage, for all mankind so that they come to you on foot and mounted on lean camels from every distant point"* (al-Hajj, 22: 27). As mentioned earlier, *hajj* in the pre-Islamic period had lost its original objective and practically became a carnival for trade, poetry competition, glorification of tribal heroes and making offerings to the idols. The House of Allah, which had been erected on an uncompromising principle of *tawhid*, became a temple with over three hundred and sixty gods.

Ḥajj as a Perfect Manifestation of *Tawhid*

The moment a believer decides to perform *hajj*, a new life cycle starts for him/her. Before boarding a plane or a ship, the pilgrim leaves behind his national dress, language, friends, and relatives. Wearing only two white unstitched sheets, he starts responding to the call for *hajj*: *"I am here my Lord, You have no associate, all Praise belongs to You; Your servant seeks Your forgiveness; You alone can forgive all my excesses. In You alone is my refuge."* The rhythmic chanting of Allah's glorification and praise creates an environment of total submission, attachment and nearness to Allah.

The One Who is All-Knowing, All-Hearing welcomes His servants to visit His House. Indeed, unless the Host does not welcome the guest (*dayf*) no one can dare enter the House. The chanting of His names and praises continues until the pilgrim gets a first glimpse of the House.

While circumambulating the Kaaba (*tawaf*) for seven rounds, the believer seeks forgiveness and makes supplications (*du'a*) including: *"Our Lord grant us what is good in this world and what is good in the world to come and protect us from the chastisement of the fire"* (al-Baqarah, 2: 201); and making this particular supplication between the *Rukn al-yamani* and the Black Stone is a Prophetic Sunnah practice.

On the 9th of *Dhu'l-Hijjah* or *wuquf* the *hajj* reaches its most important stage when the pilgrims stand at 'Arafat. Nowhere in the world does such a huge gathering take place, every year, as at Arafat. This unparalleled gathering of people in one spot reminds the believers of the Day of Judgement where all human beings shall be assembled and judged according to their conduct and behaviour in this world.

Hajj provides a yearly rejuvenation of faith, whereby people from all over the world participate and meet with other Muslims whom they never knew before and are unlikely to meet after. *Hajj* plays a vital role in developing the global brotherhood of the faithful. Like blood from all over the body flows toward the heart and, after purification, travels back, the pilgrims from across the globe, converge in the House of Allah and then return after renewing their faith.

Hajj also reminds the believers of how Prophet Ibrahim ﷺ visited one country after another when travel was extremely difficult. Just as it reminds them of the total surrender of Prophet Ibrahim ﷺ to Allah when, at the advanced age of ninety, he had his firstborn son Isma'il and when later he reached the age of adulthood, he was asked to sacrifice him for the good pleasure of his Lord. When he informed his son about his dream, Isma'il's response was amazing as he told his father to go ahead, not to hesitate and he will find him a true Muslim, obedient to Allah. The absolute obedience to Allah's command of the father and his son was so pleasing to the Lord that a sacrifice of an animal (camel, cow, goat, lamb) on the 10th of *Dhu'l-Hijjah* was ordained for every capable Muslim once a year until the Day of Judgement.

The conduct of Hajar when, out of extreme anxiety, she ran between the hilltops of Safa and Marwah was also made an integral part of the *hajj* and *'umrah*. The major objective of this global assembly at *hajj* is to experience and forge brotherhood between believers from all over the world. This spirit of brotherhood is renewed every year. And even those who cannot join personally in the performance of *hajj* or *'umrah* are given the opportunity to join in symbolically by fasting on the day of 'Arafah, the 9th of *Dhu'l-Hijjah*, and sacrificing an animal on the following day, the day of 'Eid al-Adha.

Hajj and *'umrah*, the Qur'an informs, are only for Allah and are to be performed only in the prescribed time and place. But if a situation arises, as it was at the time of Hudaybiyah when the pilgrims were stranded and not allowed to proceed further to complete the rites of *hajj*, they were commanded to make their offerings at the point where they were stopped, and complete the rites of *hajj* later on. In such unavoidable conditions, the Qur'an offers easy ways out (*yusr*). Similarly, if a pilgrim becomes sick and, on the completion of *hajj*, he cannot get his head shaved, he may either fast for a specific number of days or sacrifice an animal. Even when things are normal and the pilgrim has no resources to sacrifice an animal, he may fast for three days during the *hajj* and, upon returning to his homeland, fast another seven days. Again, this is an instance of the easiness of the *din* and an expression of Allah's Love and Compassion for His servants.

While circumambulating the Kaaba, it is not necessary to make supplications reading from a book of prayers, for Allah hears the servants' supplications in whatever expressions they are made and in whichever language. One can make any supplications from the Qur'an or Sunnah which one can remember, particularly seeking Allah's forgiveness, blessings and help in this world and the next. It is also a Prophetic practice to recite this Qur'anic, short du'a at every round of circumambulation: *"Our Lord grant us what is good in this world and what is good in the world to come and protect us from the chastisement of the fire"* (al-Baqarah, 2: 201).

During *hajj*, Allah-consciousness is increased through extensive remembrance of Allah, recitation of the Qur'an, full devotion in the performance of the *hajj* rituals and also by being honest in trade and business transactions. A *hadith* states that a truthful and honest trader shall be with Prophets (*anbiya*), martyrs (*shuhada*) and righteous people (*salihin*) on the Day of Judgement. The Qur'an elaborates: *"Complete hajj and 'umrah for Allah. And if you are prevented from doing so, then make the offering which is available to you, and do not shave your heads until the offering reaches its appointed place. If any of you should have to shave your head before that because of illness, or injury to the head, then you should make redemption by fasting, or almsgiving, or ritual sacrifice. And when you are secure, then he who takes advantage of 'Umrah before the time of hajj shall give the offering he can afford; and if he cannot afford the offering, shall fast for three days during hajj and for seven days after he returns home; that is, ten days in all. This privilege is for those whose families do not live near the Holy Mosque. Guard against violating these ordinances of Allah* and be mindful that Allah is severe in chastisement. *The months of hajj are well known. Whoever intends to perform Pilgrimage in these months shall abstain from sensual indulgence, wicked conduct, and quarrelling; and whatever good you do, Allah knows it. Take your provisions for Pilgrimage but, in truth, the best provision is piety. Men of understanding beware of disobeying Me.*

"It is no offence for you to seek the bounty of your Lord during Pilgrimage. When you hasten back from 'Arafat then remember Allah at al-Mash'ar al-Haram (i.e. Muzdalifah) and remember Him in the manner He has directed you, for before this you were surely in error. And surge onward together with the multitude of all other people who surge onward, and implore Allah's forgiveness; Allah is Most Forgiving, Most Merciful. And when you have performed your rites remember Allah as you remember your fathers; and remember Him even more.

"There are some (among the ones that remember Allah) who say: 'Our Lord, grant us what is good in this world', such shall have no share in Hereafter. And there are others who say, 'Our Lord, grant us what is good in this world and what is good in the world to come, and protect us from the chastisement of the Fire'. They shall have a portion from what they earned; Allah is quick in reckoning. And remember Allah through the appointed days. It is no sin for him who hastens off and returns in two days, and it is no sin who delays the return provided he has spent the days in piety. Beware of disobeying Allah and know well that to Him you all shall be mustered" (al-Baqarah 2: 196-203).

One major benefit of the yearly *hajj* congregation is providing the believers with a unique experience of *tawhid*. A pilgrim leaves everything behind them when they leave their homeland and commit their absolute servitude to Allah alone. At the same time, all the pilgrims interact with their brothers in faith and this global brotherhood unites the hearts and minds of the believers which the Qur'an calls a great blessing of Allah, because, during *hajj*, complete strangers become one single body of the faithful. They transcend their differences of colour, language, status, race, and nationality. They become brothers and sisters in faith as the children of Prophet Adam ﷺ and belonging to the *ummah* of the final Messenger of Allah ﷺ.

Two Types of Personality

Due to human limitations and weakness, some people, who apparently subscribe to the Islamic teachings, may continue their attachment to their pre-Islamic social customs and traditions. For example, even among the *sahabah*, a well-known person like Abdullah bin Salam ﷺ from a Jewish background, after embracing Islam kept following some of the Old Testament teachings such as avoiding the meat and milk of camels, and out of respect for *sabbath* he wouldn't hunt on Saturdays. The motive behind such actions was to seek more reward by following the Sunnah of both the Prophets of Allah– Musa and the final Prophet ﷺ. Such sincere *sahabah*, immediately abandoned following earlier practices once it was declared that now the Qur'an and the Sunnah of the final Messenger ﷺ of Allah alone constitutes the *Shari'ah*.

There were also people who did not accept Islam sincerely and looked for opportunities to harm Islam and the Muslims. Among them were some who were eloquent and impressive in their speech. But despite all this beauty in their speech, they never internalized the teachings of Islam. They kept following their pre-Islamic practices secretly while pretending to be Muslims. These were the hypocrites. In order to address this situation, the Qur'an makes general observations which allowed these hypocrites some room to improve their conduct without naming them out of the wisdom of *da'wah*: *"Among men there is a kind whose sayings on the affairs of the world fascinate you, he calls Allah again and again to bear testimony to his sincerity, yet he is most fierce in enmity. Whenever he attains authority, he goes about the earth spreading mischief and laying to waste crops and human life even though Allah (whose testimony he invokes) does not love mischief"* (al-Baqarah, 2: 204-205). Although the context of these verses is the ground reality in Madinah, during the lifetime of the Prophet ﷺ, in general, the existence of different types of personalities, is quite normal in all human societies. It is not uncommon to encounter such two-faced people in Muslim societies even today. Pre-empting this ground reality, and as a universal guidance, the Qur'an educates the believers on how to resolve such contradictions.

The *munafiqun* (hypocrites) were outwardly Muslims: they talked politely and pretended to be loyal to the Prophet ﷺ and Islam through their eloquent speech. But their real intention and objective were to gain worldly benefits and also create division and conflict within the community of the believers. The Qur'an elsewhere refers to this duplicity in the following verse: *"When you look at them their persons are pleasing, and when they speak, you pay heed to what they say... They are your utter enemies, guard against them..."* (al-Munafiqun, 63: 4). In the same *surah* it is said: *"(O Prophet ﷺ) when the hypocrites come to you, they say: 'We bear witness that you are certainly Allah's Messenger.' Allah certainly knows you as His Messenger. But Allah also bears witness that the hypocrites are utter liars"* (63: 1). This type of personality, the Qur'an informs, only looks for fame, recognition, glamour and power in this world: *"There are some (among those that remember Allah) who say: Our Lord grant us what is good in this world; such shall have no share in the Hereafter"* (al-Baqarah, 2: 200). A few verses later, the behaviour of this type of people is further elaborated on: *"Whenever he attains authority he goes about the earth spreading mischief and laying to waste crops and human life, even though Allah does not love mischief. Whenever he is told: Fear Allah, his vainglory seizes him in his sin. So Hell shall suffice for him, what a wretched resting place"* (al-Baqarah, 2: 205-207).

A believer's life and death are devoted to Allah alone and made subservient to His commands. He is not a Friday Muslim, who every Friday takes a shower, wears nice clothes, wears perfume, goes to the *Masjid* and declares Allah is Great and Most Powerful, the One and Only Lord. While the next day he declares that interest-based capitalist economy is unavoidable, and that a 'secular' democracy is 'the most perfect form of political order'. This type of person apparently wants to travel in two boats at one time. The type of people desired by the Qur'an are those who enter Islam wholeheartedly, reject all the gods of political power, financial gains, glamour, and popularity and fully submit to the One and Only God: *"On the other hand, among men there is a kind who dedicates his life seeking to please Allah. Allah is immensely Kind to such devoted servants"* (al-Baqarah, 2: 207). Such people welcome every directive from Allah and feel privileged to serve Him. Likewise, Allah is pleased with the sincerity of such servants: *"Allah is well-pleased with them, and they are well-pleased with Him. All this is for him who fears his Lord"* (al-Bayyinah, 98: 8) and their ultimate abode would be Paradise: *"O serene soul return to your Lord well-pleased (with your blissful destination), well-pleasing (to your Lord), So enter among My servants and enter My Paradise"* (al-Fajr, 89: 27-30).

> ### The Personality of the Sincere Person who Seeks *Mardat* Allah
>
> Here the term *mardat* or seeking Allah's good pleasure means an attitude of total submission to Allah's commands and directives with a pleasing, thankful, and welcoming approach, submission and gratitude. Put simply, it means that the true believer tries to find out what else he can do to please Allah and win His favour.

The expression used in the verse is *"mardat"* Allah, which refers to everything that pleases Allah. The objective of life of the true believer, therefore, is none other than to win Allah's good pleasure. Consequently, the true believer must remove all contradictions from life and do their utmost to follow the ethical directives of the Qur'an and Sunnah. These two non-variable and abiding sources provide complete guidance in all matters relating to family, society, economy, law, education, culture, and political affairs. The Qur'an and the Sunnah elaborate on how to deal with dignity, honour and respect with parents, spouse, children, relatives, friends, even strangers and the people who may be facing difficulties like those in debt or in stress, orphans, needy and the oppressed.

It is a common observation that those who are righteous and follow the Straight Path often face tests, trials, hardships and obstacles created by the evil forces of oppression. They are also often insulted and tortured but they never swerve from the path of truth. They persistently seek their Lord's help and assistance to remain steadfast and sacrifice everything to please Him. Moreover, they never complain under stress but pray: *"When will Allah's help arrive? They were assured that Allah's help was close by"* (al-Baqarah, 2: 204).

The Holistic Personality

Hajj also helps believers to transform their personality into a *tawhidic* personality with an Allah-centred vision of life which focusses all efforts on pleasing Allah alone. *Tawhid* implies the development of a unified and holistic personality. Acceptance of Allah as Lord means that the likes and dislikes, priorities in life, behaviour in private and public life and in one's profession all must be aligned with *tawhid*. It also means the achievement of moderation, fairness and balance in different dealings and the realization of an ethical socio-economic and political order founded on Allah's sovereignty. It frustrates the immoral and unethical and sexist practices such as the commercialization of women in the name of women empowerment, their unethical sexploitation in the media as well as the presence of violence, financial corruption, economic and political exploitation in society. In brief, *tawhid* implies all such unethical customs and practices to be replaced with ethical conduct and behaviour. Needless to say, there is always a constant conflict between the satanic forces and the forces of truth. They create hindrances and obstacles and, try to derail the process of ethicalization of personality and society.

The holistic personality of a believer that the Qur'an wants to build develops a behavioural pattern which reflects Allah-consciousness, steadfastness and excellence, which are indicative of Allah-consciousness, feeling of Allah's presence and doing things in the most beautiful manner (*itqan*) with a sense of servitude, i.e. serving Allah alone and not one's own desires and whims.

The life and personality of the true believer must not be fragmented or duplicitous. *Tawhid* implies renunciation of man-made gods of culture, glamour, power, and pride. It calls for the application of the teachings of the Qur'an and Sunnah in all the spheres of human life. The holistic personality created by *tawhid* also resists all temptations and traps of evil forces and social pressures. The Qur'an calls such temptations *"khutuwat al-shaytan"*, the pathways and traps of Satan, who is always ready to offer justifications for unethical conduct. The Qur'an cautions: *"Believers! Enter wholly into Islam, and do not follow in the footsteps of Satan for he is your open enemy"* (al-Baqarah, 2: 209). The believers are prompted to exercise their ethical judgement and decide whether they opt for short-term enjoyment, pleasure and entertainment, such as the use of psychedelic drugs, watching provocative movies, developing digital addiction or to resist all such temptations and become a creative person by excelling in knowledge and learning how to make life more safe and meaningful for others. In this way, one qualifies for the eternal bliss promised by the Creator and Loving Allah. The joy of defeating evil exceeds any satisfaction one can experience from worldly pleasures. This is why the Qur'an talks repeatedly about the *zakah*, *sadaqah*, charity and *infaq* spending in the way of Allah, for the more one spends in the way of Allah, the more one experiences an unquantifiable level of pleasure, bliss, and satisfaction.

The holistic personality of the believer (*mu'min*) is a recurring theme in the Qur'an, it is a personality that is fully satisfied (*nafs mutma'innah*) by serving Allah alone and experiences inner and outer peace as a result: *"Allah is well-pleased with them, and they are well-pleased with Him. All this is for him who fears his Lord,"* (al-Bayyinah, 98: 8). Apart from the tremendous reward they get in the Hereafter, a true believer gets satisfaction in this world, according to Allah's own plans: *"Worldly life has been made attractive to those who have denied the Truth. Such men deride the men of faith, but the pious shall rank higher than them on the Day of Resurrection. As for worldly livelihood, Allah grants it to whomsoever He wills without measure"* (al-Baqarah, 2: 212). This verse touches on the wisdom in providing resources to the pious who may spend out of it as much as possible in order to please Allah and get seventy times or more reward in the Hereafter. On the other hand, it also refers to the psyche of self-centred people who do not give away but keep all of it to themselves, not caring for the needy, and yet Allah does not stop providing for them due to His compassion and kindness, for the simple reason that, perhaps, one day their conscience may awaken and they may decide to spend out of what Allah has given them. No one but Allah alone with His limitless *Rahmah*, and Care could do it to even His unthankful *makhluq* (creation).

The Unity of Humankind

The Qur'an does not discriminate between human beings on the basis of their colour, ethnicity, race, or nationality. On the other hand, the modern world is rampant with prejudice, bias and discrimination on the basis of colour, race, language, and nationality. The rise of white supremacists in Europe and the US is only an expression of this global reality that inflicts most nations of the world. The Qur'an transcends all man-made categorizations and recognises just one universal criterion of faith in Allah and ethical excellence (*taqwa*) as the only basis of superiority among human beings: *"Human beings, We created you all from a male and a female, and made you into nations and tribes so that you may know one another. Verily the noblest of you in the sight of*

Allah is the most Allah-fearing (atqakum) of you" (al-Hujurat, 49: 13).

The Qur'an stresses that all human beings have a common origin (Adam and Eve), which means that all human beings are equal in the sight of Allah. The only basis for superiority amongst them is their moral conduct. It also reminds us that the original faith of all human beings was *tawhid* and all the Prophets of Allah invited people to embrace *tawhid*: *"In the beginning mankind followed one single way (was one ummah or community, later on differences arose). Then Allah sent forth Prophets as heralders of good tidings for the righteous and as warners against the consequences of evil doing. He sent with them the Book embodying the Truth so that it might judge among people in their disputes. And those who innovated divergent ways rather than follow the Truth, were other than those who had received the knowledge of the Truth and clear guidance; and they did so to commit excesses against each other. So, by His leave Allah directed the believers to the Right Way in matters on which they disagreed. Allah guides whomsoever He wills onto a Straight Way (sirat al-mustaqim)"* (al-Baqarah, 2: 213).

Two important aspects are highlighted here. First, all human beings have one common parentage. They are equal. Also, Adam and Eve submitted to Allah as Muslims. Therefore, the original faith of human beings was *tawhid*, obedience and worship of the One and Only Allah as the Creator. The Qur'an utterly rejects the theory that monotheism developed out of henotheism and polytheism. Second, it also states that Islam, submission to and obedience of the One and Only Allah, has been the original faith of all human beings, which means that Islam is a call to return to the original faith of humankind. Deviation from tawhid lead to polytheism. Islam is essentially a revival of the message conveyed by Prophet Ibrahim ﷺ and before him by Prophets Nuh and Adam. Just as the same message was delivered by Prophets Isma'il, Ishaq, Ya'qub, Musa and 'Isa.

The Islamic worldview, consequently, is not associated with a place, time or a civilizational stage. The Islamic ethical teachings are valid, relevant, and applicable to humankind today as they were applicable at the time of the advent of Islam. The universal Islamic principles of the equality of human beings, justice, truth, peace, and the dignity of man are as fresh today as they were when the Qur'an was revealed to the final Messenger, Muhammad ﷺ, fifteen centuries ago.

The verse further conveys that all human beings, irrespective of their gender, colour or race, are to be assessed and judged according to the criterion already revealed in the Book. The Qur'anic ethical norms demand the same standard from all human beings. It does not allow double standards, subjectivity, bias, or favour. In an Islamic state, Muslims and non-Muslims are to be judged with one and the same laws of the land based on universal Qur'anic principles of *'adl* or justice and fairness. Theft and loss of life have one and the same legal punishment irrespective of faith and gender. The objectives of *Shari'ah*, which are actually objectives for the whole of humanity, are the same for all people. The basic principles of protection of honour, property, life, religious and cultural freedom, and sanctity of family lineage are one and the same for all human beings, Muslims and non-Muslims alike. No discrimination can be made in matters involving human rights granted by the Qur'an and the Sunnah to all human beings.

While inviting people to the path of Truth and success in this world and the Hereafter, the Qur'an asks them to use their faculties of observation, intellect and reason in order to make a responsible judgement about their way of life and come out of blindly following the conventions of their forefathers. It also warns them about the consequences of the wilful denial and rejection of the Straight Path (*sawa' al-sabil* or *sirat al-mustaqim*).

Desisting from the customary practices of a people often leads to clash and conflict. The negative reaction to Islam's rejection of polytheism was therefore very harsh. Those who embraced the new faith were often subjected to hardships, oppression, and persecution, as happened in the case of earlier nations. A clash between the followers of the truth and those who blindly follow their forefathers' customs was inevitable. Such clash and conflict could make even the sincere believers cry out, wondering when Allah's help might come to them. The Qur'an observes: *"Do you suppose that you will enter Paradise untouched by the suffering endured by the people of faith who passed away before you? They were afflicted by misery and hardships and were so convulsed that the Messenger and the believers with him cried out 'When will Allah's help arrive?' They were assured: Behold Allah's help is close by"* (al-Baqarah, 2: 214).

The Culture of Benevolence (*Infaq*) and Social Engagement

The Qur'an wants to create a culture of benevolence among its followers. Mutual help, cooperation and support are the virtues that create solidarity and unity in any given society. A universal principle given by the Qur'an in this respect is that the believers should not think that what they earn from their hard work is theirs and belongs to them alone. Allah reminds them that whatever they earn with their skills and capacity is only possible through Allah's help and favour. He, therefore, wants them to share His favour with others: *"People ask you what they should spend. Say 'whatever wealth you spend let it be for your parents, and kinsmen, the orphans the needy and the wayfarer, Allah is aware of whatever good you do' "* (al-Baqarah, 2: 215).

The Qur'an envisions a society in which there is a high degree of benevolence and concern for other fellow human beings. Spending in the way of Allah (*infaq*) is a major theme in the Qur'an. It was mentioned at the beginning of *Surah al-Baqarah* that the true believers are those: *"Who establish prayer and spend out of what We have provided them"* (al-Baqarah, 2: 3). The same theme reoccurs again and again in the same *surah* and the believers are told to spend whatever exceeds their needs. *"They ask what should we spend in the Way of Allah? Say: Whatever you can spare"* (al-Baqarah, 2: 219), which means spending one's wealth for the sake of Allah (*infaq*) has no upper or lower limits. Earlier in the same *surah* believers were warned against miserliness (*bukhl*): *"Spend in the way of Allah and do not cast yourselves into destruction with your own hands, do good, for Allah loves those who do good"* (al-Baqarah, 2: 195). In *Surah* Ibrahim the concept is further elaborated on: *"(O Prophet ﷺ) tell those of My servants ('ibadi) who believe, that they should establish prayers and spend out of what We have provided them with, both secretly and openly, before there arrives the Day when there will be no bargaining, nor any mutual befriending"* (Ibrahim, 14: 31).

However, spending one's wealth has to be done with the intention to please Allah and Allah alone: *"The example of those who spend their wealth singlehandedly to please Allah is that of a garden on a high ground, if a heavy rain smites it, it brings forth its fruit two-fold, and if there is no heavy rain, even a light shower suffices it. Allah sees all that you do"* (al-Baqarah, 2: 265). Allah loves those believers who spend in His way and, at the same time, properly manage their emotional intelligence: *"And hasten to the forgiveness of your Lord and to a Paradise as vast as the heavens and the earth prepared for (muttaqin) the Allah-conscious (God fearing), who spend in the way of Allah both in affluence and hardship, who restrain their anger, and forgive others.*

Allah loves such good-doers" (Al 'Imran, 3: 133-134). The believers are therefore urged to spend as much as possible on social welfare and the alleviation of poverty and insecurity in society: *"And spend of what Allah has granted you by way of sustenance before death should come to any of you and he should say 'Lord, why did You not defer my return for a while so that I might give alms and be among the righteous?'"* (al-Munafiqun, 63: 10).

The Qur'an reminds the believers that spending in the way of Allah has to be with only one intention, to please Allah. It should not be done to show off (*riya'*): *"Those who, for the love of Him feed the needy, and the orphan, and the captive, (saying) 'we feed you only for Allah's sake (liwajhi Allah), we do not seek of you any recompense or thanks'"* (al-Dahr/al-Insan, 76: 8). While spending in the way of Allah, believers are also reminded that they should spend on others that which has value to them and not what is worthless: *"You shall not attain righteousness until you spend (for Allah's sake) out of what you love. Allah Knows whatever you spend"* (Al 'Imran, 3: 92). The beneficiaries, on the other hand, should not have a feeling that any favour or act of generosity has been done towards them. They must thank Allah alone for His ways of helping them from whence they never suspected.

It is also important to note that the Qur'an prioritizes spending (*infaq*) on parents and near relations. The Qur'an also differentiates between the general concept of *zakah* as an obligation due on all the believers who possess a minimum threshold and other acts of worship which are not obligatory. While almsgiving and spending (*sadaqah* or *infaq*) from what one owns are voluntary contributions, spending of whatever is beyond one's personal needs is highly recommended. Parents in Islam are not a burden or liability but one of Allah's blessings and favours. It is, therefore, an Islamic obligation to spend on them as a first priority: *"You shall serve none but Allah and do good to parents"* (al-Baqarah, 2: 83). Similar statements are made in other places such as in *al-An'am* 6: 151; *Banu Isra'il* 17: 23-25; *al-'Ankabut* 29: 8; *Luqman* 31: 15 and *al-Ahqaf* 46: 15.

One's family also has priority vis-à-vis spending of one's wealth. It is an obligation of the head of a family to spend on his wife and children from *halal*, lawful earnings. However, he cannot spend the *zakah* due on him on his wife or children. The culture that emerged consequently is of honouring, respecting, obeying parents and spending on them and other members of the family and society not as a favour, charity, or kindness but as an obligation and that too has to be done with dignity, honour, and gratitude.

This aspect of the Islamic social, ethical, and legal obligation is the opposite of the materialistic-capitalist culture in which parents are tolerated by children until they reach adulthood. As soon as children are able to take care of themselves, they become independent of their parents, who are considered the responsibility of the state or civil society; when they reach old age they are put in care homes. From an Islamic standpoint, this is an unethical and uncivilized way of dealing with one's parents which is not acceptable in an Islamic culture or social order.

The Culture of Benevolence

This culture of benevolence and social engagement creates solidarity, love and mutual trust, it consolidates the family and makes all Muslims one single *ummah*, one body. It also marginalizes hate, jealousy and mistrust while building a society wherein what is good dominates and brotherhood and sisterhood prevail.

One of Allah's qualities is His care (*'inayah*) for His creation and His providing of resources indiscriminately to human beings: *"As for worldly livelihood, Allah grants it to whomsoever He wills without measure"* (al-Baqarah, 2: 212). His generosity has no limits. The believers are also continuously reminded to pay *zakah* as an obligation while spending whatever they can afford as a voluntary and recommended act of worship (*infaq and Sadaqah*). *Nafaqa* means to sell well, to finish something, while *infaq* means spending. *Infaq fi sabil* Allah, is a recurring theme in the Qur'an as mentioned earlier. Generally, it refers to all spending excluding *zakah*. Through voluntary spending, the Qur'an wants to create an atmosphere in which people do not abstain from spending of their wealth for fear of becoming poor or experiencing a shortage in resources. The more a person gives, the more Allah promises to provide for them from unanticipated sources: *"Allah will find a way out for him who fears Allah and will provide him sustenance from whence he never even imagined, whoever puts his trust in Allah, He shall suffice him. Surely Allah brings about what He decrees, Allah has set a measure for everything"* (al-Talaq, 65: 3). It is a unique situation in which the One Who is the Real Owner of all that exists in the universe encourages His servants to spend from what He Himself has given them and guarantees that their spending will never cause any shortage to them while, at the same time, it will be rewarded abundantly in this world and the next.

The believers are prompted to spend as much as they can before death visits them: *"And spend (wa anfiqu), of what Allah has granted you by way of sustenance before death should come to any of you and he should say: Lord why did you not defer my return for a while so that I might give alms (fa-assaddaqa) and be among the righteous"* (al-Munafiqun, 63: 10).

To sum up giving in the way of Allah, *infaq*, has a wider connotation and it includes, though not limited to, giving to parents, near relations, neighbours, needy persons and for relieving people from the burden of debt, oppression, and subjugation.

Infaq (benevolence) has a great reward in the Hereafter if it is not done out of showing off: *"Those who, for the love of Him feed the needy and orphan, and the captive, (saying) we feed you only for Allah's sake we do not seek of you any recompense or thanks"* (al-Dahr, 76: 8). While *zakah* is fixed and its recipients are well defined, there is no limit for *infaq*, giving alms and spending on others. At the same time, *infaq* and *sadaqah* are to be made from what one likes for oneself. It is not giving away of things that are useless and worthless for an individual: *"You shall not attain righteousness until you spend (for the sake of Allah) out of what you love. Allah knows whatever you spend"* (Al 'Imran, 3: 92). Since there is no limit for *infaq*, whatever is more than one's needs, one may offer as *infaq*, it may be a heap of gold, or even a handful of flour or dates, in the way of Allah it brings huge reward to a person.

War Ethics

As mentioned above, *al-Baqarah* contains valuable guidelines on the socio-political, spiritual, and economic welfare of the believers and society. It deals with an array of vital themes such as social, economic, political and defence issues. In its essence, Islam is a message of peace, justice and fairness and does not encourage or favour war. But if war is imposed on the believers it makes fighting an obligation.

The Arabs of the pre-Islamic era were known for their tribal wars. Since *hajj* in the Abrahamic tradition was performed in the month of Dhu'l-Hijjah, they avoided war during the sacred months in Islam: Rajab, Dhu'l-Qi'dah, Dhu'l-Hijjah and Muharram. When the unbelievers violated the sanctity of these months, the Muslims wondered whether they should respond to them or wait until the sacred months were over. The Qur'an underscores the principle: *"Indeed fighting in the sacred months is an awesome sin but to stop and deny people from visiting the House of Allah and expelling its inmates from it are more awesome acts in the sight of Allah; and persecution is even more heinous than killing"* (al-Baqarah, 2: 217).

While allowing the believers to retaliate, even in the sacred months, the Qur'an underscores another guiding principle that sometimes the believers feel uncomfortable about certain things but, ultimately, these things may be beneficial for them. Likewise, they may dislike certain things but in the final analysis, they may derive benefit from them. Hence, instead of depending on their limited vision, they should trustingly act on the directive of the All-knowing and All-powerful. In the context of war, the Qur'an mentions: *"Fighting is ordained upon you, and it is disliked by you, it may well be that you dislike a thing even though it is good for you, and it may well be that you like a thing even though it is bad for you. Allah knows and you do not know. People ask you about fighting in the holy months, say: Fighting in it is an awesome sin, but barring people from the way of Allah, disbelieving in Him, and denying entry into the Holy Mosque and expelling its inmates from it are more awesome acts in the sight of Allah; and persecution is even more heinous than killing"* (al-Baqarah, 2: 216-217). The message conveyed is very simple: with all their knowledge, skills and capabilities human beings cannot by themselves decide what is ultimately good and beneficial for them. Human knowledge and reason have their limitations and only Allah, can guide human beings to what is good and suitable for them. The more we learn, the more we realise how little we really know. Islamic ethics and morality therefore, are not situational or relative. Their Divine origin makes them absolute and universal.

The verse also refers to the dogmatic rigidity of the agnostics, skeptics and unbelievers, and their use of oppressive measures, to deny the believers their right to worship. Pre-empting the scenario that the coercive and oppressive measures of the Makkans may pressurize those who embraced Islam to question their faith, the Qur'an cautions the believers that if they renounce Islam, for whatever reason, all their good deeds would be lost. An obvious implication of this verse is that an apostate loses all those rights which a believer has in an Islamic society. Since *iman* is the basis of social relationships, apostasy annuls even marriage between a believer and his or her apostate husband or wife. An apostate consequently can neither inherit from the believers nor the believers from an apostate:

"They will not cease fighting against you till they can turn you from your din, if they can. (So, remember well) that whoever from amongst you turns away from his din and dies in the state of unbelief, their work will go to waste in this world and in the Next. They are destined for the Fire and it is there that they will abide" (al-Baqarah, 2: 217).

The Dynamics of Faith and Migration (*Hijrah*)

The loss of (*iman*) faith, according to the Qur'an, is the greatest loss because it distances the person from their Creator, family, as well as from the community and society. An apostate person is someone who consciously denies the existence and unity of Allah or someone who does not believe in the truthfulness of Allah's Prophets and Messengers or in the Day of Judgement. These three basic articles of faith namely, belief in Allah, His Prophets and the Day of Judgement, are mostly a shared heritage in Judaism, Christianity, and Islam. A person who rebels against this common heritage and considers that he/she does not need Allah's Love and Mercy, Kindness, Care, Support and Guidance, nor needs any ideal role model in order to live a meaningful life, alienates himself/herself from the Muslim *ummah*, and society. The Qur'an cautions such a person about falling from the Grace of Allah in this world and the next.

On the other hand, those who consciously and wilfully accept Allah as their Lord and then remain steadfast in facing challenges and hardships are given glad tidings about the best of rewards which are awaiting them in the Hereafter. This is beautifully put in this verse of *al-Baqarah*: *"Those who believed and forsook their hearth and home and strove in the Way of Allah (jahadu fi sabil Allah), such may rightly hope for the Mercy of Allah for Allah is All-Forgiving, All-Merciful"* (al-Baqarah, 2: 218).

In a crystal-clear manner, the verse refers to the impact of belief on the believer's conduct and behaviour. A believer is ever prepared to sacrifice their wealth, home, country, and life for the good pleasure of Allah. Migration (*hijrah*), in its wider connotation, stands for not only physical migration but also a cultural, conceptual, and intellectual migration from a materialistic way of life to total obedience of Allah and leaving behind everything in the cause of Islam. Here, the dynamics of *iman*, or, faith become very clear for it is more than a mere verbal confession of believing in Allah as the Creator, Lord and Guide. It implies a conscious change in one's mindset, vision, and objective of life as well as a change in the nature of one's relationship with all human beings.

> ### *Hijrah* Means More Than Physical Migration
>
> *Hijrah* is a migration from a self-centred, individualistic and selfish view of life, in which one's own desires and aspirations become one's god to a total transformation of one's personality, likes and dislikes, one's association or lack thereof and one's interpersonal relations.

This aspect of faith is well illustrated in a Prophetic saying related by Abu Umamah and narrated by Imam Bukhari in which the Messenger of Allah ﷺ said: "He has perfected his faith, who loved only for (the sake of) Allah; and disliked only for (the sake of) Allah; and gave (something) for (the sake of) Allah and withheld (something) for (the sake of) Allah."

In its historical context *hijrah*, refers to the migration of the Prophet ﷺ from Makkah to Madinah when the persecution of the Makkan polytheists became unbearable for the Muslims. First, a group of unprotected Companions migrated to Abyssinia, modern Ethiopia and then all the believers were commanded to migrate to Yathrib (which was later renamed as Madinah) in 622 CE (common era).

The significance of *hijrah* lies in its concept of sacrifice, utter commitment, and the sincerity of the believer towards *din* and the Islamic way of life. *Hijrah* is a practice of many of Allah's Messengers such as Prophets Ibrahim and Musa who migrated for the sake of Allah. And definitely, the Sunnah of the Last Messenger of Allah ﷺ who emigrated to Madinah from Makkah, the city he loved and liked due to its association with Prophets Ibrahim and Ismail.

But *hijrah* as a major theme means more than moving from one location to another. It means dissociating oneself from un-Islamic economic, social, and political systems, unethical social practices, and *jahili* cultural traditions. It is a migration from pre-Islamic *jahiliyah* to Islam. The Qur'an considers all dogmatic conventions that have no Divine sanction as remnants of pre-Islamic *jahiliyah*. *Hijrah* liberates the believers from social constructs and allows them to observe the universal and Islamic ethical values of peace, love, equity, serving Allah and helping out people in order to please Allah alone.

Referring to the historical dimensions of *hijrah*, the Qur'an mentions: *"Their Lord answered the prayer thus: I will not suffer the work of any of you, whether male or female, to go to waste, each of you is from the other. Those who emigrated and were driven out from their homes and were persecuted in My cause, and who fought and were slain, indeed I shall wipe out their evil deeds from them and shall certainly admit them to the Gardens beneath which rivers flow; This is their reward with their Lord, and with Allah lies the best reward"* (Al 'Imran, 3: 195).

Leaving behind all un-Islamic attachments, rituals and ceremonies is an indication of observing and establishing of the *din*. And this becomes the most desirable form of *jihad* when the believers sacrifice their wealth and lives in their striving to establish an Islamic society that upholds social justice, peace, fairness and human rights: *"Do you consider providing water to pilgrims and maintenance of the Sacred Mosque equal in worth to believing in Allah and the Last Day and striving in the cause of Allah? The two are not equal with Allah. Allah does not direct the wrongdoing folks to the Right way. The higher rank with Allah is for those who believed and migrated and strove in His cause with their belongings and their lives. It is they who are triumphant. Their Lord gives them glad tidings of mercy from Him* and of His good pleasure. For them await Gardens of eternal bliss. Therein they shall abide forever. Surely with Allah a mighty reward awaits them"* (al-Tawbah, 9: 19-22).

A holistic understanding of *hijrah* therefore includes withdrawal from all unethical practices and behaviours. In its physical context it refers to a migration of those who are oppressed to a safe place, where they could observe *din* and their culture without any threat or danger. *Hijrah* plays a dynamic role in the transformation of the personality of a believer. Consequently, with this change in vision, the behaviours and priorities of a person also go through a change. Instead of looking for glamour, fun and enjoyment a person looks forward to a life of peace, fairness, honesty, truthfulness, and loyalty to the Creator and to His final Messenger ﷺ. The Qur'an also refers to the exemplary way in which the Helpers (Ansar) of Madinah welcomed those who migrated to them: *"Those who believe and have migrated and strove in the way of Allah, and those who gave them refuge and help, it is they who are the true believers. Theirs shall be forgiveness and honourable sustenance"* (al-Anfal, 8: 74).

The Gradual Removal of Social Evils through *Ma'ruf*

Good and ethical conduct (*ma'ruf*) is a major Qur'anic theme. *Ma'ruf* refers to a behavioural pattern of balance, moderation, ethical excellence, and virtue in all human actions. The Qur'an offers a realistic and positive solution to unethical practices. The corrective method the Qur'an puts forth is based on the principle of *ma'ruf* (good). The Qur'an wants believers to increase good in society in order to frustrate evil. Similarly, instead of introducing sudden changes, it introduces gradual and sustainable changes in human conduct and behaviour. This wise approach of the Qur'an succeeded in eliminating intoxicants within a context where people were hooked on intoxicants: *"They ask you about liquor (wine) and games of chance. Say: in both there is great evil, even though there is some benefit for people, but their evil is greater than their benefit"* (al-Baqarah, 2: 219). The Qur'an has its own ethical way of registering in the minds of its readers what is ethically good or bad. Before it uses a legal language of declaring something as unlawful, it wants people to realize for themselves its harm, thus creating in them a dislike for it.

If we look around, modern man's addiction to intoxication is similar to that in the pre-Islamic hedonistic culture. The ethical remedy the Qur'an offered to mankind over fifteen centuries ago is equally valid and applicable

The Qur'an wants human beings to make a reasoned judgement and make a conscious shift from their addiction to liquor; a better word for this transition is *hijrah*. The Qur'an recommends a gradual approach in order to unhook a people from addiction, first through informing them about its harms, even if it may have some benefits, and, in the next step, it states: *"Believers do not draw near to prayer while you are intoxicated, until you know what you are saying..."* (al-Nisa', 4: 43). Now the believer is psychologically prepared to avoid using intoxicants, to be able to observe properly the five daily prayers, he will have no choice but to avoid alcohol. But still at this stage it was not prohibited or declared to be unlawful. When the Muslim community was psychologically prepared for the prohibition of intoxicants, there was no hesitation in declaring it to be unlawful: *"Believers! Intoxicants, games of chance, idolatrous sacrifices at altars, and divining arrows are all abominations, the handiwork of Satan.*

So, turn (fa'jtanibuhu) wholly away from it that you may attain to true success (falah)" (al-Ma'idah, 5: 90).

Statistically, it is an established fact that a large number of deaths and disabilities are due to the consumption of liquor, particularly during national celebrations and while driving when drunk. Islam values the life and health of believers and all other human beings and this is why it prohibits all intoxicants. The word used with reference to drinking is *ithm* which means sin, but the full expression is *ithmun kabirun*, i.e. great sin.

The other social evils condemned by the Qur'an in the same verse are games of chance, the use of arrows for foretelling the future and other idolatrous practices. It is important to note that social evils prohibited in these verses are not only harmful to human reason (*'aql*), mental and physical health, but also lead to further harmful consequences like enmity, revenge, and violence.

The Institutionalization of Social Engagement

A Prophetic saying describes the Muslim community as one body, such that when one of its limbs is hurt, the whole body feels its pain. The presence of people who are financially better off and those who are not is normal in any human society. But an Islamic social and political order wants to alleviate poverty and makes all the believers responsible for social engagement and the elimination of poverty: *"They ask: what should we spend in the way of Allah? Say: whatever you can spare. In this way Allah clearly expounds His injunction to you that you may reflect upon them. Both in regard to this world and the Next. They question you about orphans, say: To deal with them in the way, which is to their good, is the best. And if you intermix (your expenses) with them, they are your brothers. Allah knows the mischievous from the righteous, and had Allah willed He would indeed have imposed on you exacting conditions, but He is all Powerful, Most Wise"* (al-Baqarah, 2: 219-220).

First, an important message that the verse gives is that one should spend generously *fi sabil* Allah, in the way of Allah. Here, *infaq* spending on others appears in the context of war and not in its general sense of giving *sadaqah*. In other words, not only in the normal circumstances of peace but also in war, or *jihad* in the way of Allah, social responsibility must be upheld and the believers should spend on others whatever they can afford. The word *'afw* refers to whatever is in excess of a person's needs, whether it is small or large. This excess should be spent to please Allah and protect the Muslim community from any external threats. While prompting the believers to make generous contributions for the protection and defence of the Muslim community, the verse also instructs them about how to manage the affairs of those who are orphaned, particularly those who have lost their fathers in war.

Taking care of orphans and other needy people is an Islamic social obligation. However, spending on them and managing their resource must be exercised with Allah-consciousness and a sense of accountability before Allah. If the caretaker of an orphan's property does not have his own independent source of income, he is allowed to use a reasonable amount from the resources of the orphan to sustain himself and his family. But no one is allowed to exploit an orphan's resources in the name of taking care of him or her. An orphan's rights and interests must be fully protected.

A related social issue is touched upon in the same continuation, i.e. marriage. It is declared that, as a principle, a believer cannot marry a polytheist because Islam and *kufr* or shirk (unbelief) cannot coexist. Therefore, a believing male cannot take a *mushrikah* or *kafir* woman as his life partner and vice versa. Because elsewhere, the Qur'an expounds that parents, both father and mother, are responsible for the upbringing of their children as true Muslims. This is only possible when a child does not face an ongoing conflict and clash in behavioural issues in the home. Unanimity in the belief and practice of both the mother and father alone can save a child from psychological dilemma: *"Marry not the women who associate others with Allah, in His Divinity, until they believe; for a believing slave girl is better than a (free respectable) woman who associates others with Allah, even though she might please you. Likewise, do not give your women in marriage to men who associate others with Allah, in His Divinity until they believe; for a believing slave is better than a (free respectable) man who associates others with Allah, in His Divinity even though he might please you"* (al-Baqarah, 2: 221).

Islamic social laws in the Qur'an and the Sunnah are founded on the primary principle of *tawhid*. It is *tawhid* that decides which social relationship is lawful and which kind of economic activity is allowed and what kind of political and cultural activities are permissible or prohibited.

A common misconception is the claim that love has no religion. Being a comprehensive way of life, Islam does not leave any area of human life without legislation and guidance. A person may like someone and want to take him or her as a husband or wife, but the criterion of marriage in Islam is not confined to the mere liking of another person, for piety precedes any other consideration. Therefore, no marriage can take place between a Muslim male or female and an unbeliever. The Qur'an is quite clear about this point.

The Qur'an does not hesitate in mentioning even about matters of personal hygiene because it is a complete code of conduct for all aspects of life: *"They ask you about menstruation say: it is a state of impurity; so keep away from women in the state of menstruation and do not approach them until they attain ritual purity, then come to them as Allah has commanded you. Truly Allah loves those who abstain from evil and keep themselves pure. Your wives are your tilth go then into your tilth as you wish but take heed of your ultimate future and avoid incurring the wrath of Allah. Know well that one Day you shall face Him. Announce good tidings to the believers"* (al-Baqarah, 2: 223).

The issue raised by the question is not whether the husband and wife can have intercourse when the wife is menstruating, this was known in all revealed religions as prohibited. The point was about the limits of socialisation during that period. In Judaism and Zoroastrianism, when a female was going through her periods, she was considered untouchable, while the Christians took another extreme. The Qur'an declares it a period of ritual impurity but that does not make the wife untouchable. She can participate in household activities, sleep on the same bed with her husband and share the same blanket. But until she is ritually clean, i.e. her period is over, and she has made the major ritual bath (*ghusl*), husband and wife cannot have sexual intercourse. This shows that the Divine Revelation does not confine itself to rituals, worship, and spirituality but provides comprehensive guidance and limits in all matters related to the individual, family, and social life.

The Qur'an uses a beautiful simile to emphasize the importance of marital relationships. By saying your wives are your tilth, the Qur'an allegorically encourages procreation, the observance of compassion, care, and ethical sexual practice. Furthermore, a husband is expected to value and love his wife and never consider harming their relationship. It strongly warns against swearing by Allah in family matters. Having assigned the family a central place, and marriage as a strong covenant, the Qur'an also guides regarding exceptional situations.

The Qur'an does not leave matters, such as divorce, without any guidance. To begin with, the best efforts are to be made for reconciliation, from both, husband and wife, and reconciliation is highly recommended. However, if reconciliation fails, it allows divorce. The proper way to divorce is to pronounce one *talaq* or divorce, and wait for one month, in which all possible efforts are to be made, sincerely, by both husband and wife to mend their relationship, while they stay together in the same house. If things do not improve at the completion of one month, again in a state of purity and not during a state of impurity, a second *talaq* is to be pronounced. Still both have a chance to repair their relationship. The second *talaq*, in *fiqh* is known as *raja'i* or returnable, though a renewal of *nikah* is required, without any festivities. If this second chance is lost and no reconciliation is made, at the completion of the third month the divorce becomes final and not reversible. The wisdom in this elaborate procedure is to allow both husband and wife to think coolly on the consequences, the future of their own lives and their children and the impact of their decisions on society as a whole. A Prophetic *hadith* tells us that among the things that are allowed but most disliked by Allah is the *talaq*. Therefore, a believer is expected to avoid a thing which is disliked by the Most Merciful.

A divorced wife has to wait for three periods, after that she is free to get married because it is an objective of the *Shari'ah* that believers live a family life. The Prophetic *hadith* clearly states that a person who does not desire to follow the Prophetic Sunnah of living a married life does not belong to his *ummah*. (*faman raghiba 'an sunnati fa laysa mini,*) Muslim, reported by Anas ؓ: "Who disrespects my Sunnah is not from my followers."

The Western, so-called civilized world took over nineteen centuries to start talking about the "empowerment of women" and granting them their legal rights. In Islam men and women are treated equally, not from a gender perspective but from an ethical viewpoint. What makes a female or male superior in the sight of Allah therefore are their good deeds and ethical conduct. At the same time, the Qur'an also provides both with the same legal rights and obligations: *"Women have the same rights against their men as men have against them; but men have a degree above them. Allah is All-Powerful, All-Wise"* (al-Baqarah, 2: 228).

The Building of a Compassionate Family

The Qur'an takes a realistic approach regarding family life. The family in Islam is the basic unit of society and culture. If the family is built on love, compassion and ethical conduct, human civilization progresses but if the family is marginalized, civilization and culture are also lost. The Qur'an makes the husband the custodian of the family due to obvious reasons. Just as no organization can function without an executive officer to make the ultimate decisions, the family too needs a caretaker (*qawwam*) and also a particular division of responsibilities in the family.

With great emphasis on the wellbeing of family life, as the basis of the sustainability of any society or civilization, the Qur'an also provides guidance about situations when a marriage goes through a crisis and reaches a breaking point. The guiding principle for a solid family life is following good (*ma'ruf*), excellence (*ihsan*), forgiveness '*afw*, compassion (*rahmah*) and mutual advice (*nasihah*) while avoiding arguments and conflict. Observing what is good (*ma'ruf*) is so important that even when all efforts to have a good and loving family life fail, divorce, too, has to be with good (*ma'ruf*) and in the most appropriate ethical way.

The Qur'an explains: *"Divorce can be pronounced twice, then, either honourable retention or kindly release should follow. It is unlawful for you to take back anything of what you have given to your wives, unless both fear that they may not be able to keep within the bounds set by Allah. Then if they fear that they might not be able to keep within the bounds set by Allah, there is no blame upon them for what the wife might give away of her property to become released from the marriage tie. These are the bounds (hudud) set by Allah, do not transgress them. Those of you who transgress the boundaries set by Allah are indeed the wrongdoers. Then, if he divorces her (for the third time, after having pronounced the divorce twice) she shall not be lawful to him unless she first takes another man for a husband, and he divorces her..."* (al-Baqarah, 2: 229-230).

Pre-empting any unfair conduct on the part of an ex-husband, the Qur'an underscores the following regarding the proper ethical conduct of the family: *"And so, when you divorce women and they reach the end of their waiting term, then either retain them in a fair manner (bi'lma'ruf) or let them go in a fair manner. And do not retain them to their hurt or by way of transgression; whosoever will do that will indeed wrong himself. Do not take the Signs of Allah in jest and remember Allah's favours upon you. He exhorts you to revere the Book and the Wisdom that He has sent down upon you. Fear Allah and know well that Allah has full knowledge of everything. When you divorce women and they have completed their waiting term do not hinder them from marrying other men if they have agreed to this in a fair manner. That is an admonition to every one of you who believes in Allah and the Last Day: that is a cleaner and purer way for you. For Allah knows. Whereas you do not know"* (al-Baqarah, 2: 231-232).

Often the term *halalah* used in *ayah* 229 is misinterpreted as a way of facilitating re-marriage after having pronounced *talaq* three times.

This is a total corruption of its meaning and greatly condemned by the Prophet's authentic *hadith*. Therefore, an arranged *halalah* for reconciliation is totally un-Islamic and against the Qur'an and the Sunnah of the Prophet ﷺ.

Family Ethics

The ethical revolution set in motion by Islam is not limited to certain golden principles and universal moral values, some of which have been mentioned in the earlier Scriptures of the Abrahamic tradition. The Qur'an also provides a comprehensive ethical and legal framework for the wellbeing of the individual, family and society. Being the building block of Islam's socio-economic and political order, the family is assigned a great importance. According to the Qur'an, the root cause of the global crisis in governance and economy in today's world, is essentially due to the criminal negligence shown by modern man in the application of Divine ethical directives, particularly those relating to the family as the building block of culture and civilization. Establishing a loving and caring family is an Islamic virtue: *"Marry those of you who are single (whether men or women), and those of your male and female slaves that are righteous. If they are poor Allah will enrich them out of His Bounty. Allah is immensely Resourceful, All-Knowing"* (al-Nur, 24: 32).

The Qur'an looks at family ethical issues from a socio-psychological perspective. First, taking into consideration the bioethical dimensions around the period of adulthood, it wants parents, society and the state to ensure that the youth do not indulge in extramarital relations in the name of "teen culture". And when they reach marriageable age, the parents, relatives, and society, and ultimately the state, should take the necessary measures to help them start family life. This gives them emotional, social, and economic stability and security. Being universal, Islam does not fix an age limit for the beginning of adulthood because the biological age of adulthood will always remain variable. Rationally speaking, to fix it at eighteen does not make any sense.

Second, Islam does not want even the persons in custody of others to remain unmarried when they reach a marriageable age. The Qur'anic approach to slavery is also very clear. One permanent step taken by the Qur'an is to gradually phase out slavery which was a major issue at the advent of Islam. The Qur'an declared *zakah* as an obligation on all the believers who possess a minimum threshold of wealth, and one of the eight defined avenues of spending *zakah* in the Qur'an is to liberate slaves. It also refers again and again to freeing slaves to expiate certain sins or failings. The idea is to persuade the believers that Allah does not like the practice of slavery. However, for the transition from slavery to a free society, the verse instructs that when slaves reach a marriageable age, they too should be married in order to avoid any sexual misconduct in society.

Third, one major hindrance faced by individuals and even parents is the financial responsibility that comes with marriage. The Qur'an totally rejects the concept of the deferment of marriage until a person is well-established financially. Allah takes the responsibility of providing the couple's resources through His own ways.

As discussed earlier, the Qur'an as a comprehensive way of life, guides the believers on how to live a fair and pleasant family life. However, if divorce becomes unavoidable, the Qur'an shows its concern about the welfare of children and their divorced mothers: *"If they wish that the period of suckling for their children be completed, mothers may suckle their children for two whole years. (In such a case) it is incumbent upon him, who has begotten the child to provide them (i.e. divorced women and the child) their sustenance and clothing in a fair manner. But none shall be burdened with more than he is able to bear; neither shall a mother suffer because of her child nor shall a father be made to suffer because he has begotten him. The same duty towards the suckling mother rests upon the heir as upon him (i.e. the father). And if both decide by mutual consent and consultation to wean the child there is no blame on them, if you decide to have other women suckle your children there is no blame upon you, provided you hand over its compensation in a fair manner. Fear Allah and know well that Allah sees all that you do"* (al-Baqarah, 2: 233).

A Graceful Family Life

The family ethics elaborated by the Qur'an guides a believer on how to celebrate life and how to face difficult situations. A woman who was divorced cannot remarry immediately but must wait for a duration of three periods. A widow, on the other hand, must wait for four months and ten days, but if she is expecting, then her waiting period is till the child's birth: *"The wives of men who have died must observe a waiting period of four months and ten days, when they have reached the end of the waiting term there is no blame upon you regarding what they may do with themselves in a fair manner. Allah is well aware of what you do"* (al-Baqarah, 2: 234). Islam advocates ethical and transparent conduct. It does not encourage remaining unmarried for a marriageable person nor unnecessary delay in getting remarried but at the same time it does not like a person to marry a widow during her waiting period (*'iddah*), though one can convey a proposal in a dignified way and avoid completely any secret meetings. The wisdom apparently is to allow a reasonable time for readjustment and at the same time to reform the old custom of social pressure on a widow to remain unmarried. In some extreme situations, like in Hinduism, a widow would be cremated with her husband because to be a widow was considered a curse in Hinduism:

"There is no blame upon you whether you hint at a marriage proposal to such women or keep the proposal hidden in your hearts. Know well that Allah knows that you will think of them in that connection. But do not make any secret engagement with them and speak openly in an honourable manner. Do not resolve on the marriage tie until the ordained term has come to its end. Allah knows even what is in your hearts. So, have fear of Him and know well that Allah is All-Forgiving, All-Forbearing" (al-Baqarah, 2: 235).

It further elaborates: *"There is no blame upon you if you divorce your wives before you have touched them or settled a bridal gift upon them. But even in this case you should make some provisions for them: The affluent, according to his means the strained according to his means – a provision in fair manner. That is a duty upon the good doers. And if you divorce them before you touch them or settle a bridal gift upon them, then give them half of what you have settled unless either the women act leniently and forgo the claim or he in whose hand is the marriage tie acts leniently (and pays the full amount). If you act leniently, it is closer to Allah-Fearing. And forget not to act gracefully with one and other. For indeed Allah sees all that you do"* (al-Baqarah, 2: 236-237).

The Qur'an also guides the believers regarding different scenarios relating to divorce. If a person has married but the marriage is not consummated and he divorces, he has to pay at least half of the *mehr* (gift money). But if he wants to pay more he may do so. *Mehr*, further elaborated in *Surah al-Nisa*, is not a price but a sincere bridal gift for which there is no limit. It is left to the bridegroom and according to his status or the standing of the family of the bride, it can be agreed mutually. The point made clear here is that it is a right of the bride to definitely receive a bridal gift, if not in full, at least a part of it before the marriage is consummated.

The Qur'anic ethical principle in all social matters is of encouraging that which is *ma'ruf* (good). Marriage and divorce both have to be conducted according to a proper ethical conduct. The verses 236-237 of *al-Baqarah* further instruct on fair dealing with regards to divorce. The Qur'an stipulates a two-year (maximum) period of suckling a newborn. Suckling is an ethical obligation on the mother, and yet, the Qur'an allows both husband and wife to hire someone else to breastfeed their baby if they mutually agree. In both cases, the father is instructed to be generous in taking care of the nursing mothers' welfare and pay what is required.

It is a unique style of the Qur'an to keep on reminding the believers about the importance of prayer and its role in regulating a believer's life, irrespective of the discourse. While explicating on war, financial or social matters, it keeps on reminding the believers about the importance of *salah*: *"Be watchful over the prayers, and over praying with the utmost excellence, and stand before Allah as would utterly obedient servants. And even if you face the state of fear, still perform the prayer whether on foot or riding; and when you are secure remember Allah in the manner that He taught you, the manner that you did not know earlier"* (al-Baqarah, 2: 238-239). This reference to *salah* right in the midst of a discourse on issues dealing with divorce and the nursing of children shows that, in Islam, social obligations and other acts of worship are not disconnected. Rather, they are all interlinked and synergized in a way that prevents any possible separation between what is owed to God and what is owed to other human beings. The reference to *salah* in the discourse on divorce reminds us to handle the matter with an awareness of being watched by Allah.

The middlemost prayer (*al-salat al-wusta*) refers to the prayer offered in a perfect manner as well as to the middle prayer. Some of the Companions identified it with the '*Asr* prayer. The verses also guide the believers on how to pray in an emergency situation, like war or a state of fear. In accordance with the principle of *yusr* (ease), the Qur'an recommends that, in such situations, prayer can be offered even while riding on horseback, or on a battlefield by letting a group of believers offer one unit of prayer while protected by another group of believers and then the second group takes its turn.

After reminding the believers about the rights of Allah on them, such as the strict observance of prayer, even in a state of war, the Qur'an reminds the believers about the rights of widows and their social obligations towards them. In pre-Islamic Arabia, the waiting period for a widow was one year. Later on, when the revelation came about the distribution of inheritance, this was superseded. However, in the transition period, Islam's concern for the welfare of widows is fully reflected in this verse: *"Those of you who die leaving behind your women, should make a testament of one year's provisions in favour of your wives; And if they themselves depart, there shall be no blame upon you for what they may do with themselves in an honourable manner. Allah is All-Mighty, All-Wise. Likewise, let there be a fair provision for the divorced women, this is an obligation on the God Fearing"* (al-Baqarah, 2: 240-241).

Striving to Achieve Justice and Peace

While prompting the believers to wage *jihad* against the oppressive polytheists (*mushrikin*), the Qur'an reminds the believers of Allah's favours on them, and then calls to take part in *jihad*, as it is their moral obligation to contribute generously with their wealth and lives in the way of Allah. The Qur'an then compares the attitude of the Israelites vis-à-vis *jihad*. They were afraid of death and were not enthusiastic about *jihad*. But life and death are in Allah's Hands and control and no human being can delay his or her hour of death. For this very reason, when called for *jihad*, the believers are not expected to hesitate in offering their lives. Sacrificing life is one way of thanking Allah for His countless bounties and blessings.

And if unable to participate in *jihad*, the believers can thank Allah for His Bounties by generously offering material resources. And while prompting the believers to wage war in order to establish justice, truth and peace in society, the Qur'an takes a unique approach, it says: *"So fight in the way of Allah and know well that Allah is All-Hearing, All-Knowing. Who of you will lend Allah a goodly loan which He will return after multiplying it for him manifold? For Allah has the power both to decrease and increase, and to Him will you all return"* (al-Baqarah, 2: 245). The message given is very important. Human beings are given life, capabilities, resources, knowledge, wealth, children, and reputation by none other than Allah. But, the unique generosity of the Lord is that when that same life and wealth Allah has given to His servants is offered by His servant in the cause of Islam, He considers it a loan which shall be paid back to the servants in the Hereafter in a multiplied form.

The unending mercy and forgiveness of Allah are reflected in His response to the ungrateful behaviour of the Israelites: *"(O Messenger), have you thought of what happened with the elders of the children of Israel after Moses? They asked one of their Prophets: "Set up for us a king so that we may fight in the way of Allah." He said: 'Would you possibly refrain from fighting if fighting is ordained for you?' They* said: *"And why would we not fight in the way of Allah whereas we have been torn from our homes and our children?" But when fighting was ordained for them, they turned back, except a few of them. Allah is well aware of the wrongdoers."*

"And their Prophet ﷺ said to them: 'Indeed, Allah has sent forth Saul (Talut) as your king.' They said: "By what right shall he rule over us when we are more worthy than he to dominion, for he is not very wealthy." He said: 'Allah has chosen him over you and has endowed him abundantly with both intellectual (al-'ilm) and physical (al-jism) capacities. Allah indeed has the power to bestow dominion upon whosoever He wills. Allah is All-Resourceful, All-Knowing.' And their Prophet ﷺ said to them: "The sign of his dominion is that in his reign the Ark, wherein is inner peace for you, will be brought back to you, and the sacred relics left behind by the house of Moses and the house of Aaron, borne by angels. Truly in that is a sign for you, if indeed you are people of faith" (al-Baqarah, 2: 246-248).

In Madinan *surahs*, particularly in *al-Baqarah*, the Qur'an frequently refers to the special favours of Allah on the Israelites, including providing them with the relics of Prophets Musa and Harun, to let them experience miracles such as the sudden death of thousands of them and then their resurrection. But all the favours and miracles shown to them did not turn them into humble servants of their Lord. They remained ungrateful to their Lord Who ultimately removed them from the role of the leadership of humanity and reassigned it to those who humble themselves before Allah.

The Leadership of Mankind

A major theme in *al-Baqarah* is the honouring of the human being as *khalifah*, or deputy of Allah, on earth and the harmonization of guidance and governance (*sultah*) in the person of the *Khalifah*. Earlier in the narrative of Prophet Adam's ﷺ creation, the angels were informed about his leadership role on earth. The Qur'an makes it clear that Prophet Adam ﷺ was not created to stay in Paradise but to be Allah's *khalifah* on earth. In frequent references to the episode of the rise and fall of the Israelites, the Qur'an refers to Allah's special favours on them as a people appointed to establish peace and justice as *khulafa'* or representatives of their Lord. Some of the known Prophets of the Children of Israel, Prophets Dawood, Sulayman, and Yusuf discharged their responsibilities in an excellent manner as Prophets and rulers. In several places, the requisite qualities for leadership in both domains are provided by the Qur'an.

Here in *al-Baqarah*, the Qur'an refers to a visible transgression of the Israelites, perhaps due to their long period of captivity in Egypt, namely the development of esteem and admiration for kings and considering the cow to be sacred. Consequently, when their Prophet ﷺ reached an advanced age, they requested the appointment of a strong king to lead them. On their request, Allah appointed Talut as their king. Reminded of their experience in Egypt, they made an observation: "How can a person who is not richer or more resourceful than us rule over us?" It was their belief, as it is still today in the so-called advanced and democratic countries, that a presidential candidate must show his financial standing as a prerequisite for becoming a candidate.

They are advised that the wealth of knowledge and physical strength are more important than material wealth. This attitude still exists among the general masses and in most of the secular democracies of the world: people coming from a feudal background or belonging to a ruling family are considered more suitable to rule. The Qur'an makes a paradigm shift, a total departure from the conventional concepts of leadership by birth, oligarchy, or lineage. It introduces a qualitative, transformative and ethical leadership and rejects the idea of hereditary kingship.

Elsewhere, the Qur'an further explains that: *"Allah commands you to deliver trusts to those worthy of them and when you judge between people, judge with justice. Excellent is the admonition Allah gives you. Allah is All-Hearing, All-Seeing"* (al-Nisa', 4: 58). The message is very clear, true leadership requires a combination of Allah-consciousness (*taqwa*), intellectual and physical capabilities and trustworthiness.

Qualitative Leadership

The Qur'an makes a paradigm shift, a total departure from the conventional concepts of leadership by birth, oligarchy, or lineage. It introduces a qualitative, transformative, and ethical leadership and rejects the idea of hereditary kingship.

We are told that, although their request was granted, the Israelites acted ungratefully: *"When Saul (Talut) set out with his forces he said: Allah shall try you with a river and whoever drinks of it does not belong to me; he who refrains from tasting it – unless it be just a palmful – he indeed belongs to me. Then all except a few of them drank their fill at the river. But as soon as Saul (Talut) and the believers with him went forth across the river they said: Today we have no strength to face Goliath (Jalut) and his forces. But those who believed that they were bound to meet their Lord said: How often has a small party prevailed against a large party by the leave of Allah. Allah is with those who remain steadfast. And when they went forth against Goliath (Jalut) and his forces they prayed: 'Our Lord shower us with patience and set our feet firm and grant us victory over this unbelieving people'. Thereupon by Allah's leave they put the unbelievers to fight and David (Dawood) killed Goliath and Allah granted him dominion (al-mulk) and wisdom (hikmah) and imparted to him the knowledge of whatever He willed. And were it not that Allah repelled some people with another, the earth would surely be overlaid with mischief. But Allah is Bounteous to the people of the world (and thus extirpates mischief)"* (al-Baqarah, 2: 249-251).

> ### True Leadership
>
> True leadership requires a combination of Allah-consciousness, intellectual and physical capabilities and trustworthiness.

The above verses refer to the ungrateful attitude of most Israelites. Nonetheless, they also highlight that the few who were sincere in Allah's obedience were steadfast. They followed the instructions of Talut and did not drink from the river. Allah responded to their prayer and, with His support, a small number of these believers were able to defeat a large number of the oppressors and their ruler Jalut (Goliath) who was killed by Prophet Dawood ﷺ who had volunteered to fight against Goliath.

This historic narrative shows that what counts with Allah is not large numbers of uncommitted people, but a limited number of devoted and sincere people who, with His help, can overcome a much bigger and well-equipped enemy. In other words, it is quality and not quantity that matters. A small number of believers with strength of character can achieve success over a large number of unbelieving and unethical people if they are steadfast, united and trust in Allah's help. This qualitative approach is highlighted again elsewhere, in the Qur'an: *"O Prophet ﷺ! Rouse the believers to fighting. If there be twenty of you who persevere, they shall vanquish two hundred and if there be of you a hundred. They shall vanquish a thousand of those who disbelieve, for they are a people who lack understanding"* (al-Anfal, 8: 65).

The waging of *jihad* by Talut against Jalut demonstrates that when pious and God-fearing people come forward and strive against the oppressors and evildoers, even when they are few in number, Allah grants them victory:

"If Allah were not to repel some through others, monasteries and churches and synagogues and mosques wherein the name of Allah is much mentioned would certainly have been pulled down" (al-Hajj, 22: 40). Upon reflection, one understands that the verse implies that a major objective of *jihad* is to protect the places of worship of the followers of different religions including Muslim places of worship. This dimension of *jihad* is unfortunately never highlighted. On the contrary, *jihad* is equated with the Christian concept of "holy war" which was waged by the Church to convert the Jews and Muslims by the force of the sword. This and similar misgivings have projected a negative perception of Islam and Muslims. *Jihad* is not waged for the sake of converting people to Islam but is meant to protect human rights and religious freedom of the Muslims and others.

The Role of Reason, Revelation and Miracles

The Qur'an approaches the success and failure of people from an ethical perspective. The forces of evil may be numerous while those who stand for the truth and for justice may be few in number but, ultimately truth and justice shall prevail due to the steadfastness and *istiqamah* (uprightness) of those few who commit themselves to serve Allah alone. Talut and Prophet Dawood ﷺ could not persuade most of the Israelites to join the fight, yet they were victorious over the forces of evil. Such historic events and the miracles caused by Allah are called *ayat* or signs of Allah but it is rather unfortunate that after witnessing so many signs the People of the Book as well as the *mushrikin* hesitated to believe in the Unity, *tawhid* and Sovereignty of Allah:

"These are the signs of Allah which We recite to you in Truth, for indeed you are one of those entrusted with the Message. And these Messengers (who have been designated to guide people), We have exalted some of them above others. Among them are such as were spoken to by Allah Himself, and some He exalted in other aspects and We granted Jesus, son of Mary, clear Signs and supported him with the spirit of holiness. Had He willed, those who had seen these clear Signs would not have fought one another thereafter. But (it was not the will of Allah to prevent people from disagreement by compulsion, hence) they differed among themselves whereby some attained faith and others denied the Truth. Yet had Allah so willed they would not have fought one another. Allah does whatever He wills" (al-Baqarah, 2: 252).

The Qur'anic approach is to invite and persuade people to use their power of reasoning in deciding what is right and what is wrong. It does not approve of blind belief or dogmatism and also wants its followers to achieve continuous improvement in their knowledge and behaviour. Likewise, it wants them to recognise the possibility of miracles because the One Who has created the universe and made laws to govern it, can also break or suspend these laws. He is not bound by the laws He creates. Miracles are performed by Allah's Messengers as a final argument, and by His command, to challenge, and defy the unbelievers. The message given is three-fold, first, these miracles do not make these Prophets divine nor do they share in Allah's Divinity, second, all deviations from nature are made only at the command of Allah; third, since the miracles occurred at the insistence of the people, if, even after having witnessed these miracles, they do not recognize the Truth, such people are subjected to punishment.

Encouragement of Social Engagement and the Culture of Spending on Others (*Infaq*)

The love of wealth is one of the human weaknesses, this is why spending on others (*infaq*) for the sake of Allah is a recurring theme in the Qur'an. The believers are reminded time and again about social engagement and their responsibility to spend on others from their lawful earnings, as much as possible, before they eventually meet their death. It is more appropriate to spend on others for the sake of Allah as an investment because its return, multiplied and manifold, is guaranteed by the Lord of the Universe on the Day of Judgement.

The believers are frequently reminded to spend in the cause of Allah from what Allah has provided them in order to prove that they take Allah alone as their Master and do not worship wealth or power or authority. A person whose sole purpose and aim in life is the acquisition of wealth and power or fame eventually tends to worship these and deviates from the obedience to Allah alone as his ultimate concern. The Qur'an reminds: *"O you who believe spend out of what We have provided you before there comes a Day when there* will be no buying and selling, nor will friendship and intercession be of any avail. Indeed, those who disbelieve are the wrongdoers" (al-Baqarah, 2: 254).

The way of Allah is defined by the Qur'an in several places. The highest reward is for striving in the way of Allah to liberate those who are oppressed and deprived of their basic human rights, irrespective of whether they are Muslims or not. In the way of Allah (*fi sabil Allah*), also includes support to the orphans, poor, those in debt and helping those who work full-time to spread Islam through different means. The discourse on striving in the way of Allah by offering one's life and whatever one possesses is a repeated theme in the Qur'an which indicates Islam's concern for the realization of justice, freedom, peace and security, with an uncompromising trust and faith in Allah.

The Implication of "*mimma razaqnakum*"

The phrase *mimma razaqnakum* "from that which we have provided you" is a beautiful expression which enjoins a believer to spend from what their Creator and Sustainer has bestowed upon them, because whatever is given to human beings by their Lord is a trust to be spent exactly the way the Real Owner wants it to be spent.

The Beauty of the Verse of the Throne (*Ayat al-Kursi*)

It is reported that the Prophet ﷺ once asked Ubayy ibn Ka'b about the greatest verse of the Qur'an and this Companion responded that it was the Verse of the Throne. Happy with his answer, the Prophet ﷺ said: "O Abu al-Mundhir! (Allah) bless your knowledge." The Prophet ﷺ also mentioned once that only death stands in the way of the believer entering Paradise if he recites the Verse of the Throne after each obligatory prayer. This is probably because this verse focuses on basic faith and Allah's Attributes and Greatness. The verse starts with defining *tawhid*: *"Allah, the Ever-Living, the Self-Sustainer by Whom all Subsist, there is no god but He"*. First of all, Allah exists through Himself without any prior cause; secondly, He is self-subsistent; and He is never overtaken by slumber nor does He need sleep. The Jewish concept of God assumes that after working hard for six days, He took rest on the seventh day, while the Christian concept of God presumes that Jesus shares in Allah's Divinity. The Verse of the Throne corrects these false beliefs. Allah is above all such limitations of sleep, rest, fatigue, and any other dependency whatsoever. Since He is All-Knowing, All-Hearing and All-Seeing it further clarifies that He does not need anyone to intercede or bring to His notice anything. The word used, *kursi* literally means chair, it refers to Allah's Sovereignty, control and grip on everything in the universe. It does not mean He sits on a chair like we do.

The *ayah* elaborates Allah's *tawhid* in Person (*dhat, wujud*) and *tawhid* in Attributes (*sifat*). It also removes the confusion that since He is All-Knowing, All-Seeing and All-Hearing. He does not need any pious person to intercede and bring to His notice anything. As the All-Knowing and All-Seeing, He does not need a finite human being with "high spirituality", to inform Him or recommend someone. All human beings are going to be judged by Him based on their ethical conduct and behaviour, or actions (*'amal*) and not rewarded on anyone's intermediation.

Religious Freedom

The following verse also declares that there is no compulsion in matters of faith. The Qur'an has expressly clarified the truth and made falsehood evident. It is up to the human intellect now, to decide which direction to follow. The Qur'an elsewhere states: *"Had your Lord so willed, all those who are on earth would have believed, will you then force people into believing?"* (Yunus, 10: 99); it further declares: *"And proclaim this is the Truth from your Lord. Now let him, who will believe; and let him who will disbelieve..."* (al-Kahf, 18: 29). The Qur'an further elaborates: *"O unbelievers, I do not worship those that you worship, neither do you worship Him Whom I worship, nor will I worship those whom you have worshipped, nor are you going to worship Him whom I worship, to you is your religion, and to me my way of life"* (al-Kafirun, 109: 1-6).

There is no conflict between the Verse of *Jihad* (*ayat al-jihad*) and the above Qur'anic assurance of freedom of religious practices. *Jihad* is essentially a striving and struggle against lawlessness, oppression, and denial of human rights, particularly religious freedom. It is not by any means conversion by force: *"How is it that you do not fight in the way of Allah and in the support of the helpless - men, women and children - who pray: Our Lord, bring us out of this land whose people are oppressors and appoint for us from Yourself a protector, and appoint for us from Yourself a helper"* (al-Nisa', 4: 75). The oppressed in this *ayah* are not necessarily Muslims because Islam stands for freedom from oppression for all human beings.

Not only does the Qur'an guarantee religious freedom for non-Muslims who live under Muslim rule, it also mentions very clearly that *jihad* is waged to protect the places of worship of even non-Muslims: *"If Allah were not to repel some through others (through jihad),* monasteries and churches and synagogues and mosques wherein the name of Allah is much mentioned, would certainly have been pulled down. Allah will most certainly help those who will help Him" (al-Hajj, 22: 40). It is worth mentioning that the Qur'an is the only world Scripture which refers specifically to the places of worship of the Christians, the Jews, the Muslims and others which are to be protected through *jihad*. No one can be denied access and the right to visit their places of worship irrespective of faith, race, or colour.

> ## The Legitimacy of Waging War
>
> It is not permitted to wage *jihad* against people simply because they are unbelievers or deniers of the truth of Islam. The verse makes it clear that sedition, corruption, oppression, exploitation, injustice, and persecution justify waging *jihad* and, once oppression is removed, people cannot be converted by force.

On the contrary, under Muslim rule in Spain, Jews and Christians participated in research and development without any interference. Moses Maimonides (1135-1204) Musa bin Maimun, produced in Arabic his major works, especially *The Guide for the Perplexed* which was a commentary on Mishnah and The Mishnah Torah, a codification of law.

Rushd and *Taghut*

The Verse of the Throne is followed by a reference to the fact that there is no compulsion in religion and that *rushd*, *kufr* and *taghut* have been made clearly distinct from each other. Hence, whoever rejects unbelief and *taghut* and becomes a conscious follower of the truth (*haqq*) and guidance (*hidayah*) has gotten hold of a strong, unbreakable covenant (*al-'urwah al-wuthqa*) with God.

The Qur'anic term *rushd* refers to the right course, true faith, to being well guided, and to becoming mature and sensible. Its meaning covers both physical and spiritual maturity: *"Test the orphans until they reach the age of marriage and thus if you find them mature of mind (rushdan) hand over to them their property..."* (al-Nisa', 4: 6). It also refers to the right path, the path of guidance: *"And even if they see the Right Path (sabil al-Rushd) they shall not follow it"* (al-A'raf, 7: 146). It is a special blessing from Allah to grant some of His servants wisdom and *rushd*: *"Surely We had bestowed wisdom (rushdahu) upon Ibrahim even earlier and We knew him well"* (al-Anbiya', 21: 51).

A further elaboration of the meaning of *rushd* can be understood from the story of the People of the Cave (*ashab al-Kahf*): *"When those youth sought refuge in the cave and said 'Our Lord Grant us mercy (rahmah) from Yourself and provide for us rectitude in our affairs (rashadan)'"* (al-Kahf 18: 10.) The Qur'an also uses it with reference to Allah as the ultimate Guide: *"Whomsoever Allah guides, he alone is led aright and whomsoever Allah let go astray you will find for him no guidance (waliyyan murshidan) to direct him"* (al-Kahf, 18: 17). The right way (*sabil al-rashad*) is also used to describe the Qur'an as the guide to the Right Way: *"We have indeed heard a wonderful Qur'an which guides to the Right Way (al-Rushd), so we have come to believe in it, and we will not associate* taghut *with Our Lord in His Divinity"* (al-Jinn, 72: 2). *Rashid*, therefore, means the one who follows the right path or who is rightfully guided, the term is used, for example, for the first four Muslim caliphs (*al-khulafa' al-rashidun*). The word *murshid*, from the same root, has also been used for spiritual guide in some mystical orders and by some Islamic movements for their leaders. *Taghut* stands for an excessive behaviour pattern of substituting someone or something as an object of worship and devotion apart from Allah. Not only does it refer to disobedience, it also includes attributing the authority and power, which only belong to Allah, to someone else.

The Qur'an calls itself that Truth which makes good and bad distinct and evident therefore one of the names of the Qur'an is al-Furqan, the touchstone of Truth. The two terms, *rushd* and *taghut*, in the Qur'an, symbolize two mindsets and ways of life. A way of life which is conscious and wilfully accepting of Allah, taking His Messengers as true role models, and another which is the exact opposite.

> **The Path of *Rushd* vs. the Path of *Taghut***
>
> This is the path of (*rashidun*) the rightly-guided who are promised the best reward in the Hereafter. The opposite path (the path of the *taghut*) is that of those who have a rebellious attitude and behaviour who follow their own desires, drives and instincts as their god.

Both these ways are clearly shown to human beings and they can freely choose one of the two, without any compulsion or force or *ikrah*. Freedom of will is another recurring theme in the Qur'an. The first human couple were given freedom of will, when they were kept temporarily in *Jannah* or Paradise and were told to avoid approaching a specific tree.

This freedom of will is given to every human being. One can follow the path of *hidayah* and truth, or serve the forces of evil and *taghut*. The Qur'an does not allow any forced conversion and provides full protection to religious freedom. This principle is stated in the Qur'an in a succinct manner: *"There is no compulsion in din. The Right Way stands clearly distinguished from the wrong. Hence, he who rejects the evil ones and believes in Allah has indeed taken the hold of a firm unbreakable handle (al-'urwah al-wuthqa). And Allah is All-Hearing, All-Knowing"* (al-Baqarah, 2: 256).

The task of the believer is to appropriately present the message of *tawhid* to all human beings. If they accept it, well and good; if not, no force can be used to change a person's belief system. To enjoy the benefits of embracing Islam or refusing to be a Muslim is left totally to a person's own judgement. A *Da'wah* worker is not made responsible for a person's change of faith. However, if some person freely accepts Islam, then the Qur'an promises them a great reward; and if they do not, then they shall face the consequences alone:

"Allah is the Guardian of those who believe, He brings them out of every darkness into light. And those who disbelieve, their guardians are the evil ones, they bring them out of light into all kinds of darkness. These are destined for the Fire, and there shall they abide" (al-Baqarah, 2: 257).

Experiential Truth

Out of His extreme Compassion and Bounty, Allah shows the path of righteousness to people through His Messengers and Prophets. The faith of the Messengers and Prophets of Allah is reinforced by their experience of Reality and Truth. In this respect, the Qur'an first refers to the personal experience of a person whose name is not mentioned, perhaps because it does not matter or perhaps he was a Prophet ﷺ. What matters is his observation, personal experience and realization of Allah's Transcendent Power and Authority. This person passed by a valley which was totally deserted: the houses that once stood there were utterly destroyed and uninhabited. This horrible and unimaginable destruction of a valley and its people led this person to curiously ask: How will this totally annihilated valley and the people who once lived in it be resurrected and brought back to life? Instead of verbally explaining to him how Allah can do it, Allah caused this person to die and remain dead for one hundred years, and then He resurrected him and asked him how long he thought he had been dead for. The man responded by saying that he may have been dead for a day or a few days at the most. Allah then asked him to look at the remains of his donkey to realize the limitations of human reason and experience and how wrong his guess was. He was also asked to look at his food which was still fresh. Allah wanted to let this person think and use his own intellect to compare the two states: the state of his donkey and that of his food. If he had been dead or sleeping for one day or even a few days, then how come his donkey had turned into a skeleton while his food was still fresh even after one hundred years? This made him realize how one command of Allah can cause change in the laws of nature and how in one single space and time two or more opposite laws of nature can operate simultaneously. This led him to the conviction that Allah has control over everything in the universe. The story and its message are so strong that the identity of the person to whom this episode happened becomes irrelevant.

The other episode is of a well-known historical figure who is recognised as a Messenger of Allah even by the Jews and Christians.

He is the forefather of all the Prophets of Israel. In this story, Prophet Ibrahim ﷺ is summoned by the ruler, most probably Nimrud, and in the course of dialogue the ruler asks Ibrahim about his God. Knowing the mindset of the ruler, who considered himself the god of his people, Prophet Ibrahim ﷺ mentioned two things: *"My Lord is He who grants life and causes death."* What was meant is that even a king who claims to be a god will one day die and, with all his claim to godhood, he has no power to bring a dead person back to life. But the ruler only boasted. "I, too, grant life and cause death," meaning that he could execute any of his subjects and also spare anyone he wishes to spare. Instead of following this chain of argument, Prophet Ibrahim ﷺ challenged with the following: *"But surely Allah causes the sun to rise from the East, now you cause it to rise from the West!"* This dumbfounded the ruler! The message was very clear: Not only does Allah control the destiny of human beings, but everything in the universe also is under His control: *"Did you not consider the case of the person who remonstrated with Ibrahim about who was Ibrahim's Lord just because Allah had granted him dominion? When Ibrahim said: "My Lord is He Who grants life and causes death," he replied: "I grant life and I cause death," Ibrahim said: "But surely Allah causes the sun to rise from the East now you cause it to rise from the West." Therefore, the denier of the Truth was confounded. Allah does not direct the wrongdoers to the Right Way"* (al-Baqarah, 2: 258). The two above episodes highlight Allah's Supremacy, Command and Authority over the whole universe.

This is followed by another episode in which Prophet Ibrahim ﷺ asks a question for his personal satisfaction and also in order to argue with the non-believers, as an eyewitness, on matters that caused people confusion: *"And when Ibrahim said: My Lord, show me how You give life to the dead? Allah said: Why? Do you have no faith?*

Ibrahim replied: Yes but in order that my heart be at rest. He said: Then take four birds, and tame them to yourself, then put a part of them on every hill, and summon them; they will come to you flying. Know well that Allah is All-Mighty, All-Wise" (al-Baqarah, 2: 260). This indicates that with their total trust and commitment in the Authority and Power of Allah, even Prophets were encouraged to ask questions of a critical nature.

In the dialogue of Prophet Ibrahim ﷺ with the ruler, the Qur'an highlights two attitudes regarding matters of the *ghayb* or Unseen, life and death. The ruler thought that life and death were in his hands because he could execute or spare any of his subjects and, hence, he deserved the obedience of his people. But Prophet Ibrahim ﷺ exposed the weakness of his argument. The level of faith of Prophet Ibrahim ﷺ is fully reflected in his supplication: *"My salat, my sacrifice, my life and my death all are for the Lord of all worlds"* it shows his unshakable belief in Allah's Supremacy and Power as Lord and *Rabb*, he only wanted to re-strengthen his faith by experiencing a matter of *ghayb*, because as *daiyah* he wanted to bear *shahadah* (give an eyewitness account) on matters of faith to the people. Similarly, Prophet Muhammad's Night Journey and Ascent to Heaven (*al-isra' wa'l-mi'raj*) was an experience to strengthen his total conviction in his message, to be able to inform people about certain matters of the Unseen as an eyewitness.

The Qur'an frequently uses everyday examples as an evidence of Allah's Authority and Power to resurrect people on the Day of Judgement. It is our common observation that long spells of drought can make a green valley dry and deserted. But one good shower of rain brings back life in plants and the desert becomes a green carpet. But often human beings do not look at such everyday events with an analytical mind. The Qur'an invites people to think logically and draw lessons from observable facts, to help them understand matters of a non-empirical nature (*ghayb*): *"And of His Signs is that you see the earth withered. Surely, He Who gives life to the dead earth will also give life to the dead. Surely He has Power over everything"* (Ha Mim sajdah, 41: 39).

Manifestation of Faith in *Infaq* (Spending on Others for Allah's Sake)

Infaq fi sabil Allah, spending on others to please Allah alone is also an important recurring theme throughout the Qur'an. In the early part of *al-Baqarah*, this is mentioned as a quality of those who believe in *ghayb* (the Unseen) or what is beyond people's sensory experience. Now, after referring to conviction (*iman bi'l-shahadah* and *'ayn al-yaqin*), the Qur'an turns again to the destiny of those who believe in Allah and desire to see Him on the Day of Judgement with their faces shining, and not like those who shall be resurrected with sad and gloomy faces. The Qur'an uses beautiful similes to encourage voluntary contribution, to seek the good pleasure of Allah, through working for the wellbeing of all members of society: *"The example of those who spend their wealth in the way of Allah is like that of a grain of corn that sprouts seven ears, and in every ear, there are a hundred grains. Thus, Allah multiplies the action of whomsoever He wills. Allah is Munificent, All-Knowing. Those who spend their wealth in the way of Allah and do not follow up their spending by stressing their benevolence and causing hurt, will find their reward secure with their Lord. They have no cause to fear and grief. To speak a kind word and to forgive people's faults is better than charity followed by hurt. Allah is All-Sufficient, All-Forbearing. Believers do not nullify your acts of charity by stressing your benevolence and causing hurt as does he who spends his wealth only to be seen by people and does not believe in Allah and the Last Day. The example of his spending is that of a rock with a thin coating of earth upon it when heavy rain smites it, the earth is washed away, leaving the rock bare; such people derive no gain from their acts of charity. Allah does not set the deniers of the Truth on the Right Way. The example of those who spend their wealth single-mindedly to please Allah is that of a garden on a high ground. If a heavy rain smites it, it brings forth its fruits twofold, and if there is no heavy rain, even a light shower suffices it. Allah sees all that you do"* (al-Baqarah, 2: 261-265).

The Qur'an differentiates between those who spend in the way of Allah seeking no recognition in this world and those who do so to get recognition. Spending on others and almsgiving are two major acts that are indicative of how a grateful person, whom Allah has blessed with wealth, should behave. Those who embrace a materialist view of life think like entrepreneurs, i.e. whatever wealth they accrue is due to their own hard work, planning, skills, and management of resources. While an Allah-conscious person is convinced that whatever potential and skills they possess are gifts from Allah as well as a trust to be delivered to those it actually belongs to: the needy, the indebted or those who suffer from poverty or have health problems. And since the means and resources are given by Allah, their distribution should also be as Allah desires. Those who spend of what Allah has given them solely for His good pleasure are abundantly rewarded while those who spend on others to get recognition may become known in society as generous donors but will have no share in the Hereafter: *"Would any of you desire that he should have a garden of palms and vines with river flowing beneath it – a garden in which he has every manner of fruit and it should then be struck by a fiery whirlwind and be utterly burnt down at a time when old age has overtaken him and* his offspring are still too small to look after their affairs? Thus, does Allah make His teachings clear to you that you may reflect.

"Believers spend (in the way of Allah) out of the good things you have earned and out of which We have produced for you from the earth, and choose not for your spending the bad things such as you yourself would not accept or accept only by overlooking its defects. Know well that Allah is All-Munificent, Most-Praiseworthy. Satan frightens you with poverty and bids you to commit indecency whereas Allah promises you His forgiveness and bounty. Allah is Munificent, All-Knowing, He grants wisdom to those whom He wills and whoever is granted wisdom (hikmah) has indeed been granted much good. Yet none except people of understanding take heed" (al-Baqarah, 2: 266-269).

The Gift of Wisdom

After a detailed discussion on *tawhid*, Allah's existence and the factuality of the Day of Judgement, the believers are prompted to spend in the way of Allah, not for any recognition but only to gain Allah's pleasure. A person who is short-sighted normally looks for immediate gains and profit, but a wise person looks for the ultimate end and the permanent reward of his Lord. Wisdom (*hikmah*) is an important theme in the Qur'an which has several dimensions. It indeed is a favour and gift from Allah which is shared by Allah's Prophets and a select few who are sincere and not after any personal gain or popularity.

The Arabic word *hukm* means decision while *hakama* means to pass judgement. In its general application, the word means the ability to arrive at a well-thought, well-considered, balanced and appropriate judgement. *Hakim* refers to the person who is gifted with *hikmah* or wisdom such as Khidr in the story of Prophet Musa or Luqman ﷺ after whom a *surah* of the Qur'an is named. It is a behavioural category and depicts a mature and dignified character.

The Qur'an also mentions the names of certain Prophets and Messengers of Allah who were gifted with it. With reference to Prophet Dawood ﷺ, for example, the Qur'an states: *"And We strengthened his kingdom and endowed him with wisdom (al-hikmah) and decisive judgement"* (Sad, 38: 20), and also: *"And Dawood killed Goliath (Jalut) and Allah granted him dominion and wisdom and imparted to him the knowledge of whatever He willed"* (al-Baqarah, 2: 251). Luqman was also blessed with *hikmah*: *"We bestowed wisdom upon Luqman (enjoining): Give thanks to Allah, whoso gives thanks to Allah does so to his own good"* (Luqman, 31: 12).

In several places, the Qur'an uses the word *hikmah* in the sense of the exemplary conduct of the Prophets of Allah, which illustrates the applied dimensions of the teachings of the revealed Scriptures that they were sent with or commanded to uphold. Upon raising the walls of the Kaaba, Prophets Ibrahim and Isma'il made the following supplication: *"Our Lord! Raise up in the midst of our offspring a Messenger from among them who shall recite to them your verses, and instruct them in the Book, and wisdom (hikmah) and purify their lives. Verily You are the Most-Mighty, the Most-Wise"* (al-Baqarah, 2: 129). These are four major functions of all the Prophets of Allah, as elaborated in this *du'a*, and mentioned with specific reference to the last Messenger of Allah ﷺ: *"Surely Allah conferred a great favour on the believers, when He raised from among them a Messenger to recite to them His ayat (signs) and to purify them and to teach them the Book and wisdom (hikmah) for before that they were in manifest error"* (Al 'Imran, 3: 164).

In other words, it is an integral part of Allah's final Messenger's mission to encourage and inculcate a culture of *hikmah* (wisdom), *tazkiyah* (purification of the character), and teaching the Book, including learning from the book of the universe, nature and the histories of the nations of the past, in order to learn what is right and what is wrong conduct and how to best serve Allah, Most-High.

Wisdom (*hikmah*) as a *da'wah* strategy is another recurring theme in the Qur'an: *"(O Prophet ﷺ), call to the way of Your Lord with wisdom, (hikmah) and goodly elaboration and reason with them in the best manner possible. Surely your Lord knows best who has strayed away from His path and He also knows well those who are guided to the Right Way"* (al-Nahl, 16: 125). Here, calling with *hikmah* to the path of Allah (with wisdom) refers to a variety of strategic steps needed for the proper dissemination of *da'wah* (the Islamic message). First and foremost, *hikmah* (wisdom) here means the use of politeness and leniency and penetrating speech the Qur'an calls elsewhere *qawl-e-Layyin*. Prophets Musa and Harun were advised by Allah to use polite words when addressing the Pharaoh, the tyrant of his age. Wisdom also refers to the use of one's judgement about when to stop a rational discourse and withdraw from a futile debate by saying *salam*, i.e. peace.

It also means the use of practical wisdom in not only communication of *da'wah* but also in warfare as in the case of the Battle of Uhud, the Prophetic wisdom was to track the enemy to give them a clear message that we are not defeated, we are ready to encounter with you again. And it worked.

It also means the use of the Prophetic foresight in making contracts and agreements like he did at Hudaybiah. The conditions appeared to even some senior *sahabah* as a sign of weakness. But later they discovered the *hikmah* of the Prophet ﷺ in making the treaty. The Makkans by this treaty recognized the state of Madinah and the right of Arabian tribes to become allies of the Muslim state.

The Qur'an itself has been described by Allah as full of *hikmah*: *"Ya-Sin, by the Wise (al-Hakim) Qur'an, you are truly among the Messengers on a Straight Way"* (Ya-Sin, 36: 1-4). Similarly, Allah says in the Qur'an: *"Alif Lam Ra', these are the verses of the Book overflowing with wisdom (hikmah)"* (Yunus, 10: 1). In other words, the Qur'an provides the highest possible examples of wisdom, guidance, and the way to success for the whole of mankind.

Acting wisely, therefore, means a well-reasoned, evidence-based process of reasoning, analysis, and strategic thinking while seeking help from Allah, in order to remain on the right path. The Qur'an refers, for example, to the wise Luqman who advised his son to hold fast to faith and right conduct: *"And call to mind when Luqman said to his son while exerting him: My son, do not associate others with Allah in His Divinity. Surely associating others with Allah is a mighty wrong (zulmun 'azim)"* (Luqman, 31: 13); *"Son, establish prayer, enjoin all that is good and forbid all that is evil and endure with patience whatever affliction befall you. Surely these have been emphatically enjoined. Do not (contemptuously) turn your face away from people, nor tread haughtily upon earth. Allah does not love the arrogant and the vainglorious. Be moderate in your stride and lower your voice. Verily the most disgusting of all noises is the braying of the donkey"* (Luqman, 31: 17-19). This illustrates the wisdom of sharing the *din* in the form of *nasihah* and *wasiyah*, advice and as part of one's will.

Prophet Dawood ﷺ was gifted with prophethood, kingship and wisdom: *"And We strengthened his kingdom and endowed him with wisdom, (hikmah), and decisive judgement"* (Sad, 38: 20). The latter part of the verse elaborates that giving wisdom to Prophet Dawood ﷺ was necessary because he had to act as Allah's Prophet ﷺ as well as a ruler: *"O Dawood, We have appointed you* vicegerent (Khalifah) on earth. Therefore, rule among people and do not follow (your) desire lest it should lead you astray from Allah's Path" (Sad, 38: 26). The final Messenger of Allah ﷺ was commissioned with four major responsibilities, referred to earlier. One of these, i.e. teaching wisdom, which in this context, means calling to Islam as a role model of perfect behaviour or wisdom in the form of his *qawl* and *fa'il* (his most eloquent and precise words and his conduct and behaviour). This is why the pearls of wisdom of the Prophet ﷺ are called *jawami'l kalam*.

The word *hukm* coming from the same root also means verdict, judgement and decision: *"We bestowed the same favour upon Dawood and Sulayman. Recall, when they gave judgement (hukman) regarding the tillage into which the sheep of some people had strayed at night and We were witnesses to their judgement. We guided Sulayman to the right verdict and We had granted each of them judgement (hukman) and knowledge ('ilman)"* (al-Anbiya', 21: 78-79). It is also used in the Qur'an to refer to the wise judgement of Allah: *"Do they desire judgement according to the law of ignorance. But whose judgement can be better (ahsan) than Allah's for those who have certainty of belief"* (al-Ma'idah, 5: 50). Prophet Yahya ﷺ (John) was given wisdom even as a child: *"O Yahya! Hold the Book with all your strength. We had bestowed wisdom (al-hukma) upon him while he was still a child"* (Maryam 19: 12). Similarly, Prophet Lut ﷺ was given wisdom: *"We bestowed upon Lut sound judgment (hukman) and knowledge ('ilman) and We delivered him from the city that was immersed in foul deeds. They were indeed a wicked people, exceedingly disobedient. And We admitted him into Our Mercy, verily he was of the righteous"* (al-Anbiya', 21: 74-75). In the light of these few Qur'anic references, the general meaning of *hikmah* can be taken to mean seeking to resolve any issue with foresight, maturity and practical wisdom, which is a great gift from Allah to His servants. The best source of wisdom is the *uswah* or perfect example of the final Messenger ﷺ. This is why the Qur'anic exegetes and *Hadith* scholars are of the view that the Prophetic actions (*'aml*), statements (*qawl*) and endorsements (*taqrir*), taken together, are what constitute real wisdom (*al-hikmah*). A deep understanding of the Prophetic Sunnah (role model) alone can guide a believer to make appropriate judgements on personal, social, legal, and national issues.

The Culture of Almsgiving (*Sadaqah*)

Sadaqah, as mentioned earlier, is a voluntary contribution to please Allah which should be a matter between the believer and his Lord. The root word of *sadaqah* is from *sidq* or truthfulness and, hence, *sadaqah* means giving to others voluntarily and with sincerity, truthfulness, willingness, pleasantness, purity of heart and pure intention to please Allah and not to show off or expect a reward or recognition in return.

Sadaqah, just like *infaq*, has a wider connotation, while *zakah* is specific as defined in *al-Tawbah*, even though *sadaqah* is sometimes used as a synonym of *zakah*: *"(O Prophet ﷺ)! Take sadaqah out of their riches and thereby cleanse their riches and bring about their growth (in righteousness) and pray for them..."* (al-Tawbah, 9: 103). The word *sadaqah* is also used in the sense of *zakah* when referring to the eight legal disbursements of *zakah*: *"The sadaqat are meant only for the poor and the needy and those who are in charge thereof, those whose hearts are to be reconciled and to free those in bondage and to help those burdened with debt and for expenditure in the way of Allah and for the wayfarer. This is an obligation from Allah, Allah is*

All-Knowing, All-Wise" (al-Tawbah, 9: 60).

A culture of seeking reward (*ajr*) only from Allah through *sadaqah* is highly encouraged by the Qur'an and the Sunnah. An authentic Prophetic *hadith* states: "Protect yourselves from the Fire even if through just half a date (given in *sadaqah*)." Similarly, another Prophetic saying reported by Muslim states: "*Sadaqah* never decreases wealth." The Prophet ﷺ is also reported to have said "*Sadaqah* is proof (*Burhan*)." In other words, anyone who is sincere and does not want to be known as a generous person is expected to give *sadaqah* in secret and such an act then becomes a *burhan* or proof of their *iman*.

One could give *sadaqah* as a voluntary act just to help someone else or it could be to expiate one's sins: *"Are they not aware that it is Allah who accepts the repentance of His servants and accepts their sadaqat and that it is Allah who is oft Relenting, Ever-Merciful"* (al-Tawbah, 9: 104). The beauty of Islam and Allah's bounty are such that, according to a Prophetic saying, a smile of the believer to another believer is considered a *sadaqah*. Though a single penny has not been spent, even the simple act of smiling at another person, for the pleasure of Allah, is rewarded as a charity.

A society in which people hasten to give *sadaqah*, not to get fame, reward, or recognition, but to please Allah, can easily alleviate poverty, diseases, illiteracy, and insecurity. It is in this sense that Islam envisions a society which takes care of the welfare of people as its primary duty: *"If you dispense your charity publicly, it is well, but if you conceal it and pay it to the needy in secret, it will be even better for you. This will atone for several of your misdeeds, Allah is well aware of all that you do"* (al-Baqarah, 2: 271).

The Qur'an creates a direct relationship between Allah and His servants who, out of forgetfulness or weakness, may commit wrongs, whether serious or not so serious. The Qur'an wants the believers to ask Allah directly for forgiveness through the culture of *sadaqah* and *infaq*. This impacts a believer in three ways, first, a person is relieved of any psychological pressure on his/her mind. Second, one's direct relation with Allah is solidified because the Most Benevolent and The Gracious loves His servant when he returns to Him for forgiveness, His Forgiveness has no limits, He Calls Himself: **"The Forgiver of sins, the Acceptor of repentance..."** (al-Mu'min/Ghafir 40: 3). Third, *sadaqah* and *infaq* cause increase in wealth and resources because Allah has promised that when a person gives *zakah* or *sadaqah* and makes *infaq*, this act is like planting corn where one seed develops into seven ears and each ear carries a hundred corns. This is how the reward for whatever is spent in the way of Allah is multiplied. This, however, does not mean that a person may become relaxed in doing wrong and take for granted that *infaq* and *sadaqah* will compensate for habitual wrongdoings: *"You are not responsible for setting these people on the Right Way. Allah sets on the Right Path whomsoever He wills. Whatever wealth you spend in charity is to your own benefit for you spend merely to please Allah. So, whatever you spend in charity will be repaid to you in full and you shall not be wronged"* (al-Baqarah, 2: 272).

While encouraging the believers to embrace a culture of *sadaqah*, *infaq* and *zakah*, the Qur'an also touches on real life situations whereby a person or a group of people are wholly involved in the dissemination of the Islamic message but, due to their sense of dignity and self-esteem, they do not ask for any financial assistance to meet their personal needs. The Qur'an advises those who are affluent to come forward and meet the needs of such sincere and humble people. These persons, out of self-respect, do not stretch out their hand therefore those who have means should generously provide them with resources in a dignified way and make life easy for them: *"Those needy ones who are wholly wrapped up in the cause of Allah, and who are hindered from moving about the earth in search of their livelihood, especially deserve help. He who is unaware of their circumstances supposes them to be wealthy because of their dignified bearing but you will know them by their countenance, although they do not go about begging of people with importunity. Whatever wealth you spend on helping them, Allah will know of it"* (al-Baqarah, 2: 273).

The Secular Concept of Corporate Social Responsibility vs. The Culture of *Infaq* and *Sadaqah*

Everywhere in the world, there are people who feel their corporate social responsibility and contribute toward welfare projects. But generally, such acts of charity are motivated by a desire for recognition and even for the sake of deriving political benefits. Many rich corporations sponsor sports, healthcare and other projects with their brand name projected for all to see. Individuals, too, may have a hidden desire to be recognised as philanthropists for the work they do in society. The culture of *sadaqah* and *infaq* that the Qur'an advocates is different: *"Those who spend their wealth by night and by day secretly and publicly will find that their reward is secure with their Lord and that there is no reason for them to entertain any fear or grief"* (al-Baqarah, 2: 274).

Establishing an Interest-free Society

The culture of *sadaqah* and *infaq* prompts the believers to help the needy only for Allah's good pleasure. By contrast, the culture of materialistic societies inspires the entrepreneurs to aim for as much profit as possible for themselves. Such people are not prepared to grant loans to the needy without imposing interest on them. In all materialist-capitalistic economies, the curse of interest exacerbates the situation of the needy. This is why Islam prohibits all forms of usury and economic exploitation: *"As for those who devour interest, they behave as the one whom Satan has confounded with his touch. Seized in this state they say: Buying and selling is but a kind of interest, even though Allah has made buying and selling as lawful, and interest unlawful. Hence, he who receives this admonition from his Lord, and then gives up (dealing in interest) may keep his previous gains and it will be for Allah to judge him. As for those who revert to it, they are the people of the Fire, and in it shall they abide. Allah deprives interest of all blessing whereas He blesses sadaqat with growth. Allah loves none who is ungrateful and persists in sin. Truly the reward of those who believe and do righteous deeds and establish prayer and give zakah is with their Lord; they have no reason to entertain any fear or grief"* (al-Baqarah, 2: 274-277).

An economic system based on interest or usury (*riba*) makes the rich richer and the poor poorer and more miserable. The Qur'an condemns usury in the strongest terms and Allah declares war against those who deal with usury:

"Believers! Have fear of Allah and give up all outstanding interest if you do truly believe. But if you fail to do so then be warned of war from Allah and His Messenger. If you repent even now you have the right of the return of your capital; neither will you do wrong nor will you be wronged (la tazlimuna wa la tuzlamun). But if the debtor is in straitened circumstances let him have respite until the time of ease; and whatever you remit by way of charity is better for you, if only you know. And have fear of the Day when you shall return to Allah and every human being shall be fully repaid for whatever (good or evil) he has

done and none shall be wronged" (al-Baqarah, 2: 275-281). According to the Qur'an, the prohibition of *riba* has been a part of the teachings of all the earlier Messengers of Allah.

While guiding the believers about managing their finances and providing a model of an interest-free economy, the Qur'an also directs them about how to observe transparency in contracts, agreements, and covenants. It is important to note that although the pre-Islamic Arabs traded with Asia, Africa, and parts of the Mediterranean, they conducted their business through verbal agreements. The Qur'an encourages a tradition of writing down business contracts and having them witnessed by others: *"Believers! Whenever you contract a debt from one another for a known term commit it to writing. Let a scribe write it down between you justly, and the scribe may not refuse to write it down according to what Allah has taught him; so, let him write and let the debtor dictate; and let him fear Allah, his Lord and curtail no part of it. If the debtor be feeble minded, weak or incapable of dictating let the guardian dictate equitably (bi'l-'adl), and call upon two of your men as witnesses, but if two men are not there, then let there be one man and two women as witnesses from among those acceptable to you so that if one of the two women should fail to remember, the other might remind her. Let not the witness refuse when they are summoned (to give evidence). Do not show slackness in writing down the transaction whether small or large, along with the term of its payment. That is fairest in the sight of Allah, it is best for testimony and is more likely to exclude all doubts. If it be a matter of buying and selling on the spot it is not blameworthy if you do not write it down but do take witnesses when you settle commercial transactions with one another. And the scribe of the witness may be done no harm. It will be sinful if you do so. Beware of the wrath of Allah. He teaches you the Right way and has full knowledge of everything"* (al-Baqarah, 2: 282).

> ### The Benefits of an Interest-Free Economy
>
> An interest-free economy is bound to bring economic benefits, growth, and development. Even in capitalist societies, lowering interest rates results in more investments, economic growth, and the creation of jobs. A human-friendly, Islamic system of economy goes a step further and builds the best ethical practices in the economy, finance, and banking through a total prohibition of *riba*. It offers more opportunities for trade, industry, and agriculture through the encouragement of interest-free partnership and profit and loss sharing agreements.

No Gender Disparity in Legal Matters

This above Qur'anic verse is often generalized and a principle is drawn from it that the evidence of a woman is half that of a man. This literalist approach does not agree with the overall approach of justice and fairness held throughout the Qur'an. Justice and not equality is the Qur'anic basis of dealing with all behavioural issues, whether they relate to *'ibadat* (worship) or *mu'amilat* (transactions) or *'uqubat* (legal penalties and punishments).

The Qur'an itself is an evidence of the fact that it does not equate two women with one man. While dealing with a situation in which there is no witness but only two people accusing each other, the Qur'an does not say that the husband should take an oath four times while his wife should take an oath eight times: *"As for those who accuse their wives (of unchastity) and have no witnesses except themselves the* testimony of such one is that he testify swearing by Allah four times that he is truthful (in his accusation) and a fifth time that the curse of Allah be on him if he be lying. And the punishment shall be averted from the women if she were to testify swearing by Allah four times that the man was lying, and a fifth time that the wrath of Allah be on her if the man be truthful"* (an-Nur, 24: 6-9). Moreover if the *ayah* of (al-Baqarah, 2:282) is considered in a live situation say Zaid has taken from Bakr a loan of five hundred million and on it Ahmad and Saimah and Sa'diyah are the witnesses. And after five years a dispute arises and in the law court, Ahmad and Saimah testify that the amount was five hundred million, while Sa'diyah thinks it was fifty million, what shall be a fair judgement? Naturally the evidence of one male and one female shall lead the judge to decide in favour of five hundred million. In other words, when we apply the *ayah* in a live situation the *ayah* conveys a different meaning. Therefore, one cannot draw from just one verse of the Qur'an a general principle that two women are equal to a man. There is also strong evidence from the Sunnah which supports the view that even the evidence of a single believing lady is conclusive. For example in the case of a *sahabiyah* who in the early morning hours was on her way and was attacked by someone, she shouted, the accused was caught and was brought in front of the Prophet ﷺ, and he asked the *sahabiyah*, was this the person, and on her evidence and testimony alone, the Prophet ﷺ ordered his execution. Similarly, in situations where the parentage of a newborn is disputed the evidence of a single midwife who helped in the delivery of the child is considered stronger than four heavyweight male witnesses. The *ayah* also puts great responsibility on the scribe and the witness, they cannot excuse themselves when they are called to testify.

The following verse deals with the situation whereby a business agreement is reached during a journey and there is no scribe available to write down the contract: *"But if you are on a journey and you cannot find a scribe, then have a security on hand. But if you trust one another, then let him who is entrusted deliver his trust and let him be ever Allah-Fearing and conscious of God, his Lord. Nor shall you ever wilfully suppress a testimony, for whoever suppresses it, then most surely his heart is sinful. And Allah is All-Knowing of all that you do"* (al-Baqarah, 2: 283).

> ### Why does the Qur'an Instruct about Economic and Financial Matters?
>
> The Qur'anic instructions on money matters and what is meant by a just economic order remove the basic confusion created by the systems of life whereby religion stands for spirituality and personal piety, while the economy, political system, and governance are to be run on the principles of material benefit and control. This concept has no place in the Islamic worldview. Life in Islam is one whole and all human activities are to be synergized under *tawhid*. Allah is not a ceremonial god who is welcome in the mosque but not allowed to guide people in law courts and other economic, commercial, cultural, and political domains.

The believers are asked to seek Allah's Forgiveness and Support in their striving for ethical living at the personal, social, economic, political, and cultural levels. The supplication at the end of *Surah al-Baqarah* is loaded with optimism, humility, repentance, hope and trust in the Compassion, Kindness, Magnanimity, Forgiveness and Power of the Lord of all created beings.

Having re-confirmed the articles of faith, the believers humble themselves to Allah while requesting Him not to burden them with that which is beyond their capacity, not to take them to task when they forget or commit a mistake, but to be kind to them, have mercy on them and bless them: *"All that is in the heavens and the earth belongs to Allah. Whether you disclose whatever is in your heart or conceal it, Allah will call you to account for it, and will then forgive whomsoever He wills and will chastise whomever He wills. Allah has power over everything.*

The Messenger believes and so do the believers, in the guidance sent down upon him from his Lord: each of them believes in Allah and His Angels, and in His Books, and His Messengers. They say: we make no distinction between any of His Messengers. We hear and obey. Our Lord! Grant us Your Forgiveness, to You we are destined to return. Allah does not lay a responsibility on anyone beyond his capacity. In his favour shall be whatever good each one does, and against him whatever evil he does. (Believers pray thus to your Lord) Our Lord Take us not to task if we forget or commit mistakes. Our Lord! Lay not on us a burden such as You laid on those gone before us. Our Lord! Lay not on us a burden which we do not have the power to bear. And overlook our faults, and forgive us, and have mercy upon us. You are our Guardian, so grant us victory against the unbelieving folk" (al-Baqarah, 2: 284-286).

The message of *al-Baqarah* is very simple: be honest, truthful, and dutiful to the Creator, the Merciful Lord of the Universe; remove contradictions in your life and let the One and Only Allah be followed in all human activities. Do not follow the gods of power, race, colour, wealth, land, glamour, and popularity. Follow the role models of Allah's true Prophets

Nuh, Ibrahim, Musa, 'Isa and others as well as the exemplary conduct of the final Messenger ﷺ. His role model provides a balanced, moderate, fair, fully preserved, and compassionate imitable example. Depend on only Allah's help in building a world where fairness, justice, freedom, dignity, honesty, and truth may prevail and rule. Strive against racism, oppression, exploitation, and all forms of colonialism, (economic, political, social, cultural, and legal); eschew ethical relativism, individualism, and materialism.

As an *ummah* appointed by Allah to invite mankind to the right path, the path of success in this world and the life to come, strive for *ma'ruf* (what is good) and fight against *munkar* (unethical practices and what is evil), be prepared to uphold the leadership role (*khilafah*) to establish justice, peace, security, and welfare in society. Be thankful to Allah for His countless blessings and avoid ungrateful behaviour.

The *surah* also provides a blueprint for a successful socio-economic, political, and cultural order which gets rid of any exploitative interest-based economic systems and governance. It also shows how the message delivered by the Book and the Prophet ﷺ is no different than what was delivered by Prophet Ibrahim ﷺ and all earlier Messengers and Prophets of Allah. It is due to its comprehensive treatment of faith, acts of worship and righteous works that the Prophet ﷺ is reported to have said that this *surah* protects the residents of any household, in which it is recited, from misguidance and also guides them to success.

The *surah* around its end invites believers to seek forgiveness from Allah, for any unintentional and forgetful violation of His commands, to request Him not to put an unbearable burden on us and if a situation of test arises to bless us with steadfastness, perseverance, and moral courage to face the test and trial and permit us to lead humanity to a state of dignity, honour, cooperation, selflessness and make us succeed in the life Hereafter and life in this world by following the Divine Guidance given in the form of the Qur'an and the role model of the Final Messenger ﷺ.

Alhamdulillah wa ma tawfiqi illa bi Allah.

March 23, 2023